THE JEWISH COMMUNITY
OF SALONIKA

This publication was made
possible through grants from the
Edmond J. Safra
Philanthropic Foundation
and Lisa and Bernard Sabrier

The Jewish Community of Salonika

History, Memory, Identity

BEA LEWKOWICZ

VALLENTINE MITCHELL
LONDON • PORTLAND, OR

First published in 2006 in Great Britain by
VALLENTINE MITCHELL
Suite 314, Premier House, 112–114 Station Road,
Edgware, Middlesex HA8 7BJ

and in the United States of America by
VALLENTINE MITCHELL
c/o ISBS, 920 NE 58th Avenue, Suite 300
Portland, Oregon, 97213-3786

Website http://www.vmbooks.com

British Library Cataloging in Publication Data:

Lewkowicz, Bea
    The Jewish community of Salonika : history, memory,
    identity
    1.Jews - Greece - Thessalonike - History 2.Jews - Greece -
    Thessalonike - Identity 3.Holocaust, Jewish (1939-1945) -
    Greece - Thessalonike 4.World War, 1939-1945 - Greece -
    Thessalonike
    I.Title
    305.8'924'049565

ISBN 0-85303-579-2 (cloth)
ISBN 0-85303-580-6 (paper)

Library of Congress Cataloging-in-Publication Data:

A catalog record for this book is available
from the Library of Congress

Printed in Great Britain by
MPG Books Ltd, Bodmin, Cornwall

to my parents

and in memory of my grandparents
Alexander and Margit Friedmann
Moses and Regina Lewkowicz

Contents

List of Tables

List of Maps and Illustrations

Maps

Illustrations

Abbreviations

AJDC	American Joint Distribution Committee
CJMCAG	Conference on Jewish Material Claims Against Germany
EAM	National Liberation Front (Communist)
EDES	National Republican Greek League (non-Communist)
EEE	*Trie Epsilon* National Union of Greece
ELAS	Military Wing of EAM
FYROM	Former Yugoslav Republic of Macedonia
JCRA	Jewish Committee for Relief Abroad
KIS	Central Board of Jewish Communities
OPAIE	Organisation for the Relief and Rehabilitation of the Jews of Greece
PASOK	Panhellenic Socialist Movement
RSHA	*Reichssicherheitshauptamt*, a subdivision of the SS
SS	*Schutzstaffel*, Hitler's personal guard and special security force

Note on the Use of Names and Translation

All the names that appear in the text are abbreviated or changed to protect the anonymity of the interviewees. The anthropologist Meyerhoff writes that 'there are circumstances which call for identification rather than disguise' (Meyerhoff 1978: x). I feel that in the light of the nature of the narrated historical experiences, the circumstances do call for identification. Most interviewees would probably agree with this view and would wish to be mentioned by their full names. After many hours of contemplating this issue, I decided that it was necessary to abbreviate the names of people who appear in this text, despite my great reluctance to do so. This is for two reasons: firstly, I do not have the explicit consent of all the interviewees for the publication of their surnames. Secondly, I cannot be sure that each interviewee would accept my theoretical framework and thus might object to appearing by name in this piece of research.

The interviews that appear in this text have either been conducted in English or have been translated from French, German, Hebrew or Greek. I edited the interviews as little as possible and the translations remain close to the original statements. Words in Greek, Hebrew, French, or German appear in italics. The transliteration of Greek and Hebrew words in the text reflects the sound of these words rather than their spelling (*Kinotita* rather than *Koinotita*). Further explanations and additions have been given between square brackets.

Acknowledgements

This study would not have been possible without the help and support of many people.

I would foremost like to express my deep gratitude to all of the interviewees for sharing their life histories with me and to all the people who welcomed me with open arms, 'adopted' me, and made me feel at home in Thessaloniki. I also wholeheartedly thank the former president of the Jewish Community of Thessaloniki, Mr Andreas Sefiha, for the generous help and co-operation I received from the community throughout my fieldwork, the late Mr Albertos Nar for helping me to access community records and for providing me with insightful information, and the Director of the Saul Modiano Home for the Elderly, Mrs Viktoria Benozilio, for tolerating my many visits and for introducing me to some of my interviewees.

My special thanks go to Professor Anthony D. Smith and Professor Peter Loizos, my supervisors at the LSE. Professor Smith's expertise in the field of nationalism and ethnicity has guided and inspired me; his thorough reading of my writing and continuous support have been invaluable. Professor Loizos has listened and responded; his sound advice and unwavering encouragement spurred me on and stimulated my curiosity in Mediterranean anthropology. I would also like to express my gratitude to the late Professor Ernest Gellner for introducing me to the study of nationalism and culture and to Professor Waltraud Kokot for acquainting me with the anthropology of Greece and Salonika. Further thanks go to Professor Mark Mazower, Dr Charles Stewart, Dr Margaret Kenna and Dr Rena Molho for their constructive comments and helpful insights. I am also grateful to my colleagues from the Association for the Study of Ethnicity and Nationalism for the lively and fruitful exchanges on nationalism and ethnicity.

I owe a great debt to everyone who helped to ensure the completion of this book:

Dr Gertrud Friedmann for her enthusiasm and commitment in transcribing interview tapes and in proof-reading the entire manuscript; Christine Garabedian for 'being there' from the very beginning and for supplying me with intellectual, editorial, and emotional support; Ellen Germain for her generous and detailed editorial contributions to my first publication on the Jewish Community of Salonika and to the final draft of this book; and Donatella Bernstein, Daisy and Charles Hoffner and Louise Pennington-Legh for proof-reading.

I am very grateful to the Economic and Social Research Council for giving me a doctoral scholarship and to the University of Tel Aviv for the Research Fellowship on the 'Rethinking Nationalism' Program at the Institute for German History. I would like to thank the American Joint Distribution Committee, Yad Vashem, and the Wiener Library for allowing me access to their archives.

It is with great pleasure that I thank all my friends and *pareas* in Cologne, Salonika, Jerusalem, and London for providing me with encouragement and distractions at the various stages of this project. Above all, I want to thank my family for their love, patience, and support throughout this interesting journey.

My final thanks go to Vallentine Mitchell for publishing this book and to my husband Malcolm Miller and our sons Alex and Benjamin for being my new source of inspiration.

Preface

As this book is being published in 2006, we need to be aware of the time frame in which it was written. This manuscript was finished in the year 2000 and my main fieldwork took place in 1994. Many things have changed since I described the memory landscape of Salonika. In 2005, 60 years after the liberation of Auschwitz, where so many Salonikan Jews were killed, the Holocaust has become a matter of national remembrance. The 27 January 2005 was the second time Greece marked the official National Day of Remembrance of the Greek Jewish Heroes and Martyrs of the Holocaust. The commemoration ceremony in Salonika was attended by the German Foreign Minister Joschka Fischer. It was a high-profile event which received national and international press coverage. In 2000 a plaque was put on the site of the old railway station which recalls the deportations of the Salonikan Jews in 1943. The year 2004 also saw the publication of Mark Mazower's book *Salonica: City of Ghosts*, an extensive and eloquent overview of the history of the city and its multicultural population. At the outset of our research, Mazower and myself were both confronted with the absence of Jews in the histories of Greece and the histories of Salonika. While he set out to write the much-needed history of the city, which encompasses the experiences of Christians, Jews, and Muslims and incorporates the radical historical discontinuities of deportations, evictions, forced resettlement, and genocide (Mazower 2004: 10),[1] the aim of this book it to get a glimpse of the past through the voices of the Salonikan Jews who experienced some of these radical upheavals in their own lives.

As the whole world remembered the sixtieth anniversary of the liberation of Auschwitz in January 2005, one commentator noted: 'The battle of amnesia is over. The battle of memory has just begun'.[2] Through the study of personal testimonies, it has been my aim to preserve and interpret individual and collective memories and identities and thus bring to life the history of the remarkable Jewish community of Salonika.

Bea Lewkowicz
February 2005

NOTES

1. Mazower, M., *Salonica. City of Ghosts. Christian, Muslims and Jews 1430–1950*. Harper Collins: 2004.
2. Stephen Smith (Chairman of Beth Shalom Holocaust Centre) *Jewish Chronicle* 21 January 2005, p. 25.

Introduction

This study is an ethnographic account of the Jewish community of Salonika and a description and analysis of oral histories gathered during my fieldwork in 1994.[1] My aim is to look at the intersection of history, memory and identity. In what follows I will analyse how identities and memories are shaped by historical experiences and conversely how identities shape memories of historical experiences.

The focus of my interest has evolved over time: through ethnicity I discovered memory, and through exploring the impact of nationalism on identity I became aware of the impact of the Holocaust.[2] Through the present I discovered the past.

I first went to Salonika[3] in 1989 with a group of undergraduate anthropology students from the University of Cologne (results are published in Kokot 1990). In the course of my fieldwork preparation I read, among other things, Albert Cohen's *Solal*, Elias Canetti's *The Tongue Set Free*, and Primo Levi's *The Truce*. I learnt about the history of the Sephardi Jews in Salonika and about multicultural life in the Balkans.[4] I learnt that until 1922/23 the Jews constituted the majority population of Salonika and that during the German occupation almost the entire community[5] (96 per cent of the Jewish population) was deported and killed.

A few days after my arrival I was taken to a dinner where I met a Salonikan Jewish family which was very proud of its family history and of the history of the community. They told me that their family carried 'important names for the Jewish history of the city' and that 'this community had a continuous Jewish life for 2,300 years, which makes it different from all other communities'.

During the weeks that followed I did not find many other expressions of this 'sense of history', so strongly conveyed to me at that dinner (neither in the memory-scape of the city nor in the community). Jewish history was not mentioned in tourist guides or in official history books, there were no monuments recalling anything Jewish. None of the former

Jewish schools, hospitals, or other remaining Jewish buildings in Salonika carried any explanatory plaques. There were no traces of visible Jewish history in the urban landscape of Salonika.

My own initial research, perhaps also in reaction to this 'absence of Jewish history', focused on the contemporary Jewish community, and in particular on young Greek Jews and how they perceive of themselves as members of a minority group in contemporary Salonika. I considered that making a contemporary account would be an important contribution to the scholarly field since most descriptions of the Jewish community ended with the Second World War[6] and finished with one or two sentences about today, such as 'today, Salonika is home to little more than 1,000 Jews' (Messinas 1997).

Another reason for my focus was the difficulty in dealing with the traumatic history of the Holocaust. Although I interviewed older and younger people I hardly used any of my interviews with the older informants in my initial account nor did I write extensively about the Holocaust. One statement I did quote was:

> My daughter thinks the sun is bright in Salonika, she adores the sea and loves coming to Greece. I say, the sun is beautiful and I love the sea, but Greece is a terrible wound in my heart. Greece for me is the death of generations of people. (Lewkowicz 1994: 234)

What I did not quote was the continuation of this statement, where Lili M. says: 'It took me years of hard work … to forget and to be able to feel like a human being.' (Af8). In one of my first interviews with an older man who had survived Auschwitz, he turned to me and said: 'I cannot speak much because this story makes me sick, do you understand?' (Am26).[7]

After Sam P. made this remark I immediately changed the subject. It was not my intention to cause pain or discomfort to the people I spoke to. I did not want to make people remember a time which they had tried to forget. I therefore chose not to concentrate on the Holocaust[8].

The theme of the Holocaust was nevertheless present during my initial research. After meeting me, some people immediately started talking about their Holocaust experience and showed me their tattooed number on their arm. In almost every encounter I was confronted with the question of how I, as a Jew, could live in Germany. When I communicated in German I was aware that some people had learnt this language in the concentration camps. I was also very conscious of the fact that my own presentation of my personal and family history was of the utmost importance in my communication with most community members. Since the history of the community, of the pre-war, war, and post-war periods, did not seem to be a pertinent communal concern, I concentrated on the issue of minority identity in a nation-state.[9] When I returned for my main doctoral fieldwork in 1994 there was a noticeable difference: following the 500th anniversary of the expulsion of the Jews from Spain (*'Sepharad*[10] 1992'), the community had become more interested in its past. This was expressed through public events and a project which began to gather testimonies in the community,[11] and a plan to create a Jewish museum. The 'Society for the Study of Greek Jewry' had organised its first major conference in November 1991.

This change of attitude in the community did not reflect a more general change regarding the Jewish presence in Salonika. As in 1989, the community was still 'invisible'. Jewish history was still absent from the urban Salonikan landscape and from the consciousness of the majority of the city's population. When I told young Christian-Orthodox Greeks that I was doing research on the Jewish community of Salonika they often asked: 'What Jewish Community? Were there ever any Jews in our city?' I should add that sometimes I had the opposite reaction, 'Oh yes there are many, many Jews here, at least 50,000.'

The only public 'Jewish site' at the time was the 'Platia Evreon Martyron' (Jewish Martyrs' Square) which the municipality of Salonika had dedicated to the memory of the Jews in 1986; however, the existence of such a square was not common knowledge among Salonikans. Some months into my 1994 fieldwork I decided it was time to look at the Platia Evreon Martyron, which some community members had mentioned to me. Since the square is located outside the city centre I took a taxi to get there. When I asked the driver to take me to the square, he got very offended when I, being a *xeni* (foreigner), insisted that such a square existed, even after he had assured me that he had never heard of it in all the 30 years he had been driving a taxi through Salonika. After ten minutes of arguing he agreed to let me direct him. When we finally got there we were both proved right. The square did exist but the name-plaque was sprayed over with black paint. The only legible thing on the signpost was *Platia* (see Figure 1).[12]

This episode exemplifies the general approach one needed to adopt in the late 1980s and early 1990s in order to find out about the Jewish presence in contemporary Salonika: one had to know what to look for and where to look for it in order to find the various manifestations of Jewish life. The community centre, the synagogues and the Jewish school could not have been recognised by most non-Jewish Salonikans. Jewish tombstones,[13] which could be found as part of paths, courtyards and walls in various parts of the city (in 1989 they were also clearly visible on the paths of the University), could not be identified by most of the city's inhabitants (see Figures 27, 28, and 29). I could not have found any of the buildings or places on my own, which I was shown when I was taken on a 'Jewish history tour'.

Since some years have passed between the time of my main fieldwork and the writing of this text, we need to be aware that this situation has since changed: a Holocaust monument was erected in 1997,[14] and the Jewish Museum of Thessaloniki[15] opened its doors in May 2001 (see Figures 5 and 6). Furthermore, in the last couple of years a considerable number of Jewish testimonies and autobiographies have been published in Greek (for a good discussion of recent publications see Varon-Vassard 1999).

On my last visit to Salonika in May 1999 I was eager to find out whether these developments have made a noticeable difference. While sitting in front of the Holocaust monument on Nea Egnatia Street, an elderly woman started talking to me. Although she lived locally she did not know what the monument we were looking at was about, nor had the taxi driver who drove me back to my friends heard about this monument. A day later I sat at the hairdresser's reading some magazines. In one of the glossy magazines called *Close Up* I found an article entitled 'Families of Salonika: The Howell Family' (Tentokali 1999: 128) which described in great detail the history of one Jewish family. During the week of my stay another article was published in the daily Salonika newspaper, entitled 'Jakovos Handeli, Auschwitz Survivor', which was an interview with Handeli, a Salonikan Jew who now lives in Israel (*Salonika*: 25 May 1999).

These encounters illustrate that on the one hand an awareness of the Jewish presence in Thessaloniki is still not part of a general urban memory, but on the other hand it has become more common to read and hear about Salonikan Jews through the media and academic publications. While in 1989 the memory of a Jewish past was mostly 'family memory', what Jan Assman (1997) calls 'communicative memory' (references to the past which are communicated within two or three generations in the realm of the family), in 1994 the Jewish past had become a communal memory focus and by 1999 it has become a part, if only a small part, of what Assmann calls the wider Greek 'cultural memory'. It is thus important to bear in mind that memory processes are subject to time and that my analysis is situated in the 'anthropological time' of my main fieldwork, 1994, when Jewish history was clearly not an element of Greek 'cultural memory'.

The aim of this thesis is thus to describe and uncover notions of identity and memory among Jews in Salonika which have been formed in agreement, opposition, confrontation, discussion and competition with other discourses about the past and the history of the Jews in Greece. The narratives of individuals to be described thus form part of other historical narratives, which are 'the means whereby competing stories about the past are organised to give credibility to actions in the present and future' (Herzfeld 1992: 62).

Chapter 1 of this book provides a general overview of my theoretical and methodological framework. Chapter 2 discusses the theoretical concepts and issues pertinent for this study. Chapter 3 deals firstly with the history of Salonika and its Jewish community, with reference to the general history of Greece, and secondly with the topic of Greek nationalism and minorities in contemporary Greece. In Chapter 4 I will describe the Jewish community and its institutions and look at some demographic figures concerning Salonikan Jews, and the following four chapters describe and analyse the narratives of the interviewees. These four chapters cover three broad periods: the pre-war era (Chapter 5), the war time (Chapters 6 and 7), and the post-war era (Chapter 8). In each section I will discuss the events which were of historical significance and the issues which seemed of significance to the interviewees. Each period is clearly characterised by a general theme: for the pre-war period it is the pre-catastrophic 'normality' of family, religious and communal life; for the war period it is the experience of the German occupation and survival (either in the concentration camps, with the partisans, or in hiding in Greece); and for the post-war period it is the reconstruction of private lives and the reconstruction of a decimated community. Chapter 9 deals with the issue of identities and boundaries and looks at constructs of 'self' and 'other' in the narratives of the interviewees.

NOTES

1. Most interviews were gathered during 1994 but I also include interviews from my previous fieldwork in 1989 and from visits to Salonika in 1995 and 1997.
2. The term 'Holocaust' as a name for the Nazi genocide of the Jews was introduced in the late

1950s. The term *Shoah* (the Hebrew word for catastrophe), which is also used to describe the Nazi genocide, can be found in writings of the early 1940s in Palestine (see Young 1988: 84–8).

3. The Greek name of the city is Thessaloniki. As Thessaloniki was known as Selanik in Turkish and Salonique in French, many refer to the city as Salonika or Saloniki.

4. Elias Canetti describes in his autobiographical novel *Die Gerettete Zunge* (*The Tongue Set Free*) the city of Rustschuk, where Sephardi Jews lived alongside Turks, Greeks, Albanians and Armenians. He writes: 'Rustschuk where I was born was a wonderful place for a child. If I said that it was in Bulgaria I would give an insufficient image of the city because people of different origins lived there and one could hear seven or eight languages a day' (transl. Canetti 1989: 8).

5. Whenever I use the words 'community' or 'communal' in the text I refer to the Jewish community of Salonika.

6. I will often refer to 'the war', as will my interviewees. The reader can assume that 'the war' always refers to the Second World War.

7. All interviewees were categorised into three groups: interviewees born before and during the war (group A), interviewees born in the post-war years (group B), and interviewees born after 1956 (group C). This means that the letter A,B, or C refers to the age group of the interviewee, the letter m or f denotes the gender of the interviewee, and the number indicates the number of the interview (1–53).

8. In a different context, I later interviewed people for the 'Survivors of the Shoah Visual History Foundation' (1996–99). In these interviews the situation is very different because the interviewees who came forward had decided beforehand that they wanted to talk about their Holocaust experience.

9. See Lewkowicz 1994.

10. The word *Sepharad* means Spain in Hebrew. The Jews who lived in Spain and Portugal before the expulsion in 1492 are referred to as *Sephardim*.

11. The interviews which were conducted by Erika Kounio-Amariglio and Albertos Nar have subsequently been published (see Kounio-Amariglio and Nar 1998).

12. I had a very similar experience in Athens. I was invited to a wedding which took place in the synagogue of Athens. The aeroplane was delayed and I was in an extreme hurry to get there in time. After I jumped into a taxi I told the driver where I wanted to go, and he started arguing with me. He had never heard of a Jewish synagogue. I told him to drive to Melidoni street. He had never heard of that street either. He made it quite clear that he thought I was a confused foreigner and even when we got there he still looked very doubtful. One thing was clear, this was not a language problem. He simply had not heard of such a thing as a Jewish synagogue before.

13. These are tombstones which were used as building material, following the destruction of the Jewish cemetery by the German Wehrmacht in 1942.

14. The monument was erected as part of the 'European Cultural Capital Programme' in 1997. The artist who created the sculpture was Professor Nandor Glid from Belgrade, whose memorial sculptures are also exhibited at Yad Yashem in Israel, in Dachau and in Budapest.

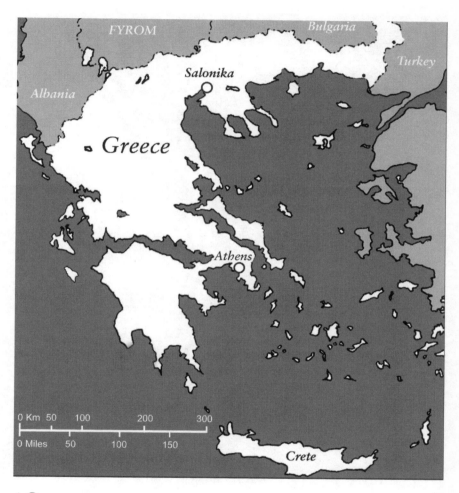

1 Greece

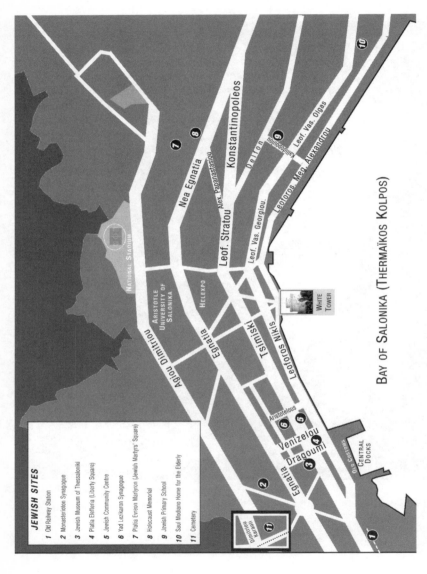

JEWISH SITES

1 Old Railway Station
2 Monasterioton Synagogue
3 Jewish Museum of Thessaloniki
4 Platia Eleftheria (Liberty Square)
5 Jewish Community Centre
6 Yad Lezikaron Synagogue
7 Platia Evreon Martyron (Jewish Martyrs' Square)
8 Holocaust Memorial
9 Jewish Primary School
10 Saul Modiano Home for the Elderly
11 Cemetery

BAY OF SALONIKA (THERMAÏKOS KOLPOS)

2 City of Salonika and Jewish Sites

1

Background

The aim of this chapter is to provide an outline of this book in terms of its theoretical and methodological orientation. The first part of this section will offer some of my fieldwork observations as an introduction to the themes to be discussed throughout this study. The second part will review some of the previous research on the Jewish community of Salonika, and finally I will present the general methodology on which this research is based. Three events which took place soon after my arrival in Salonika in February 1994 take us right into the middle of the dominant themes of this book, namely memory and identity.

The first communal commemorative event I experienced in Salonika was the *Mera Mniminis Tou Olokavtoma Ton 50,000 Evraion Tis Thessalonikis*, the annual Holocaust Memorial Day for the 50,000 Jews of Salonika, which took place on 20 April 1994. The commemoration ceremony consisted of two parts which took place in different locations. The first part was a religious service and ceremony in the main synagogue, the second part consisted of prayers and the laying of wreaths at what was then the only Holocaust monument in the Jewish cemetery. The first part was a public event to which local and national politicians were invited, the second part was mostly attended by community members. The synagogue was decorated in black and white with the words *Aionia H Mimni* (Eternal Memory) displayed in large letters (see Figures 17, 18 and 19a). The core of the ceremony consisted in the lighting of the candles of the menorah (the seven-branch candlestick). The first one was lit by the president of the community and the remaining six were lit by six concentration camp survivors who were asked to come forward by their concentration camp number (see Figure 20). The atmosphere was very sombre and at the end of the ceremony the Greek national anthem was sung. The ceremony in the afternoon was on a much smaller scale. After the rabbi recited prayers for the dead, representatives from the different sections of the community laid down wreaths at the Holocaust memorial[1] inside the cemetery (see Figures 21 and 22). At the end, both the Israeli and Greek anthems were sung. After leaving the cemetery, I noticed an elderly man wearing a kippa (skullcap) on the street. When other people saw this, they immediately ran up to him to tell him that he had forgotten to take off his kippa. It was clearly considered very inappropriate to wear a kippa outside the cemetery or the synagogue.

Several weeks later I attended another community event, the *Makedoniki Vradia* (Macedonian Evening), organised by the Jewish school. I found myself in the hall of the community youth centre. The children wore white T-shirts with a golden star, the star of Vergina,[2] and performed Greek dances and songs (see Figure 10). Next to the stage was a display of traditional Macedonian costumes. Proud parents watched the performance of their children.

The third and biggest event took place on 29 May 1994. The community had organised a special ceremony to honour the Christian Orthodox Greeks who helped Salonikan Jews to survive during the German occupation.[3] The hall at the Aristotle University was filled with about 1,000 people: community members, politicians, and family members of the people who participated in the ceremony. After the president of the community and six Jewish children lit the seven candles in memory of the death of the Salonikan and all other Jews who died in the Holocaust, medals and certificates were handed out to honour the anonymous Greek, the anonymous Salonikan, and specific individuals and families. When it came to the individuals, the 'saved' or their family representative was called up to present the medal to the 'saviour' or their family representative. The ceremony lasted about two hours and closed with the singing of *Eli, Eli*[4] in Hebrew and Ladino[5] as well as the Greek anthem (see Figure 25).

All three events relate to memory of the past and all reveal something about the present identity of the community as well as exemplifying the close connection between memory and identity and between the past and the present. They also represent the different ways of negotiating the 'different histories' of the Jews of Salonika. The annual Holocaust Day commemoration points to the centrality of the experience of the Holocaust, which almost extinguished the entire community. But it also points to private and public aspects of this memory in which official public commemoration (in the synagogue) is juxtaposed with private mourning (in the cemetery for community members). Both memory spaces, the synagogue and the cemetery, clearly indicate the 'Jewishness' of the commemorated past. At the time, no other publicly accessible memory spaces existed in the city of Salonika.

The second event commemorated a more general 'Greek' past. Such an event could have taken place anywhere in Greece in 1994 or 1995, in a city or a village school, on an island or in the province, at a time when Greece wanted to assert the 'Greekness' of its northern province, Macedonia, and contest any other claims to this name by the neighbouring FYROM (Former Yugoslav Republic of Macedonia), often simply referred to as Skopje.[6] This event was widely discussed in the community, with different opinions being voiced. Some people were enthusiastic about it, some felt that it was necessary to have organised such an event ('it had to be done'), some people thought it was not appropriate for a Jewish school to get involved in contemporary politics, and some people remained indifferent. In contrast to the Holocaust Remembrance Day, it was certainly the contemporary Greek identity of the community and the position of the community in overall Greek society which accounted for the organisation of the *Makediniki Vradia*. The event was a clear 'identity statement'. As one of my interviewees put it: 'the loudspeakers were on high volume' (Bf32). It was important for the community to publicly demonstrate its commitment to the 'Greek cause'.

The third event, the award ceremony for the non-Jewish Greek saviours, is interesting because it contains elements of both previous events: it commemorates the experience of the Holocaust but it commemorates it through one specific theme, the theme of Christian heroism and help. Through this looking-glass the commemoration of the Holocaust, for many years restricted to the 'inside' of the community, became a large public event held in a public space. The ceremony thus brought together different themes from different realms of memory, the Jewish communal memory of the death of almost 50,000 Salonikan Jews and the Greek 'official' memory of the Second World War, stressing resistance and heroism.

The three events are significant in understanding two important aspects of the nature of memories and identities and their complex relationship. First, memories and identities are shaped and expressed by different (more and less powerful) agencies such as the state, communal organisations, families and individuals. Second, memories and identities reinforce each other, that is to say there is a two-way relationship. On the one hand, memories of particular experiences shape current identities; on the other hand, current identities shape our memories of particular experiences. As Antze and Lambek put it: 'Memories are produced out of experience and, in turn, reshape it. This implies that memory is intrinsically linked to identity' (Antze and

Lambek 1996: xii). Gillis also points to the close connection between the notions of identity and memory:

> The parallel lives of these two terms alert us to the fact that the notion of identity depends on the idea of memory, and vice versa. The core meaning of any individual or group identity, namely the sense of sameness over time and space, is sustained by remembering; and what is remembered is defined by the assumed identity. (Gillis 1994: 1)

We can thus conceptualise identity and memory a) within a continuous process in which links are forged between the past and the present and b) within a continuous process of negotiation between the different agencies which formulate the very notions of identities and memories. In the latter process individual formulations of 'self', 'other' and the 'past' are formed in dialogue with other social agencies which claim the right to establish authoritative versions of 'who we are and who we think we are'. The transfer between the individual and the collective is mediated through state education, state ceremonies, official commemorations, museums, scholarship, media representations and so forth (Antze and Lambek 1996: xvii). Irwin-Zarecka uses the notion of 'framing' to describe the process of 'memory work' in which 'we all make sense of the past with the help of a whole variety of resources ... This making sense is motivated by our personal experiences but facilitated (or impeded) by public offerings, and that such public offerings are a mixture of presences and absences' (Irwin-Zarecka 1994: 4). She concludes that we need to look at the dialectic process between publicly articulated and privately held views of the past. It follows that expressions of individual and communal identity and memory can a) converge (overlap), b) diverge (contradict), or c) co-exist (in different contexts and situations). This allows us to situate the various expressions of memories and identities in relation to each other.

Looking at the above ceremonies, we saw that the communal 'memory strategy' was characterised by a distinction of 'private' and 'public' memory, by a wish to participate in Greek official state memory, and by a focus on the common historical experience of the German occupation by Christian Greeks and Jewish Greeks. In the above terminology we could speak of memory processes of convergence (between the communal and the state realm) and co-existence (in terms of the 'private' memory of the community). We could also look at the different events and see them as 'representative' of two different processes: one in which the historical particularity of a group's experience is expressed in communal commemoration ceremonies and another, in which the particularity of a group's contemporary identity is expressed in the display of 'shared memories' of the past.

One of the main aims of this work is to analyse how individual Salonikan Jews make sense of their lives and their pasts. Individual Jewish narratives of the past and expressions of identity will be described and situated within the overall memory–identity framework outlined above, and it will be argued that the two aspects which clearly dominated the described communal events shape individual narratives as much as they shape communal memory. These aspects are a) the experience of the Holocaust and b) the wish to converge, or at least not to challenge Greek 'official memory'. The analysis of individual narratives rests mainly on the life histories I have collected during my fieldwork. As the oral historian Paul Thompson (Thompson 1988: 148) and others have pointed out, oral history provides access to the experience of often 'forgotten' or 'silenced' histories and to the nature of memory itself.

The aim of this book is thus two-fold: on the one hand to reconstruct historical experiences, on the other to consider the 'texture of memory'. The first context gives the reader an idea about important events and processes of Salonikan Jewish history. The second context will provide an understanding of 'how people make sense of their past, how they connect individual experience and its social context, how the past becomes part of the present, and how people use it to interpret their lives and the world around them' (Frisch 1990: 188). Having said that, there is a strong emphasis on the 'reconstruction' of history through the voices of the interviewees, as a 'history from below' and a 'counter history'. The lack of academic literature on the history of Salonikan Jews contributed to the need to communicate the interviewees' experiences through a historical framework. Consequently, a more in-depth analysis of aspects of the life histories which did not fit into this framework needs to be the subject of future research. Another theme which needs to be explored elsewhere is the difference between two or three life histories produced by the interviewees over a time-span of years.

PREVIOUS RESEARCH ON THE JEWISH COMMUNITY OF SALONIKA

It is remarkable how little research has been carried out on the Jewish community of Salonika and the Jews of Greece in general.[7] As Steven

Bowman remarks in the *Bulletin of Judeo-Greek Studies*: 'Books specifically on Greek Jews … are rare, perhaps a few dozen in a handful of languages' (Bowman 1995: 24). One should stress that this refers to general research about Greek Jewry.[8] Research about Jewish communities in Greece after 1945 is even harder to come by. There are a few unpublished dissertations (Asser 1983 and Fromm 1992), a number of articles and papers (Elazar 1984, Sitton 1985, Vassiliadis 1997), and Plaut's study of the Jewish communities in the provinces (Plaut 1996). Social and oral history has only very recently been introduced, mainly through the research of Rena Molho on the Jewish community of Salonika at the end of the nineteenth and beginning of the twetieth centuries (Molho 1993a, 1993b, 2001) and through the work of Frangiski Abatzopoulou on survivors' testimonies (Abatzopoulou 1993). The dearth of research in all the relevant disciplines, namely history, sociology and anthropology, goes hand-in-hand with the virtual non-existence of Greek Jewish history in Greek historiography (see Marketos 1994), Greek school books and Greek tourist guides.

One of the reasons why the Holocaust of the Greek Jews remains largely unknown is due to the fact that Holocaust studies tend to focus on the experience of Ashkenazi Jews.[9] Salonika is one of the few Sephardic communities which was severely affected by the Holocaust. On the other hand, studies of Sephardic Jewry often focus on folklore and linguistic issues[10] and thus do not encompass social and political history. It is because of this 'division of labour' (in Jewish Studies) that the story of Salonikan Jews has not been brought to attention.

Since Jews in contemporary Greece are mostly an urban population, the 'rural bias' of Mediterranean anthropology would seem to be one of the most important factors in explaining the lack of anthropological attention. Being more closely related to the 'traditional' field of study of anthropology, it is hence not surprising that the first relevant ethnographies of Greece deal with rural and marginal areas (such as Friedl 1962 and Campbell 1964). Since these ethnographies emerged a shift has taken place, and today there are a number of studies which were conducted in cities (Hirschon 1998, Faubion 1993, Kokot 1995) which attempt to link the local village level to the wider Greek context (see especially Herzfeld 1991, 1992). However, urban minorities such as Armenians and Jews have so far not attracted much attention.

It is very interesting that, for totally different reasons, urban minorities and their histories have not entered Greek historiography, neither on the national nor on the local level. This is also true for literary (see Abatzopoulou 1997) and other forms of representation (see introduction). As Rena Molho puts it:

> Today, at the university in Salonika, there is not a department, not a course, nothing about the Jews – or about the Turks or other communities either. There is nothing in the historical institutes. Nothing in the city's museums. Hardly a book in the Greek bookstores. Nothing. As if we were never here. (Molho quoted in Kaplan 1994: 237)

The omission of Jews in the public memory of Salonika has to be seen in the wider context of historical discourse adopted in Greece which stresses historical continuity and ethnic purity, that is, 'single ethnicity'. An article which appeared in the newspaper *Elefterotipia* summarises a study which analysed Greek schoolbooks and interviewed teachers. The results were summarised as follows:

> In the narration of the historical course Hellenism ... any indications of the existence of different groups within the national group are suppressed and passed over in silence, as are all concrete acts of suppression of difference and diversity. (quoted in Varouxakis 1995: 14)

Mark Mazower suggests that the historiographical silence concerning the Jews of Salonika and the only very recent publications of survivors' testimonies cannot exclusively be explained by Greece's national identity and official memory but also by the development of the discipline of history in Greece after the war. Modern history developed very slowly in post-Civil War Greece, and the discipline as a whole remained rather conservative, concentrating on political and diplomatic rather than on social history (see Mazower 1995: 42). Consequently, Greek historians have not written a great deal about Jewish social history but neither have they written much about the Civil War. Mazower also notes that a change has taken place in recent years and that a wave of interest in Greek Jewry has swept the Greek public, manifested in the publication of books (for example Megas 1993), journals, and newspaper articles, which can be attributed to a general feeling of nostalgia for 'a lost world', 'the world destroyed by the nation-state' (Mazower 1995: 40).[11]

Having established that the history of Greek Jewry, that is, Salonikan Jewry, has been – for the different reasons mentioned above – largely ignored, this work will, it is hoped, contribute to a number of recent anthropological studies which have focused on 'alternative histories' in Greece, such as Hirschon's work on Asia Minor refugees in Piraeus (1998), Kokot's study of a refugee quarter in Salonika (1995), and Voutira's work on the Russo-Pontic migration (1991). All these studies have illustrated how people perceive of themselves and their social world in negotiation with notions of the past and identity put forward by a powerful nation-state, which ignores or neglects the 'social experience' of a specific group. The link between the theme of Jewish ethnicity and other anthropological studies of Greece is relevant and therefore will be made more explicit in the next chapter.

RESEARCH CRITERIA

Salonika, like other cities in the Mediterranean and Middle East, has undergone tremendous changes in the twentieth century. The demographic, political, and architectural landscape has altered radically. In the context of this work the most relevant changes concern the ethnic and religious composition of Salonika's population, its incorporation into a nation-state (1912), the subsequent introduction of nationalism (for example, through centralised state education and the introduction of national celebrations), and the annihilation of almost 50,000 Salonikan Jews during the Second World War.

The most important themes of my thesis, memory and identity, are clearly linked to these historical changes. The questions I set out to answer were:

a) how are these historical changes and 'events' represented in individual narratives of Jews in Salonika and in the realm of the communal memory;
b) how have these historical changes affected formulations of Jewish identity and memory; and
c) how does Jewish memory fit into the general 'memory-scape' of the contemporary Greek context?

One of the aims of this work is to illustrate how the Jews of Salonika express their identity and memory in contemporary Greece. We need to bear in mind that identity and memory formulations are an outcome of an interactive process of constant negotiation between various levels of society, and that we are dealing with different representations of identity in different domains which influence each other.

As seen above, memory cannot be analysed without looking at identity, which requires the clarification of certain assumptions concerning the nature of minority identity:

1) The overall political system and the majority culture shape minority identity. That is not to say that minorities, that is, members of minorities, do not have choices, but that the choices they make on a collective and individual level need to be explained in terms of the dominant political system and the majority culture.

2) The Greek state and Greek nationalism, which fits all the characteristics of an 'ethnic nationalism', provide the framework in which members of a minority experience and construct their particular identity.

3) Remembering the past is a crucial element of every nationalism and 'official memory' therefore plays an important role in the construction of identity (both of the majority and the minority populations).

4) The expressions of minority identity and memory – in cases of conflicting memory and conflicting ideas of identity between the 'dominant' and the 'subordinate' groups – can be understood as a strategy, or rather strategies, to accommodate contradictory discourses, both on a communal and individual level. These strategies reveal present individual and collective self-images.

5) Minority identity, seen as an adaptive strategy – adopted by groups and individuals – in a 'monocultural' nation-state, is expressed differently in the 'private' and the 'public' realm.

6) Private and public ethnicities seem to be of particular importance in societies which have developed very elaborate notions of the private and public realms. I would like to suggest that the formulation of public and private ethnicities is linked to a broader cognitive system through which people perceive themselves and others. If notions of 'us' and 'them' operate on many different levels of identity formation, religious and/or ethnic identities can become another form of private identities. However, this does not happen in cases of politicised minorities.

7) The notion of private ethnicity in the context of the Jewish community of Salonika needs also to be looked at in the context of the impact of the war. Although the survivors had returned to 'their city' they had become 'internal refugees' because their 'home' no longer existed because friends and families were absent and because

most references to the Jewish past had disappeared in the post-war landscape of the city. The war had thus transformed a heterogeneous and settled population group (who had developed a very strong notion of their Salonikan identity) into a homogeneous, vulnerable and uprooted minority group. In light of this experience, a 'low public profile' and the notion of private ethnicity need to be seen as individual and communal post-war strategies to cope with a situation of extreme loss and vulnerability.

METHODOLOGY

The general methodology applied in order to answer the questions raised consisted of ethnographic fieldwork and in-depth interviewing.

Fieldwork

As a method or a way to study people and cultures, fieldwork has been defined in different ways. The 'fieldwork pioneer' Bronislav Malinowski postulated that the aim of fieldwork is 'to grasp the native's point of view, his relation to life, to realise his vision of the world' (Malinowski 1961: 25). In a standard anthropology textbook 'fieldwork' is conceived as the 'intimate participation in a community and observation of modes of behaviour and the organisation of social life. The process of recording and interpreting another people's way of life is called ethnography' (Keesing 1981: 5).

The fieldwork method has also found its way into other disciplines. Judd, Smith and Kidder (1991: 299), for example, equate 'fieldwork' with 'participant observation' and distinguish it from other forms of qualitative research (such as open-ended questions embedded in a structured interview or questionnaire). Fieldwork is considered to be an

> open-ended exploration of people's words, thoughts, actions, and intentions. Fieldworkers enter the world of the people they study instead of bringing those people to a laboratory or asking them to answer a structured interview or questionnaire ... Some fieldworkers are intensely immersed as participants in the lives of the people they are studying: others remain more nearly observers. (Judd, Smith and Kidder: 299)

The last sentence of this quotation is very important. The difference between the fieldwork method and other methods is the crucial role of the researcher in the fieldwork process and in the collection of data, a role which is partly consciously chosen but partly ascribed to the researcher through the context of the research. While early anthropology often excluded personal accounts from its academic writing, today reflections of the researcher's position, role and status in the field form a normal part of ethnographic writing (see Marcus and Fisher 1986, Rosaldo 1986, Golde 1970).[12] Today's ethnography acknowledges that we 'do fieldwork by establishing relationships, and by learning to see, think, and be in another culture, and we do this as persons of particular age, sexual orientation, belief, educational background, ethnic identity, and class' (Bell *et al.* 1993: 1).

In contrast to non-ethnographic research, the ethnographic endeavour is not tightly restricted to specific locations, and boundaries (social, personal and professional) are not well defined. In fact, it is inherent to the concept of fieldwork that boundaries are commonly crossed.[13] This process is problematic because it blurs the private and the professional sphere. Informants might not consider that informal discussions are written down in fieldnotes and might eventually appear in a thesis or a book, and they might disapprove of 'private' matters being brought to the 'public'.[14]

The fieldwork method constitutes one of the best ways to examine people's ideas, values, and perceptions because fieldwork provides a context for the analysis of 'what people say about themselves', in the case of this book the context for the interviews conducted, and a context which creates personal relationships (and, it is hoped, trust) between the researcher and their informants.

Although the focus of this work lies in the presentation and analysis of interviews, for reasons which will be explored below, it needs to be understood that the interviews were an integral part of the fieldwork. Most of the interviewees were people I met in the community and continued to meet (either at communal events or in private) after the 'formal' interview. 'Making sense' of the interviews and of communal identity and memory is very much shaped by fieldwork observations, therefore a few words about the general fieldwork and about my role in 'the field' are needed here.

During my first fieldwork visit in the summer of 1989 I met mostly younger Salonikan Jews, partly because it was summer and the main collective activity of the community was the summer youth camp (*Kataskinosi*), and because my main contact was the Israeli teacher of the community whose main social group (*parea*) consisted of younger people. When I decided to go back to Thessaloniki in 1994, I contacted one of the persons I met in 1989 and had remained loosely in touch with. The help and support I subsequently received made my landing in Salonika much softer and facilitated personal access to the community. 'Being adopted' by one family who were very involved in the life of the community provided me with many insights and, equally important, with the emotional support of a 'home'.

The three biographical aspects of my life which seemed relevant for the definition to my role in the field are a) that I am Jewish; b) that I had grown up in Germany as a child of parents who are Holocaust survivors; and c) that I was an unmarried young girl/woman (*Kallo Kouritsi*).[15] The fact that I came from Germany aroused considerable suspicion and unease among some community members, especially during my first visit in 1989.[16] This seemed less of an issue on my second visit in 1994, partly because I had come from London to Salonika, because people got to know me personally, and also because it was my Jewish identity which was considered most important. My Jewish identity, reinforced by my speaking Hebrew and a knowledge of Jewish customs and religion, gave me the status of an 'outside insider'. It made it easier to participate in synagogue services and communal events and 'explained' my interest. Within a framework of clear public and private boundaries it was important that I was considered *diki mas* (which translates as 'one of us').[17] This was also true for the interview context. Here, it was probably equally important that I was not Greek and one could therefore discuss more freely 'sensitive' matters of Greek–Jewish relations and Jewish identity.

In the non-Jewish environment the perception of me as a Jew made me often feel uneasy. I sometimes had to deal with comments about the wealth, power and stinginess of the Jews. On one occasion, I was sitting in the office of the acting rabbi. As he was busy, I started talking to a Christian friend of his, who was also in the office. In the casual chat which followed this young man told me that he thought the Jews are very good businessmen because they are so stingy. Apparently, he did not find it strange to say something like this in the office of the rabbi. This kind of discourse seemed very normal to a lot of people.[18] On other occasions people insinuated that I was biased in my research. In one instance, I was told when discussing a particular issue 'you should ask your people'. Other people insinuated that my real *patrida* (fatherland) must be Israel. These kinds of comments made me cautious and I consequently adopted a 'low public Jewish profile'.

It is difficult to judge to what extent my gender and age influenced my research. At the time, I felt that my age enabled me to relate both to people my age and the older generation and my gender made contact with other women easier. The exchange with other women, as friends and interviewees, was more open and intimate than my exchanges with men, and can partly be explained in terms of the sensitivity of gender relations between persons of different sex unrelated by kinship, in the Mediterranean and in a small Jewish community.

Fieldwork activities consisted in attending most social communal events and religious services, regular visits to the Jewish school and the Jewish Home for the Elderly, visits to the summer youth camp (*Kataskinosi*) and ENE seminars (*Evraiki Neas Elladas*, Jewish Youth of Greece), the collection of statistical data from the community archive, and the conducting of interviews.

The Interviews and the Profile of the Interviewees

The interviews conducted in Salonika can either be classified as 'life histories' – defined as a 'retrospective account by the individual of his or her life in whole or part, in written or in oral form, that has been elicited or prompted by another person' (Watson and Watson-Franke 1985: 2) or as semistructured life world interviews, 'whose purpose is to obtain descriptions of the life-world of the interviewee with respect to interpreting the meaning of the described phenomena' (Kvale 1996: 5). This kind of interview can also be conceptualised as a conversation which has a structure and purpose (Kvale 1996: 6).

Fifty-three interviews were conducted with Salonikan Jews of different generations who were divided into three groups: 30 interviews with people who were born before and during the war (group A), eight interviews with people born in the post-war years (group B), and 15 interviews with people born after 1956 (group C).[19] The interviews which receive most attention in this volume are the 30 life histories of group A, who at the time of interviewing were aged between 51 and 91.

With the exception of two persons, I initially met all the interviewees in the community context, either in the synagogue, the community club, or in the Home for the Elderly. While I approached people whom I met in the synagogue or in the community myself, in the Home for the Elderly I was introduced to the interviewees by the director of the home, because only she knew who was willing and able to talk to me.

The interviews varied considerably in form and content. The interviews with the younger generations were more theme-oriented than the interviews with the older generation. The general aim was to ask open questions to enable the interviewee to offer their own 'analytical framework'. I would therefore often start an interview by saying something very general, such as 'Could you please tell me something about yourself and your family?' or 'Could we talk about Salonika before the war?'. In some instances it was necessary to conduct more directive interviews and ask more specific questions. The 'narrative quality' varies greatly from interview to interview. Some people had a very clear idea of 'their story' and others felt more comfortable answering concrete questions. In some interviews there was a dominant theme to which the interviewee returned, in others the interviewee did not seem to 'have an agenda'. When I had the impression that someone was uncomfortable or did not want to discuss a specific topic I did not pursue it. This is methodologically important because it sometimes required a shift in the focus of the interview if the memories evoked were too painful. It was necessary to be sensitive to this issue as some people had not wanted to be interviewed because they did not see themselves as fit enough to talk about their war-time experiences.[20]

The task of the interviewer in this process is quite difficult because the interviewees often send out contradictory messages. The first thing, for example, Lili M. (Af8) told me after I asked a very open question about her memories of the Jewish community of Salonika was: 'Don't ask me that. Don't make me go back. I can't.' However, she then proceeded to give me a very detailed account of her whole life in which she talked openly about the pre-war period, her experiences during the war and her return to Salonika. Depending on my reactions to her initial remark the interview could have taken a different direction. However, we should also bear in mind that the questions of the interviewer are of less relevance in what Niethammer calls, '*Erinnerungsinterviews*' (memory interviews), in which the narrator remembers quite independently from the interviewer (Niethammer 1995: 34).

The length of the interviews also varied greatly. They ranged from a 20-minute interview to a six-hour interview, conducted on several occasions. Some interviewees I met only once, some I met numerous times. I also incorporated interviews from my first fieldwork visit in 1989 and from visits after 1994. I conducted three interviews with people in 1989 who had died by 1994 and three interviews with people whom I re-interviewed in 1994 and thereafter. As a result, there are six people whom I interviewed several times in the course of the ten years since first starting my research; they constitute my 'main informants'.

The 30 interviewees of group A come from different educational, professional, and family backgrounds. This is not intended as a 'representative' sample of Salonikan Jews from that age group (since this was not the criterion by which they were chosen) although they probably do represent most of the different pre- and post-war experiences. Two aspects 'biased' the interviewee selection: language and community involvement. I was not likely to meet somebody who did not live in the Home for the Elderly and had nothing to do with the community and I could not have interviewed somebody who only spoke Greek and Ladino. Although I learnt basic Greek during my stay I did not feel confident enough to interview exclusively in Greek. The interviews were conducted in either French, English, Hebrew or German. German was used when it was either the informant's mother tongue or second language, English and Hebrew constituted the language learnt in the country of post-war emigration (four interviewees had emigrated to Israel, four to the United States), while French was widely learnt and spoken by the older generation in school (especially in the Alliance schools and the French Lycée). Since the French language and French culture played a more significant role, and was spoken more fluently among the Salonikan middle and upper classes, the interview sample might have a slight class and urban bias because French was not at all or not as fluently spoken among the working classes and in places outside Salonika.

Among the 30 interviewees 12 were women and 18 men. The age divisions are as follows: seven were born under Ottoman rule between 1902 and 1911; eight between 1912 and 1920; nine between 1921 and 1930; three between 1931 and 1935; and two between 1941 and 1944. Twenty interviewees were born in Salonika, two in Athens, two in Larissa, one in Kavalla, one in Karditsa, one in Cairo, one in Germany, one in another part of the Ottoman Empire, and one in the Austro-Hungarian Empire. Among the ones not born in Salonika, three came there as children in the inter-war period, two came as adults in the 1920s, three as children in the post-war period, and two came as adults in the 1960s.

THE POST-FIELDWORK PROCESS

Analysis

Between the fieldwork and post-fieldwork process a shift of emphasis occurred: in the first phase interviewing was an integral part of my ethnographic research but in the second phase the interviews themselves moved to the centre of my focus. My engagement with the interviews through months of listening, deciphering and transcribing produced a thesis not envisaged at the time of the fieldwork.

My reading of the interviews as texts started to focus on the historical experiences of the interviewees. In the light of the strong presence of the themes of the German occupation and the Holocaust in the interviews, either through articulations or silences, it seemed to make sense to focus on history and memory, although this meant sacrificing many other issues in the context of this thesis, especially the ones which deal with the younger generation, whom I had already discussed in earlier work (Lewkowicz 1990, 1994). This shift was an outcome of the complex process of conducting oral histories during the fieldwork and analysing them during the process of transcribing and writing up. Skultans suggests that her project was 'hijacked by the narrators' and oriented in a direction which overrode her research plans (Skultans 1998: 13). The shift of emphasis during my post-fieldwork can also be described by the notion of 'hijacking', a 'hijacking' which involved both the narratives and my reading of the narratives. Reading the transcripts led to the development of a strong sense of responsibility towards the narratives of the interviewees. Being aware of the fact that life histories are 'doubly edited' (Skultans 1998: 1), first through the encounter in the interview and then through the (re)encounter with the transcribed text, I felt a sense of obligation to present the stories of my interviewees within the historical framework.

Skultans problematises her relationship to the narratives she collected in the field. She quotes Vincent Crapanzano who wrote: 'The life history is often a memorial to an informant-become-(distant)-friend, a commemoration of a field experience, and an expiation for abstraction and depersonalisation – for ruthless departure' (Crapanzano in Skultans 1998: 14).

The distance from the interviewees which emerged in the post-fieldwork process clearly changed my role as a researcher. Being involved in the community and in the lives of people turned into being involved predominantly with their narrative texts. Through this distance my role as 'witness' (of memory of the past) emerged, a role which I had not acknowledged during my fieldwork.[21] Through recording and listening to the life histories I became, in Dori Laub's terms, 'party to the creation of knowledge de novo' (Laub 1995: 57) and the interviews became 'testimonies' (see Chapter 4). Using a historical framework as an analytical framework seemed to be less 'tampering' with the 'texts' than other anthropological forms of analysis. As a consequence, much more space is given to the narrations of the interviewees than to ethnographic observations. This shift needs to be seen as an outcome of the confrontation with the textual interviews and the development of the interpretative framework.[22]

If we follow Crapanzano's notion of 'life histories as memorials', then every writer will – in the process of writing – decide (consciously or unconsciously) what kind of 'memorial' they want to produce, as has the person who narrated their life. In this way, this book becomes also a 'narrative memorial' which reflects an engagement with people who recounted their lives and my engagement with the interviews as texts which have been put into a theoretical and historical framework.

CONCLUSION

In outlining the theoretical, methodological and ethnographic content of this study the shifts which occurred at specific stages of the research have been examined. Individual, communal and national memory processes are my main concern. The focus in this analysis is the use of the past in the present. The aim of this work is not to establish an authoritative version of 'what really happened' but to describe the interviewees' experiences of historical processes and events.

NOTES

1. This memorial was erected in 1962 (Nar 1997: 293). It is a structure which consists of a marble base and a marble top in the form of a menorah (seven-branched candlestick). Psalm 7: 6 is inscribed in Hebrew beneath the menorah: 'The generations to come might know them, even the children that should be born, who should arise and declare them to their children.'
2. This sun-like star was found in the excavations of Pella and Vergina in the tombstone of Philip II. At the time of my fieldwork the star was widely used as a symbol of the 'Greekness' of Macedonia (in jewellery, as car stickers and posters, in company logos and so on).
3. This event was called *'Timitikes Diakrisis Stous Sotires Kai Efergetes Ton Evriaon Tis Thessalonikis'* (Honorary Award of the Saviours and the Benefactors of the Jews of Salonika).
4. The main text of this prayer (Psalm 22: 2, Hebrew version) reads: *Eli, Eli lama asawtani* (My Lord, My Lord, why did you forsake me?).
5. Ladino or Judeo-Spanish is the written and spoken language of Jews of Spanish origin. Some scholars insist that the term Ladino should only refer to the 'sacred' language of Bible translations and prayers. I follow the usage of my interviewees who do not seem to differentiate between Ladino and Judeo-Spanish (sometimes also referred to as Spaniolit or Spanish).
6. As the Greek state insisted that the name Macedonia and the symbol of the star of Vergina are Greek and hence 'stolen' by FYROM, one could see signs throughout the city saying 'Macedonia has been Greek for 3,000 years' or 'Macedonia is Greek'. When I arrived for my second fieldwork trip in 1994 the airport of Salonika had been renamed 'Macedonia Airport'.
7. This was certainly true at the time. For a good discussion of recent publications, which have drastically increased over recent years, see Varon-Vassard 1999.
8. The most substantial books on the history of the Jews of Thessaloniki, the *Histoire des Israélites de Salonique* by Joseph Nehama and *In Memoriam* by Michael Molho, were written before and shortly after the war (and were re-published by the Jewish community in 1978).

9. The term 'Ashkenazi' refers to the descendants of Jews who settled in Germany (and later migrated to many other countries).
10. This becomes apparent when looking at the programmes of conferences, such as the programme of the Conference 'Hispano-Jewish Civilisation after 1492', organised by the Misgav Yerushalaim in 1992.
11. In 1998 the Greek Foreign Ministry published a volume entitled *Documents on the History of the Greek Jews*. There is not space to discuss this volume in detail, but it does need to be pointed out that the selection of documents seems to be biased towards presenting a 'positive' view of Greek–Jewish relations. The back cover of the book reads: 'Documents on the History of the Greek Jews ... represents the intertwined history of the two peoples which began in the era of Alexander the Great, was resumed after the mass arrivals of the Sephardic Jews from Spain in the Balkan peninsula and tragically interrupted by the Holocaust. It was on this dramatic occasion that the Greek people, laity and clergy, and the Greek governments of the day demonstrated their determination to take risks and make sacrifices for their fellow citizens of Jewish faith.' (*Documents on the History of the Greek Jews* 1998, edited by P. Constantopoulou and T. Veremis).
12. This new trend in ethnography is called 'reflexive' or 'post-modern' anthropology. In acknowledging the role of subjectivity in the fieldwork, the sexual identity and sexual conduct of the fieldworker can also become the focus of academic scrutiny. See Kulick and Willson (1995) *Taboo. Sex, Identity and Erotic Subjectivity in Anthropological Fieldwork*.
13. Davis claims 'that anthropology is an intrusive endeavour' and illustrates how difficult it was for her to deal with the negative response to her research by the village community (see Davis 1993).
14. Herzfeld talks in this context about the danger of informants being offended because 'the ethnographer had foregrounded what the people studied wish to maintain in the background' (quoted in Brettell 1993: 14).
15. People often use the phrase '*kallo kourizi*' in a complimentary manner (meaning you are a 'good girl').
16. One person told me for example that his uncle had advised him not to meet me since I was German. But his aunt had said that he should meet me because I was Jewish. It becomes clear from reading my early fieldnotes that I had to struggle with the issue of my German–Jewish identity in the field.
17. The case of a Dutch researcher illustrates how lucky I was to have had access to the community. During my fieldwork I met a Dutch woman who was interested in Ladino. Since she was not introduced by anyone, the community was very reluctant to inform her about communal activities. She also had problems persuading people to be interviewed.
18. The discourse about the stinginess of Jews is not restricted to the private sphere as the following episode, which was told to me by a friend, shows. In a court case which dealt with an employment issue, one witness accused the employers of being 'stingy Jews'. The lawyer of the employers replied that this could not be pertinent because only one of the employers was Jewish.
19. I also conducted 12 interviews with other people who are more difficult to categorise (group D). They were Athenian Jews, Jewish and non-Jewish educators, Armenian and other Salonikans.
20. In one case a man continued to change the date of the planned interview. Finally he told me that he was not feeling well and that he therefore could not talk about his experiences in the *Lager* (concentration camp). He had assumed that I was only interested in this topic. As it became clear to me that the possibility of being interviewed was very stressful for this man, I of course did not ask him again for an interview.
21. I did see myself though as a witness to the present of the Jewish community. This was clearly expressed with the photographic lens through which I tried to capture and document Jewish 'sites', social and religious communal events, and the lives of individual people.
22. Hirsch coined the term 'post-memory' (Hirsch 1999: 8). This concept refers to the powerful relationship of children of survivors of cultural or collective traumas to the experiences of their parents. It might also have to do with my post-memory that I first chose not to concentrate on the Holocaust and later developed a strong sense of 'responsibility' towards the Holocaust accounts of the survivors.

2

Theoretical Framework

This chapter will outline the most relevant theoretical terms of reference for this study. The intention is not to give an exhaustive account of the theoretical debates on 'culture', 'ethnicity', 'nationalism' and 'memory' but to discuss the contexts which form the framework of this thesis. The first part of the chapter deals with the analytical 'frames' (see Irwin-Zarecka 1994) which have informed my thinking about the issues concerned, and the second part discusses the themes which emerged from my reading of the 'anthropology of Greece'.

CULTURE, ETHNICITY AND IDENTITY

This study is concerned with memory and identity. As discussed above, these are contextualised within a continuous process in which identities are produced and sustained by memories, and memories are shaped and 'edited' by present identities.

Both memory and identity are constituent parts of a culture, and through culture they are expressed and mediated. In her research on Latvian life-histories Skultans set out to describe 'the cultural resources used to make sense of the past and incorporate it into a personal history' (Skultans 1998: 27). She points out that 'narrative experience necessarily draws upon shared cultural values and representations' but at the same time it 'retains a historical value as a window to the past' (Skultans 1998: 28).

Antze defines culture as 'memorial practice' and argues that 'our memory of the past is always culturally mediated' (Antze and Lambek 1996: 147). In the more recent anthropological literature the focus shifted from 'culture' to 'ethnicity' and 'ethnic group' and we thus need to look briefly at the history and definitions of these analytical concepts.

The term 'culture' has played a central role in the development of social anthropology, a discipline which made 'the understanding of the cultural other' (Jenkins 1999: 85) its primary focus. Kroeber and Kluckhohn (1952) listed nearly 300 definitions of the term 'culture'.

One of the classical, very general definitions of culture is that of Tylor (1871): 'Culture or civilisation, taken in the wide ethnographic sense, is that complex whole which includes knowledge, belief, art, morals, law, custom, and any other capabilities and habits acquired by man as a member of society.'

Some anthropologists use definitions of culture which focus more on cognitive aspects, that is to say on meaning rather than on behaviour. Fox, for example, suggests understanding culture as 'a set of understandings and a consciousness under active construction by which individuals interpret the world around them' (Fox 1990: 10). Eriksen includes behaviour in his definition of culture. For him culture refers to 'those abilities, notions and forms of behaviour persons have acquired as members of society' (Eriksen 1995: 9). The social agents in these definitions are 'individuals' or 'persons' who engage in a 'system of shared meaning'. These conceptualisations of culture point us a) to the complex interplay between the social and the individual spheres, between the 'complex whole' and 'persons'; b) to an understanding of culture which can refer both to 'practice', that is, behaviour, and cognition, that is, knowledge; and c) to an understanding of culture which emphasises 'sharedness'. Recent debates about culture have emphasised heterogeneity and diversity (see Govers and Vermeulen 1994: 5). As Rudolph points out: 'not every member of a culture group possesses the knowledge of all the details of this culture ... not everybody has to agree with everything. Finally, not everything needs to be conscious on the individual level' (transl. Rudolph 1988: 43). If culture is not homogenous, neither is 'ethnicity': 'People differ in the way they imagine the ethnic community. The ethnic group is an aggregate of selves, each of whom produces ethnicity for itself' (Govers and Vermeulen 1994: 5).

Let us take a closer look at the notion of 'ethnicity'. Since Glazer and Moynihan published their book *Ethnicity* in 1975 stating that 'ethnicity seems to be a new term' (Glazer and Moynihan 1975: 1), the words 'ethnicity', 'ethnic group',[1] and 'ethnic conflict' have become common terms in the English language and a major concern for the Social Sciences (see Eriksen 1993: 2). In particular in Social Anthropology the study of ethnicity and ethnic groups has attracted much attention. This had to do a) with the growing importance of ethnic conflicts, the break-up of poly-ethnic empires and states and the rise of nationalist movements all over the world; and b) the shift from 'tribe' to 'ethnic group', in which groups are seen in interaction with other groups and not as fixed entities.

Similar to the notion of culture, many scholars have tried to define and re-define the concept of 'ethnicity' (see Williams 1989). Different theoretical orientations shape different understandings of these concepts. As with the concept of culture, 'ethnicity' can refer to practice and cognition. Ethnicity has been seen as a 'rational choice' (Bell 1975), an 'emic category'[2] of ascription (Moerman 1965), a 'subjective sense of belonging' (De Vos and Romanucci-Ross 1975), and has been analysed in the context of race relations (Rex and Mason 1986), the economic opportunity scheme (Hannerz 1989), the expression of group boundaries (Barth 1969), interests groups (Cohen 1969), and the socio-psychological needs of individuals (Epstein 1978). These approaches vary to the extent in which they view ethnicity as a 'natural given', a primordial phenomenon, or as a more situational phenomenon which should be studied in respect of its instrumental function. Another way of classifying the various approaches to ethnicity is to differentiate between the levels of analysis. Marxist and 'conflict-oriented' approaches of ethnicity focus on the grand structure of society, the 'boundary' and 'interest' approaches focus on the interaction between groups, while the socio-psychological approaches focus on the individual.

In the context of this study we will follow Macdonald's broad definition of ethnicity; she views ethnicity as a specific form of social identity, understood as an 'allegiance to people, group and often place, and past' (Macdonald 1993: 6). Since ethnicity emerges in different social contexts (urban ethnic minorities, indigenous people, minorities in nation-states, groups in 'plural societies'[3] and so forth) it does not seem necessary to reduce the function and practice of ethnicity to one specific sphere, nor does it seem necessary to conceive of ethnicity as either malleable or fixed. We can thus conceive of both malleable and more fixed ethnic identities. Verdery makes this point very clearly:

> Identities will be less flexible wherever the process of modern nation-state formation has the greatest longevity and has proceeded the furthest; wherever long-standing nationalist movements have effectively inculcated the sentiment of a single kind of belonging. (Verdery 1994: 37)

It follows that one can study 'the ways and circumstances in which people define themselves and are defined by others' (the process of ascription and prescription) and 'the ways in which identities are defined and experienced by various people' (Macdonald 1993: 6), without neglecting structural factors which are crucial for identity formation.

Verdery introduced in the above quotation the state as the crucial factor regarding the fluidity of identities. It is an important conceptual point to bear in mind that individuals give meaning to their various identities within a specific society with specific structures. The state is an important variable in this structure because it assigns and defines national, ethnic, religious and other social identities.[4] It follows that ethnic identities play different roles in different societies. In societies in which ethnic divisions and cleavages are incorporated in the political and legal system, the overall importance of ethnic identity is very different from its importance in societies in which ethnic categories or collective group membership does not appear in the political and legal realm.

NATIONALISM, MINORITIES AND THE STATE

As in the debate about ethnicity there are many different approaches which tackle the phenomenon of nationalism. Smith classifies these approaches as 'perennialist', 'modernist' and 'post-modernist' (see Smith 1995: 18) and states that the role of the past in the creation of the present is one of the areas which has created the sharpest differences among nationalism scholars. While perennialists stress the immemorial nature of the past, modernists focus on nationalism as a modern phenomenon which emerged along with capitalism, and post-modernists stress the imagined character of the nation. Respectively, perennialists relate national identity and nationalism to pre-ethnic identities, while modernists and post-modernists do not make this connection and stress the 'invented' (Hobsbawm and Ranger 1983) and 'imagined' (Anderson 1991) nature of the nation and the nation's past.

The Greek nationalist movement, the emergence of the Greek state, and the role of the past in the Greek nationalist discourse would certainly make an interesting case study to illuminate some of the above issues (see Blinkhorn and Veremis 1990). This, however, is not the major concern of this thesis. What is relevant to this study, and this brings us back to Verdery's argument, is the nature of the contemporary Greek state and of Greek nationalism as the general framework, or rather context, in which members of a minority experience and construct their particular identity. Verdery not only stresses that nation-states have a great impact on the fluidity of identities but she also underlines that 'identity choice varies with different kind of states' (Verdery 1994: 39).

This is a very crucial argument in terms of this work. It is not only the kind of state with its political and legal structure which influences identities and group boundaries but also the kind of nationalism which has been adopted by the same state which determines the range and importance of minority identities, that is, the distinction between 'ethnic' and 'civil' nationalism, which goes back to Meinecke's distinction between '*Kulturnation*' and '*Staatsnation*' (1969: 17).[5] The '*Kulturnation*' and its ethnic nationalism stresses the common origins, the common heritage and the common culture of its members, while the '*Staatsnation*' and its civic nationalism stresses the territorial and political aspects of nationhood. Although one should bear in mind that every nationalism contains civic and ethnic elements in varying degrees and varying forms (Smith 1991: 13), we can classify Greek nationalism as an ethnic nationalism, in which ideas of common origin, common culture and historical continuity have been asserted by nationalist historiography and nationalist ideology (Kitromilides 1990: 33). Moreover, the Orthodox Church is now closely associated with 'Greekness' and the idea of a homogenous *ethnos* (see Just 1989: 85). Greekness is defined by the Christian Orthodox religion, by language and common history. Here, we can go further and introduce another term which is useful in the Greek context, that of 'monocultural nationalism'. 'Monocultural nationalism' underlines the stress on one culture (and on one historical discourse) and the implicit denial of multiculturalism (and multicultural history). It is the wider Greek context in which Jewish identity and memory is formulated and, in Verdery's terms, which shapes the identity choices of a community and of individuals.

Bearing in mind that the nature of the state and the nature of the specific nationalism are pertinent to identity formation, the city of Salonika is a very interesting case study because over the last 90 years it has belonged to two very different 'states', the Ottoman Empire and the Greek nation-state. In the process of Greek nation-building Salonika has been ascribed particular importance as the capital of Greece's most contested region, Greek Macedonia. Since its incorporation into the Greek state in 1912 Thessaloniki's population changed dramatically, first after the arrival of about 100,000 Asia Minor refugees in the 1920s and second after the deportation of almost the entire Jewish community in 1943. In the attempt to build a Greek Macedonian identity, Salonika has been projected as a Byzantine Greek city whose multicultural past has been forgotten (Mackridge and Yannakakis 1997: 15). This of course affected the Jewish population. At the outbreak of the First World War Jews, like Greeks, were a distinct ethno-religious group within the political structure of an empire which, according to M.G. Smith's notion of 'plural societies', 'differentially incorporated' ethno-religious groups into the larger social system (Smith 1969: 429). Jews perceived themselves as Salonikan, Sephardi and Levantine, with an Italian, Spanish, Greek or Turkish citizenship.[6] Today Salonikan Jews are citizens of the Greek nation-state and are considered a religious minority (*Thriskeftiki Mionotita*). Although Greek Jews in official Greek publications are referred to as 'Jewish Greeks', or 'Greeks of the Jewish faith' (*Evraion Ellinon*) (see, for example, Ministry of Foreign Affairs of Greece and University of Athens 1998), in popular discourse 'Greeks' and 'Jews' are often referred to as two different 'people' or 'races'.[7]

Within the community the question of self-categorisation is a contested topic. In the light of the 'accusation' of not being 'properly Greek', the community also stresses the notion of 'Greeks of the Jewish faith'. In private discussions, opinions on this topic are divided. During a discussion about the notion of 'Greek Jews' or 'Jewish Greeks' somebody asked me: 'What do you think? Are we [Greek Jews] just a religious group or are we an ethnic group?'[8]

In order to understand this dilemma we need to turn to history, and more importantly to memory. Looking at memory will help us to a) gain understanding of the historical processes out of which categorisation of 'us' and 'them' emerges; and b) gain understanding of present collective and individual self-images since states, communities and individuals 'select and maintain particular memories in order to construct and reaffirm collective self images' (Doumanis 1997: 14). By using the notion of memory as a frame of analysis we can leave aside the central question of nationalism scholars about the 'real', 'invented' or 'imagined' nature of the past, and focus instead on the contemporary significance of the past for states, communities and individuals.[9] In doing so, we are extending Verdery's framework by situating minority identity and minority memories within the boundaries of a state, which sustains its particular nationalism by particular memories of the past.

MEMORY

As shown above, references to the past are considered to be an intrinsic part of the notions of 'culture', 'ethnicity' and 'nationalism'. The past is accessed through memory which is shaped by historical experiences (of groups and individuals) and by present identities. This process invariably links identity to memory. Images of 'self' (on the individual and group level) are clearly connected to images of the past (and possibly the future).

In recent years the topic of memory has received renewed scholarly attention and has been widely discussed in various disciplines, mainly in history, anthropology, sociology, psychology and cultural studies. Scholars have set out to study 'the connective structure of society' (Assmann 1997: 293) and have focused on 'sets of practices like commemoration and monument building and general forms like tradition, myth, or identity ... in simple and complex societies, from above and from below, across the geographical spectrum' (Olick and Robbins 1998: 106). The fact that social memory studies are transdisciplinary and non-paradigmatic has to do with the nature of memory, defined by Fentress as a 'complex process, not a simple mental act; even the words we use to describe the act (recognise, remember, recall, recount, commemorate...) show that memory can include anything from a highly private and spontaneous, possibly wordless mental sensation, to a formal public ceremony' (Fentress 1992: x). As with culture and ethnicity, memory lies at the meeting point between the individual and society and is expressed by different social agents. As with culture and ethnicity, memory refers both to the realm of 'action' (expressed, for example, in commemorative ceremonies) and of 'representation' (sets of ideas about the past).

Due to the overwhelming growth of literature in recent years it is only possible here to sketch out some of the broader developments in the field of memory. These have been classified into three different 'schools' (leaving out the vast psychological literature) of memory, which partly represent different disciplines: a) Halbwachs and his successors; b) Oral History and Life Histories; and c) Cultural Recall, Memory and Trauma (of which a sub-group deals exclusively with Holocaust research).

Halbwachs and his Successors

Maurice Halbwachs is often considered the 'founding father' of collective/social memory theories. Halbwachs was a French sociologist and a disciple of Durkheim. His *Social Frameworks of Memory* (*Les Cadres Sociaux de la Mémoire*) was published in 1925 in which he applied Durkheim's notion of 'collective consciousness' (defined as 'the totality of beliefs and sentiments common to average citizens of the same society', 1964: 79) to the field of memory. He contended that the composite collective memory provides the 'social frameworks' (*cadres sociaux*) in which individual memory is located (see Hutton 1993: 9). In other words, the structure of the collective memory is such that individual memory will conform to its model. Halbwachs bases his assumption on the premise that living memory involves an interplay between repetition and recollection. Through repetition an idealised image has been created, an 'agreed version' of a particular event, so to speak, which homogenises all individual memory (Halbwachs 1980: 120–7).

His second hypothesis concerns the durability of collective memory. The durability of collective memory is linked to the social power of groups. This implies that all memory is structured by group identities and that the survival of memories is linked to the survival of the group:

> that one remembers one's childhood as part of a family, one's neighbourhood as part of the local community, one's working life as part of a factory or office community... that these memories are essentially group memories, and that the memory of the individuals exists only in so far as she or he is probably the unique product of a particular intersection of groups. (transl. Halbwachs 1980: xii)

In this argument Halbwachs opposes the psychological, individualistic approach of memory by emphasising that memories are acquired and recalled in society, that is, in groups. Halbwachs used the analogy of sea waves breaking on a rocky shore to illustrate his idea of collective memory and social frameworks. With the rising tide the rocks are covered by the sea. When the water retreats what remains are 'miniature lakes nestled amidst the rocky formation'. In this image the advancing sea represents the living memory, while the pools of water which remain are the recollections which are left behind, shaped and contained by the rocks, representing the social framework (Halbwachs 1925: 18). Halbwachs distinguishes 'autobiographical memory', 'historical memory', 'history', and 'collective memory'. 'Autobiographical memory' refers to the memory of events experienced by the people who remember, 'historical memory' refers to memory which is transmitted through historical records, and 'collective memory' refers to the active past which forms the present identity of a group. Halbwachs viewed 'history' as the 'dead past' which is not relevant any more for the present of the group (see Olick and Robbins: 110). 'History' is thus juxtaposed to 'collective memory' which aims to construct an image of the past which corresponds to the present (that is, the present identity of society).

Apart from sporadic interest in memory (for example, by art historian Aby Warburg and sociologist G.H. Mead, see Olick and Robbins 1998: 106) the study of collective memory lay dormant until the early 1980s when it became again the focus of public and academic discussions. One of the most prominent historical studies in this 'memory revival' was the work of the French historian Pierre Nora. In *Les Lieux de Mémoire*, published between 1984 and 1992, Nora and his collaborators set out 'to unlayer French commemorative traditions to see how they were originally constructed' (Hutton 1993: 9). According to Nora it is the historian's task to identify and classify the imaginary schemes in which the nation's past has been conceived. In addition to collective memory, Nora speaks of historical memory, produced by historians and scholars. Nora locates four places, or sites, of memory: symbolic sites, monumental sites, functional sites and topographical sites. Symbolic sites consist of ceremonies and commemorations, monumental sites of architecture, functional sites of history textbooks, 'official history', and topographical sites of libraries and archives. These *lieux* of memory are contrasted to earlier *milieux* of memory. 'The former are impoverished versions of the latter: if we were able to live within memory, we would have not needed to consecrate *lieux de mémoire* in its name' (Nora in Olick and Robbins: 121). It is thus the decline of (natural) memory which, according to Nora, leads to the creation of 'memory sites'.

Although Nora's study stands out among the wealth of empirical material, other historians and anthropologists have also embarked on the study of commemorative practices, mostly in the context of the nation-state (for example, Hobsbawm 1983, Lowenthal 1985, Gillis 1994, Spillmann 1997, Assman 1997). The focus of these studies is the 'politics' of memory (and forgetting). Gillis argues:

> we are constantly revising our memories to suit our current identities. Memories help to make sense of the world we live in; and 'memory work' is ... embedded in the complex class, gender, and power relations that determine what is remembered (or forgotten), by whom, and for what end. (Gillis 1994: 1)

An important contribution to memory theories which cannot be overlooked forms the work of two German scholars, Jan and Aleida Assmann. Their conceptual framework presents a creative elaboration of Halbwachs' ideas.

In his introduction to *Das Kulturelle Gedächtnis* Jan Assmann states:

'Societies construct [*imaginieren*] self images and identities across different generations through a culture of memory.' The aim of his study is to analyse 'how societies remember and how societies imagine themselves through memory' (Assmann 1997: 18). By introducing the notion of '*Kulturgedächtnis*' (cultural memory) and '*Kommunikationsgedächtnis*' (communicative memory) Assmann introduces a framework which differentiates between different kinds of collective memories and allows us to look more closely at the process of memory transmission (see also Chapter 5). As Halbwachs, Assmann is interested in the social 'framing' of memory. He asserts that the content and organisation of memory is largely dependent on 'outer dimensions', that is to say on the social and cultural framework. *Kommunikationsgedächtnis* and *Kulturgedächtnis* are important parts of the 'outer dimensions' of memory (Assmann 1997: 20). The former kind of memory refers to memories of the recent past which are shared among contemporaries and among three to four generations. The life of the *Kommunikationsgedächtnis* is bound to its carriers: after their death other memories will replace the old ones. This distinguishes it from *Kulturgedächtnis* which represents 'fixed' and 'embodied' memory. Here Assmann refers to material and immaterial embodied memory, such as texts, rituals and monuments. The objects of this memory are often fixed points in the past and it is thus characterised by 'sacredness' and *Alltagsferne* (distance from day-to-day reality). But it is not only the time-frame which differentiates the two forms of memory (recent past versus distant past) but also the nature of their agency. *Kommunikationsgedächtnis* is transmitted by many, *Kulturgedächtnis* by an elite of specified carriers (such as priests, artists, scholars and so on) who canonise 'traditions' and memories regarded as worthy of being transmitted. Canonised 'cultural memory' is present-oriented because it keeps memories alive which are relevant for the present of the group, that is to say for the present identity of the group.[10] Translated to the memory of the individual Assmann talks of two memory processes, the one of 'founding memory' (*fundierende Erinnerung*) and the one of 'biographic memory'. It needs to be underlined that Assmann clearly states that the subject of remembrance and memory is always the individual (Assmann 1997: 36). But individual memory is always dependent on cultural practices and external 'storage facilities', such as the media (Assmann 1999: 19). Aleida Assmann sees parallels between individual and 'cultural memory', both shaped interactively through communication, that is to say through language, images and ritual repetitions (Assmann 1999: 19).

Similar to the Assmanns, Irwin-Zarecka also uses a memory approach which focuses on the social framework of memory in her study of the Jews in Poland entitled *Frames of Remembrance* (1994). She introduces the notion of 'framing' as an appropriate analytical device for looking at memory because in her view 'framing' points us to the dialectics between publicly articulated and privately held views of the past and implies that there is something outside individual memory which shapes and limits the scope of possible interpretations of the past. Irwin-Zarecka writes:

> We all make sense of the past with the help of a whole variety of resources ... This making sense is motivated by our personal experience but facilitated (or impeded) by public offerings, and such public offerings are a mixture of presence and absences. A 'collective memory' – as a set of ideas, images, feelings about the past – is best located not in the minds of individuals, but in the recourses they share. (Irwin-Zarecka 1994: 4)

What Assmann calls 'cultural memory' she refers to as the 'infrastructure' of collective memory, consisting of spaces, objects, 'texts'. This kind of 'memory work' secures a presence of the past and makes an engagement with the past possible. In this framework memory is part of a conflictual process in which diverse agents struggle for its possession and interpretation.

Other recent studies which look at the social processes through which memory is channelled include Connerton's *How Societies Remember* (1989) and Fentress' and Wickham's *Social Memory* (1992). They use the term 'social memory' rather than 'collective memory' because they object to the notion of a 'collective' which renders the individual 'a sort of automaton, passively obeying the interiorized collective will' (Fentress and Wickham 1992: 7). Their approach does nevertheless focus on the social transmission of memory:

> For students of society, past or present, memory is everything, both tools and material, both the means and the goal of their labour. But even individual memory is not simply personal: the memories which constitute our identity and provide the context for everyday thought and action are not only our own, but are learned, borrowed and inherited, in part and of a common stock, constructed, sustained, and transmitted by the families, communities, and cultures to which we belong. (Fentress and Wickham 1992: viii)

A study which grounds this understanding of memory in ethnographic fieldwork is Zonabend's book *The Enduring Memory*, in which she and other researchers looked at time and history in a French village. Between 1968 and 1975 Zonabend and four other researchers conducted fieldwork in the village of Minot, questioning and listening to the inhabitants of the village. Their main focus was to write an ethnography of 'village time', so to speak, and to find out how people perceive their past. One of the interesting findings of the book was that: 'the individual in a village lives first of all in family time, and his kinship structures his memory of this time' (Zonabend 1984: 199). 'So history is dated in the village through family events. Family time organises historical time' (Zonabend 1984: 198). Zonabend captures the experiences and discourses of individuals and groups and combines individual accounts with a structural analysis of the social and economic history, thus relating biographies to the wider village framework and making them a means and an important tool to understanding society. In contrast, oral histories constitute an approach which is less concerned with the social framework of memory and more with individual narratives of lives and past events.

Oral History and Life Histories

Various definitions have been used to describe 'oral history' which can be both a method of research and the object of research. Roper defines 'oral history' as 'the recording and interpretation of spoken testimonies about an individual's past' (Roper 1996: 579), Perks suggests that 'oral history – the interviewing of eye-witness participants in the events of the past for the purposes of historical reconstruction – has had a significant impact upon contemporary history as practised in many countries' (Perks and Thompson 1998: x).

    The oral history approach was developed in the discipline of history and needs to be distinguished from the 'life-history' or biographical approach developed in anthropology and sociology in the 1920s and 1930s which used life-histories (defined as 'any retrospective account by the individual of his life in whole or part, in written or in oral form', Watson and Watson-Franke 1985: 2) to understand culture through individual experience. One of the most famous pioneering studies in the use of personal documents is Thomas and Zaniecki's work *The Polish Peasant in Europe and America*, first published in 1920. By using personal documents, mainly letters, the authors aimed at describing the life of a social group (see Watson and Watson-Franke 1985: 6), namely of Polish immigrants in the United States.[11] The aim of the early life-history approach was to 'relay experiences and events as the subjects themselves perceive them' (Melhuus 1997). With a changing theoretical paradigm in anthropology (see Marcus 1992) life-histories were not regarded any more as a direct representation of an informant's life but a 'text' constructed and 'edited' by the anthropologist. The focus shifted to 'meaning' and 'representation'. From this perspective explorations of life-histories lead to explorations of individual and collective memory and cultural representations expressed in the narration of lives.

The development of oral history is clearly linked to the development of *Alltagsgeschichte* and 'history from below' which attempted to give voice to marginalised groups, to 'give history back to the people in their own words' (Thompson 1988). It was the aim of oral historians to challenge traditional historiography and to 'recover' evidence of non-elite groups. In this vein, many studies were published based on interviews with women, immigrants and the working classes (Roper 1996: 579). By writing about non-dominant memories (which some scholars call 'counter-memory') the historian transforms the standing and character of these memories because they then become, in Assmann's words, part of the *Kulturgedächtnis*.

The work of the 'Popular Memory Group' has further developed this kind of approach to oral history by looking at memory as an ongoing process of contestation and resistance in which 'reading and reaction, official and unofficial, public and private' inter-penetrate (Olick and Robbins 1998: 127). Its focus is not the memory consensus but the struggles over the construction of the past which are attributed significance for contemporary politics and individual remembering (see Popular Memory Group 1998). The Popular Memory Group focused on struggle because it recognised the differential power of different memory agencies, such as the dominance of 'national memory' over other memories.

At the end of the 1970s and beginning of the 1980s some oral historians challenged the pure 'recovery' and 'gathering' focus of oral history and asserted that 'memory – personal, historical, individual, and generational' should be moved to the centre stage of analysis and not only remain the method of oral history. Frisch writes in 1979:

> Used in this way, oral history could be a powerful tool for discovering, exploring, and evaluating the nature of the process of historical memory – how people make sense of their past, how they connect individual experience and its social context, how the

past becomes part of the present, and how people use it to interpret their lives and the world around them. (Frisch quoted in
Perks and Thompson 1998: 2)

In recent work of oral historians, for example in the studies of
Alessandro Portelli (1991) and Luisa Paserini (1987, 1996), the aspects
which distinguish oral sources from other sources, namely subjectivity, orality and the narrative form, are woven into the framework of
analysis. Paserini's study on 'Ideology and Consensus under Italian
Fascism' (1987) demonstrates that the influence of public culture and
ideology can be revealed in the silences, discrepancies and idiosyn-
crasies of personal testimony. Portelli highlights the question of dis-
crepancy between 'historical facts' and memory. He states:

> The discrepancy between fact and memory ultimately enhances
> the value of the oral sources as historical documents. It is not
> caused by faulty recollections ... but actively and creatively gen-
> erated by memory and imagination in an effort to make sense of
> crucial events and history in general ... Beyond the event as such,
> the real and significant historical fact which these narratives high-
> light is memory itself. (Portelli 1991: 26)

As oral historians discovered the 'different credibility' (Portelli
1991) of the subjective in memory (as have social scientists) it drew
some towards another field which is very concerned with memory,
namely psychoanalysis. In her recent book on the 1968 generation
Paserini intertwined the text about the narratives of her interviewees
with a text of her own psychoanalysis (Paserini 1996). This, however,
does not seem to be the overall trend of oral history today. There is a
third 'school' of memory for which insights of psychoanalysis and psychology are indeed very relevant, which can be described as 'Cultural
Recall, Memory and Trauma'.

Cultural Recall, Memory and Trauma

This last area of memory studies is the most recent and most interdisciplinary. This is not the place for an extensive review of the vast literature in this field. The aim of this section is to convey a rough idea
about this kind of memory research, embedded in a post-modern, literary paradigm.

Looking at the book *Acts of Memory: Cultural Recall in the Present* (Bal,
Crewe and Spitzer 1999) we can see that its contributors come mainly

from the disciplines of cultural studies, literature and history. In the introduction Mieke Bal sketches out which assumptions on memory the authors share: firstly, 'cultural memory' signifies that memory can be understood as a cultural phenomenon, as well as an individual and a social one; secondly, 'cultural memory' is 'neither remnant, document, nor relic of the past, nor floating in a present cut off from the past' (Bal *et al.* 1999: vii) but it links the past to the present and the future; thirdly 'cultural memory' is the product of collective agency; and fourthly the process of 'cultural recall' is something which people 'perform' (this understanding differs considerably from Assmann's notion of 'cultural memory'). Leo Spitzer's paper on Austrian Jewish refugees in Bolivia exemplifies this new approach to memory. He looks at acts of memory, performed by individuals in a cultural framework. He also includes his own memories mediated by photographs into the analysis (Spitzer 1999). The author thus situates himself as an integral part of the analysis.

Throughout the book a very broad notion of memory is used which includes unconscious 'habitual memories', 'narrative memories' and 'traumatic memories'. Traumatic memory seems of particular relevance for this memory approach, indicated by the attention trauma is given in the introduction and in the individual contributions. In cases of traumatic recall we deal with events of the past which have a persistent presence and resist 'narrative integration' by the subject.[12] Bal links the theme of traumatic recall to the emergence of literature on Holocaust testimonies and memory, such as Langer's *Holocaust Testimonies, The Ruins of Memory* (1991), Feldmann's and Laub's *Testimony: Crises of Witnessing in Literature, Psychoanalysis, and History* (1992)[13] and LaCapra's *Representing the Holocaust: History, Theory, Trauma* (1994). While Langer is concerned with the nature of survivors' memories, Feldmann and Laub and LaCapra deal with the wider implications and the process of acts of remembering and acts of witnessing.

Langer emphasises the 'divided self', a self which cannot integrate 'deep memory' of the traumatic past and 'common memory' directed at closure and coherence (Langer 1991: xi). Feldmann and Laub discuss the need for traumatic memory to be legitimised and narratively integrated. They also address the question of what testimony can teach us in the post-traumatic century. Laub argues that the Holocaust was an event which, during its historical occurrence, produced no witnesses and created a world 'in which one could not bear witness to oneself' (Laub 1995). He therefore thinks it is essential for the narrative which could not be articulated to be told, to be transmitted, and to be heard.

By the experience of giving testimony the narrator reclaims their position as a witness and thus reclaims their life-story. LaCapra tackles the 'transferential' relationship between survivor and therapist or interviewer and argues that there are two 'memorial positions' when dealing with the Holocaust or other traumatic experiences: 'acting out' (melancholia) and 'working through' (mourning). 'Acting out' is based on identification and victimisation, 'working through' involves self-reflexivity and some amount of distance (LaCapra 1994). It is interesting to note that research about the 'second generation', that is to say children of Holocaust survivors, is predominately conducted by psychologists who are interested in the transmission of trauma (see Epstein 1979, Wardi 1992, Rosenthal 1998).[14]

Returning to the general 'cultural memory approach', it needs to be emphasised that this is not one coherent approach but rather a 'meeting point' for scholars from several disciplines. Antze's and Lambek's book *Tense Past. Cultural Essays in Trauma and Memory* illustrate this point (1996). What seems to unite the contributors is the understanding of 'memory as practice', 'not the pre-given object of our gazing' (Antze and Lambek 1996: xii), a commitment to reflexivity (about the creation and mediation of 'texts' and the positioning of the author) and an interest in the application of psychological concepts, such as 'working through' and 'closure', to the production and analysis of narratives. The notion of 'memory as practice' is complemented by the notion of 'memory as a process', a continuous process in which personal and social memory (and narratives) are linked through a complex web of interactions. Antze and Lambek state this view very clearly:

> Experiences of nationhood and ethnicity [are] linked to popular narratives and ceremonies, which are linked to newspaper accounts and thence to official histories, museums, boundary disputes, and sponsored ceremonies which are linked to theories propounded by historians, political scientists, and other experts. (Antze and Lambek 1996: xx)

The conference on 'Frontiers of Memory', held in September 1999 in London,[15] demonstrated that although the discourse on memory started in different disciplines and with different concerns, a new field of memory studies seems to have emerged which brings the various schools together. This overview of three exclusive memory approaches serves to highlight the background for the emergence of the different memory discourses.

THE ANTHROPOLOGY OF GREECE

This section will consider some anthropological studies of Greece and explore their relevance to some of the issues discussed above.

Due to the 'rural bias' of the anthropology of Greece it seemed rather difficult to link a study of an urban minority to previous anthropological work. In my first account of the Jewish community of Salonika (Lewkowicz 1994) I therefore did not make any reference to other anthropological studies. Only during my second period of fieldwork did I realise that one can, and indeed should, relate aspects of Jewish identity and memory to a very important field of the anthropology of Greece, namely the study of kinship and the family.

During the first period of fieldwork one aspect of the Jewish community which was striking was the low public profile it had adopted in Salonika. Along with this low public profile went a notion of 'private Judaism', of Jewish ethnicity expressed in the private realm. I interpreted this expression of ethnicity as a minority strategy in a nation-state which views 'other loyalties' with great suspicion. On returning to Salonika I realised that the division between private and public seemed to play an important role in other aspects of social life in Greece. Among my first observations was the difference of appearance regarding the clothing worn 'at home' and when 'going out'. Another example of the strong public/private divide which comes to mind is the existence of a '*Saloni*' which used to be utilised only for entertaining guests and thus represents the most public area of a private home. Although the distinction of private and public is not as clear cut in modern apartments as in village houses (Wente 1990: 24) and '*Salonis*' are often integrated into the common living space, notions of the house (*to spiti*) as something private with limited access for visitors are still of significance today. In the literature the division between the private and public realm features quite prominently and is often related to gender roles:

> Investigation of the domestic (or private)/public dichotomy and its relationship to gender roles is especially important in Greece where, as in other Mediterranean societies, the dichotomy is highly developed and strongly gender linked. Within any Greek village (and to a great extent, in town and cities also), there is a sharp physical demarcation between the private sphere, bounded by the walls of the house, and the public areas – the street, the 'platia', and the shops ... The division between private and public is

behaviourally demarcated as well, particularly with respect to gender roles ... The house, the centre of domestic life, is both physically and morally associated with women ... Conversely, the public sphere is open freely to men, and ostensibly it is men who shape events in this sphere. (Dubisch 1986: 10,11)

What is significant here is not so much the extent to which this description is still applicable to the modern Greek urban situation, but the fact that the public/private divide, in whatever changed form, is an important symbolic system through which people perceive themselves and others and formulate boundaries of inclusion and exclusion. Dubisch acknowledges that only by moving 'beyond gender' can we fully explore the oppositions of public/private, male/female, inside/outside, self/other (Dubisch 1986: 36) and understand the different ways in which these concepts help people 'to make sense' of their experiences. She acknowledges that 'the separation between "private" and "public" is paralleled socially by concepts of "insiders" (*diki mas*) and "outsiders" (*xeni*)' (Dubisch 1986: 35). Kokot illustrates this point very clearly in her study of Asia Minor refugees in Salonika. She suggests that the notions of 'us' and 'them' are powerful concepts employed on all levels of identity formation. The Asia Minor refugees in her study perceive of themselves, for example, as 'urban' opposed to 'rural', 'refugees' opposed to 'indigenous inhabitants', 'leftists' opposed to 'rightists' (Kokot 1994: 250).

If we think of the public/private opposition in terms of spatial and social boundaries it is not at all surprising that we can find variations of this conceptual opposition in other processes of boundary creation, such as nationalism and ethnicity. This leads me to propose the argument that a particular kind of nationalism, and a particular kind of minority ethnicity, developed very successfully in Greece because it could build on the cultural concepts of private and public.

Nation-building in Greece, and in particular in the northern territory of Macedonia, entailed a very strong emphasis on assimilation. Due to the 'contested' character of Macedonia the Hellenisation process in this area was implemented quite forcefully. In the inter-war period names of places which were of Slavonic or Turkish origin were changed to Greek ones and individuals were encouraged to change their names as well (Mackridge and Yannakakis 1997: 10). The usage of the Slavonic language was strongly discouraged. The ideal of the 'homogenous nation-state' thus imposed a certain notion of 'Greekness' which stressed ethnic purity and historical continuity and did not leave any room for the expression of 'other' traditions or histories. This is what was referred to above as 'mono-cultural' or ethnic nationalism. On the public level, the hegemony of this specific discourse seems widely accepted. But, as some anthropologists have documented, in the private realm the situation is different. Here, there is room for the expression of identities which might be considered problematic or sensitive 'outside'. Asia Minor refugees on Lemnos, Slav-speakers in the Florina region, and inhabitants of a town in Greek Macedonia, Aghios Dimitrios, all practise customs or say things 'at home' or 'among themselves' which seem to be restricted to the 'private realm'. Tsimouris describes that the Anatolian traditions in the practices of daily life constitute an important part in the articulation of a sense of belonging. But at the same time these practices are viewed with a high degree of ambivalence because these 'folk habits' challenge the self-presentation of the inhabitants of Aghios Dimitrios in other domains (Tsimouris 1995: 17), which are more in line with the 'official' historical discourse of the nation-state. Similar patterns were observed by Karakasidou and Cowan. Cowan recounts that in the town of Sohos 'polyglot local codes' are used in everyday situations, such as the use of Bulgarian or Turkish in nicknaming, wedding rituals and musical experiences. But in public contexts Sohoians feel quite reluctant to acknowledge these practices:

> They had been instructed for many years by people originating outside the community – school teachers, public officials, visiting folklorists – as well as some from within, that the 'non-Greek' elements of the tradition were 'not relevant, 'not important', 'something they should forget'. (Cowan 1997: 163)

The reluctance to acknowledge certain parts of one's identity, even at home, is much greater among the Slav speakers Karakasidou researched. On account of the thorough Hellenisation policy in the region which was facilitated greatly by state-guided public education (especially after the First World War), many Slavo-Macedonians identified themselves very strongly with Hellenism. In many instances, parents decided not to discuss (or even to hide) their Slavo-Macedonian identity at home. Thus many children were not aware of their 'non-Greek' background (Karakasidou 1997: 102).

The first two case studies discussed illuminate that the notion of private and public, in particular as an emic notion, facilitates what could be called private and public ethnicities or social identities. These

enable individuals and groups, on the one hand, to adhere to the official nationalist discourse but, on the other hand, to formulate their own
discourses and practices. The case of the Slavo-Macedonians is different. It is different because the question of identity among Slavo-
Macedonians is much more political. In contrast to the Asia Minor
refugees and the inhabitants of Sohos, whose 'Greekness' was never
challenged, the Slavo-Macedonian population became a much bigger
target of national enculturation because of its perceived 'foreignness'
and the fear of the Greek state of an irredentist movement backed by a
neighbouring state. The political consequences of acknowledging any
kind of Slavo-Macedonian identity are thus much more far-reaching
than the other identities discussed above, even when only expressed at
home. In such cases of political sensitivity even the private realm does
not seem to offer a secure place for the formation of 'alternative' identities. To put it in Karakasidou's words, this illustrates a 'near hegemony' of the Greek nation.

What Tsimbouris and Cowan have illustrated for practices and customs is described by Doumanis for the private and public realm of
memory (Doumanis 1997). He researched the memory of the Italian
occupation among Dodecanese islanders and found that there was a
huge gap between privately articulated memories and publicly
expressed representation of this period. Since the islanders want to
present themselves as 'good Greek citizens' they stress the themes of
the Greek *'Kulturgedächtnis'*: the oppression of the Italian occupation
and the manifestations of local resistance. Other themes, such as
friendship and marriages between the Italians and the Greeks, are only
addressed in the private realm. (For a more detailed discussion of
Doumanis' study see Chapter 10.)

The contrast between private and public also played an important
role during the political periods in Greece when the articulations of
left-wing political views could result in being exiled to an island. In her
study of the 'Social Organisation of Exile' (1991) Kenna points to the
adverse effect the presence of people who were punished by the state
for their publicly articulated views had on the islanders. The 'islanders
learned to keep their political and other ideas to themselves and not to
discuss them with "outsiders"' (Kenna 1991: 76).

It could be suggested that in some instances the private realm
enables groups and individuals to defy the official nationalist discourse,
and argued further that the cultural notion of 'private–public' contributed to the success of Greece's nationalism. Firstly, it provided a
pre-nation-state concept of 'us' and 'them' and secondly, it provided a

concept for the formulation of private identities which does not pub-
licly challenge the official discourse. Herzfeld's suggestion, that
Greeks see themselves internally as *romiosines* (in reference to their
Byzantine and Ottoman past) and as *Hellines* (in reference to classical
Greece) to outsiders, is another illustration of the impact of the pub-
lic–private on formulation of identity (Herzfeld 1987: 102).

The conceptualisation of the private–public has clear ramifications
for minority ethnicity. A private ethnicity could be like another seg-
mentary layer among many other private identities. It does, however,
restrict certain identities to the private realm, which expressed in public might cast some doubt on the 'loyalty', 'allegiance', and *syneidisi*[16]
(conscience and consciousness) of the person or group. It will therefore
be argued here that this case study, the Jewish community of Salonika,
can be examined within the general context of private and public identities in Greece. Because of the shifting nature of these two spheres,
diki mas (one of us) denotes many different levels of inclusion and
exclusion.

CONCLUSION

If we follow Halbwachs' notion of collective memory, we conceive of
memory not as a mere individual capacity but as embedded in and
reflecting the wider culture of a group. Memories of the past form a
crucial part of individual and group identities: 'We experience our present world in a context which is causally connected with past events and
objects ... And we will experience our present differently in accordance with the different pasts to which we are able to connect'
(Connerton 1989: 2).

Thus groups and individuals create their identities, in other words,
create a sense of themselves, by linking their present experiences to a
perceived past and a foreseen future. In doing so they attribute meaning to past experiences as part of a general 'web of significance'. From
this point of view, 'memories are part of a group's culture, the fabric
from which a group's language, values, norms, and rituals are drawn'
(Rapaport 1997: 24) and at the same time culture provides the language
and cognitive concepts of remembering. Memory therefore is, as are
culture and ethnicity, both practice and cognition and, to follow Fox,
the 'outcome of a constant process of cultural production' (1990: 2). A
large part of this thesis deals with individual narrative memories.
Narratives can be understood as 'discourses with a clear sequential

order that connect events in a meaningful way' (Hinchman and Hinchman 1997: xvi). In order to understand fully these narratives we need to look at the larger system in which remembering takes place, at the socially shared 'frames of remembrance' in which discourses about the past are created and transmitted, that is to say at the general 'infra-structure' of memory. The particular 'frames' of individual memory and identity, which seem of relevance here, stem from the literature presented above: nationalism and dominant memory (expressed in the dominant *Kulturgedächtnis*), community memory (expressed in com-munal commemorations and memory practices), and the traumatic experience of the Holocaust. The cultural notion of private and public is another frame through which we can analyse minority identity and memory, because the memory of a Jewish past has largely been con-fined to the boundaries of the community. Jewish history has, until very recently, not been part of the wider Greek national history. The disappearance of the Jews from Salonika did not constitute a collective trauma for Greek society, similar to the post-war situation in Poland (Irwin-Zarecka 1994: 49), where the destruction of Polish Jewry did not constitute a collective trauma for Catholic Poland.

With the emergence of a more public Jewish memory in Salonika, we have to ask which particular 'past' the community wants to connect to and what kind of self-image this connection implies. Further, we need to establish how the interviewees connect to their past and whether their connection corresponds to the communal (and other) representation of the past.

NOTES

1. 'Ethnic group' has also been defined in many different ways. Some scholars stress the cultural content of ethnic groups and see them as 'a self perceived group of people who hold in com-mon a set of traditions not shared by others with whom they are in contact' (De Vos and Romanucci-Ross 1975: 9). Smith characterises an 'ethnic community' with the following six attributes: 1) A collective proper name. 2) Myth of common ancestry. 3) Shared historical memories. 4) One or more differentiating elements of common culture. 5) An association with a specific homeland. 6) A sense of solidarity for significant sectors of the population (Smith 1991: 21). Others hold a broader definition and describe 'any group of people who set themselves apart and are set apart from other groups with whom they interact' as an 'ethnic group' (Seymour-Smith 1986: 95).
2. The term 'emic' is used in conjunction with the word 'etic'. While 'emic' refers to concepts, notions and ideas used by 'the natives', 'etic' denotes the concepts and analytical framework used by the researcher (Eriksen 1993: 11).
3. The concept of 'plural society' was developed by J.S. Furnivall and later extended by M.G. Smith and P. van den Berghe. It refers to societies in which different groups are differential-ly incorporated into the state (Smith, M.G. 1969).
4. This does not necessarily mean that the citizens of the state accept and internalise the pre-scribed roles.

5. The German historian Friedrich Meinecke introduced this distinction in 1908.
6. In Edgar Morin's *Mémoirs* these multiple identities are wonderfully described (see Morin 1994: 335).
7. It is interesting to note that the introduction to the 'Documents of Greek Jews' refers first to 'Jewish Greeks' but then to the Jews and the Greeks as 'two peoples' and 'two nations' (Ministry of Foreign Affairs of Greece and University of Athens 1998: 38).
8. The Greek word *ethnos* blurs the English distinction of 'ethnic' and 'national' because it refers clearly to the nation. Due to the lack of another term, minority groups can thus be easily seen as 'rival bidders for national loyalty' (Mazower 1996: 24).
9. In his study 'Memories Cast in Stone' David Sutton is critical of analytical approaches which attempt to replace invented or imagined past by 'truer' scholarly accounts. He advocates an approach which focuses on the meaning attributed to the past by groups and individuals. The central question of his book is: 'What does a given population believe to be the general relevance of the past for present-day life, and how is this played out at the national, local, and personal levels?' (Sutton 1998: 7).
10. Assmann differentiates between three identities, individual and personal 'I' identities and a collective 'us' identity. Individual and personal identities are made up of the images a person has of themselves with regard to their singularity as a member of society and as an individual. The collective identity is constituted of the image which a group propagates and with which its members identity (Assmann 1997: 131).
11. For a detailed discussion of the use of life histories in anthropology see Watson and Watson-Franke (1985), Langness and Frank (1981).
12. For an overview of recent literature on trauma see Caruth 1995 and Herman 1992.
13. Langer, Feldmann and Laub refer in their work extensively to the video testimonies of the Fortunoff Video Archive at Yale University.
14. Rapaport's sociological analysis of 'second generation' Jews in Germany (Rapaport 1997) is a notable exception.
15. The speakers on the concluding panel included Paul Antze, Michael Lambek and Luisa Paserini.
16. For a discussion of the historical and current usage of the concept of *syneidisi* see Stewart (1998: 8).

3

The Historical and Political Background: Salonika, Greece and the Jews

THE HISTORY OF SALONIKA AND THE JEWISH COMMUNITY: AN OVERVIEW

This chapter will provide an overview of the history of Salonika and the Jewish community in the general context of the history of Greece.[1] The war, the German occupation, and the post-war period will be discussed in greater detail in Chapters 7, 8, and 9.

Salonika was founded in 315 BCE and named after Thessalonikeia, the half-sister of Alexander the Great. Due to its strategic location in the Aegean Sea and in the trade crossroads of the central Balkans, Salonika became the capital of the Roman province of Macedonia in 146 BCE and the second most important city in the Byzantine Empire. It is believed that the first Jews settled in Salonika in 140 BCE. In 48 CE St Paul visited Salonika and preached in the synagogue for three consecutive Saturdays. By that time Jewish communities were established all along the coast of Asia Minor, in Athens, Corinth, Verroia and Phillipi (Stavroulakis 1986: 1). The Jews of the Byzantine Empire became known as 'Romaniot Jews'. The Romaniot Jews spoke Greek and developed their own special customs. The first detailed account about the lives of the Romaniot Jews was given by Benjamin of Tudela who travelled through Greece in the twelfth century. In his account the Jewish community in Salonika numbered about 500.

In 1430 Salonika was taken by the Ottomans Turks and in 1453, with the fall of Contstantinople, it was incorporated in the Ottoman Empire, together with the rest of Greece. Under Islamic Law Jews were guaranteed the same rights as other non-Muslim groups and Jews and Christians were considered *dhimmis*, 'People of the Book'. This *dhimmi* status gave them specific rights and privileges and under the *millet* system of the Ottoman Empire 'each community (i.e. religious community) was allowed to function with a considerable degree of internal autonomy' (Angel 1978: 28).

The expulsion of the Jews from Spain in 1492 by the Catholic monarchs Ferdinand and Isabella and the subsequent decision by Sultan Bayazid II to open the borders of the Ottoman Empire to the exiled Jews was a crucial turning point in the history of the Jews of Greece.[2] With the settlement of the Spanish Jews, the Sephardim, in the major cities of the Ottoman Empire – Constantinople, Adrianople and Salonika – two very different kinds of Jewish communities were confronted with each other. The Sephardim came from a more urban Jewish culture than the Romaniotes. In places where a massive number of Sephardim settled the Romaniotes adopted Sephardi customs and language (Judeo-Spanish).[3] This is what happened in Salonika where about 20,000 Jews arrived in 1492/93.

By the beginning of the sixteenth century Jews constituted the majority of the city's population. The Sephardic Jews organised themselves around synagogues, each named after their town or province of origin, Calabria, Majorca, Lisbona, Catalonia and so forth. Each community was autonomous and had its own leaders, rabbis, schools and tribunals. The Ottoman authorities designed a tax specifically aimed at the Jewish community, which each Jewish household had to pay. Although the Ottoman administration treated the Jewish community of Salonika as one group it took almost 300 years for Salonikan Jews to create and accept one central Jewish administration. In the fifteenth and sixteenth centuries the Jewish community, or more precisely communities, flourished and attracted more Jewish settlers from Northern and Southern Europe. With more than 30 synagogues, talmudic schools, and libraries Salonika became known as 'the Mother of Israel'.[4] The Sephardi Jews soon developed commercial networks in the Mediterranean and the Middle East. Salonika became a centre for the export of tobacco and textiles, in particular cotton and silk.

In the seventeenth century the Jewish preacher Shabbetai Zewi (1626–76) came to the city. He and his followers believed that he was the true messiah and the rabbinical authorities expelled him from Salonika. In Istanbul he converted to Islam and some of his followers did the same. They formed the 'Donme' sect (Turkish for 'turned'), practising a syncretic mixture of Jewish and Muslim rituals and beliefs.[5] In their fight against new sectarian movements the different synagogues united in 1680 and elected one supreme council which was composed of three rabbis and seven dignitaries.

At the beginning of the nineteenth century, and in some parts of Europe and North America already at the end of the eighteenth century, a new political idea was developed which became one of the most powerful political concepts of the nineteenth and twentieth centuries, the notion of the nation and the nation-state (Alter 1985: 10). Nationalist movements began to appear in the Ottoman Empire in a world of increasing political and military rivalries. In 1821 the Greeks began their struggle for independence. Following the intervention of the Great Powers – Russia, Britain, France and Germany – Greece became independent in 1830. Salonika was not part of the newly formed political entity which covered the southern and central regions of today's Greece, often referred to as Palia Ellada. In 1833 Bavarian Prince Otto was named the first King of Greece.

By the middle of the nineteenth century Salonika underwent a 'renaissance'. English, Dutch and French merchants 'discovered' the Balkans and the Middle East and soon European culture and technology began to flow into Salonika. In his autobiography, *Vidal et les Siens*, Edgar Morin claims that the modernisation which then occurred in Thessaloniki needs to be ascribed to a group of Jews from Livorno who had settled in Salonika at the end of the eighteenth century and who had brought with them the 'seeds of modernisation'. Subsequently, Salonika attracted German, Austrian, Dutch and Spanish commercial interests. Herman Melville, the American writer, describes his impressions of Salonika as follows:

> An Austrian steamer from Constantinople just in, with a great host of poor deck passengers, Turks, Greeks, Jews, etc. came ashore in boats … Great uproar of the porters and contention for luggage. Imagine an immense accumulation of the rags of all nations, and all colours rained down on a dense mob all struggling for huge bales and bundles of rags, gesturing with all gestures, and wrangling in all tongues. (quoted in Molho 1991: 114)

With the industrialisation in the nineteenth century a number of wealthy Jewish families played an important role in the city's development, the most famous ones being the Alatini and the Hirsch families. In 1858 Moses Alatini, whose family owned a large bank, founded the Alatini Flour Mills (this building still exists in Salonika today). In 1871 Baron Hirsch, an Austrian Jew, funded the construction of a railway line between Salonika and Skopje. Besides the construction of an industrial infrastructure, these families also financed the creation of an urban welfare structure which provided housing and help for the poor. The famous Baron Hirsch Hospital was built in 1907 and the Alatini Orphanage in 1911. This modernisation of Salonika went hand in hand with the opening of schools where languages of instruction were

Italian, French (Alliance Israelite Universelle, Mission Laique Française), or German. Together with this cultural expansion came the expansion of daily and weekly newspapers and magazines. The first newspaper, *El Lunar*, was published in 1856 in Ladino, and by the end of the century Salonika had six daily Ladino newspapers and three French ones. Considering the rapid change the city was undergoing as well as the the rapid growth of a Jewish working class,[6] it is not surprising that in 1909 Avram Benaroya, a Bulgarian Jew, founded the socialist organisation *Federation Socialiste Ouvrière* and thus introduced socialism to Salonika. Benaroya's Federation was also a reaction to another political force which had been emerging, the force of nationalism. After the 'Young Turk Revolution' in 1908 the new Turkish army drafted men of all nationalities into the army and it became clear that Turkish and Greek nationalism was going to affect the future of the Jews of Salonika. As a result of the political uncertainty, a first wave of Jewish emigration to the United States, Argentina and the United Kingdom occurred around 1910. Two years later, when Salonika became Greek, a much more substantial number of Jews decided to leave the city. Many settled in France. Although the Greek government assured equal rights to its Jewish citizens there was a strong feeling of mistrust towards the Greek government, based on the positive experience of Jews in the Ottoman Empire and perhaps on the fear of possible anti-Semitic incidents.[7]

Another response to the dilemma of Salonikan Jews was the emergence of Zionist organisations which were founded between 1899 and 1919 (such as *Kadima, Bnei Zion, Maccabi*). In contrast to the situation in eastern Europe, Zionism in Salonika was not a reaction to fierce anti-Semitic persecution by a majority population. Zionism and Zionist organisations became part of an intra-communal struggle in which Zionists fought against the 'assimilationists' by introducing Hebrew and a new way of secular Jewish education. Since all nationalistic organisations were banned by the Ottoman administration in 1904 and due to the feeling that Zionism might be seen as an unpatriotic political idea, the community council issued a statement anouncing that it neither supported nor participated in the Zionist movement (Molho 1997a: 331).

In 1912, with the outbreak of the Balkan Wars, Greece acquired the territories of Epiros, Macedonia, Crete and Western Thrace. In 1913 Salonika was officially declared to be part of the Greek state. A large part of the Greek population remained outside the borders of the Greek state (especially in Istanbul, Smyrna and Alexandria).

After 1912 all Jewish parties in the community (Zionists, socialists and assimilationists) displayed similar distress about the national redrawing of the borders. They decided to lobby for Salonika to become an international, denationalised city. The fact that Salonikan Zionists submitted a memorandum to the central Zionist organisation concerning the issue of internationalisation illustrates that Zionism in Salonika was not mainly concerned with the emigration of Salonikan Jews to Palestine. In fact Thessaloniki attracted leading Zionist attention because it seemed like a model for a Jewish state (Molho 1997a: 341). It was significant that Zionists in Salonika were prepared to take a critical stance towards the Greek authorities. It was mainly the Zionists who criticised the government for the discriminatory way in which it dealt with the re-housing problem after the great fire of 1917. The fire had destroyed mainly Jewish areas in the centre of town. Venizelos' liberal Cabinet expropriated large parts of the destroyed areas. The relocation of Jewish neighbourhoods to the outskirts of the city was the beginning of the Hellenisation and modernisation of Salonika (see Chapter 6).

Looking at the first Pan-Hellenic Zionist Congress, which took place in Salonika in 1919, Molho comes to the conclusion that Salonikan Zionism functioned as a vehicle for modernisation and democratisation within the Jewish community. Its focus was 'not on Zion but on Salonika' (Molho 1997a: 349) and it was a response to the political instability of that time.

The incorporation of Salonika into the Greek nation-state meant that the Jewish population was expected to change its cosmopolitan orientation and its language preferences. However, just after 1912, it was the aim of the Greek government to gain the trust of the Jewish population of Salonika and therefore the authorities allowed the Sabbath to be kept in the city and exempted Jews from military service. The Jews presented a different problem from that of other minorities because they were perceived as *apatris*, without a homeland. In the description of the Tobacco Strike in 1914, Efi Avdela illustrates that the Jewish workers were portrayed as 'antihellenes' by the Greek press not because they were socialists, but because they were 'bad Socialists' (Avdela 1993: 201). In this view nationalist Venizelist socialism ('Greek, patriotic, masculine') was contrasted with cosmopolitan socialism ('foreign, homeless, stateless, feminine') (Avdela 1993: 197), the latter associated with Benaroya's Federation.

The following decades in Greece, and in particular in Salonika, are characterised by severe clashes between followers of the king (royalists), who advocated neutrality in the First World War and followers of Prime

Minister Venizelos[8] (nationalists), who wanted to fight on the side of the entente powers. The conflict became known as the 'National Schism' in which Venizelos was associated with an aggressive irredentist policy of the 'Megali Idea', the plan to re-establish the borders of the Byzantine Empire, and the king and his supporters with 'a small but honourable Greece' which should first consolidate its hold over the new territories (Clogg 1992: 89). In Salonika, the most important city of 'new Greece', Venizelos was very popular, while the King found his supporters in many regions of 'old Greece'. In 1919 Greek troops occupied Smyrna (Izmir). The treaty of Sèvres, signed in 1920, provided that Greece would be in administrative control of the Smyrna region. However, this treaty was never ratified by the Turks. The Greek army then launched a major offensive in southern West Anatolia but was defeated by Turkish troops in 1922. The capture of the city by the Turks was accompanied by the massacre of about 30,000 Greeks and Armenians. The Greek quarters of the city were destroyed. Greek troops and the Greek population fled the city. The massacre and the expulsion of Greeks from Smyrna and its aftermath became known as the *mikrasiatiki katastrophi*, the Asia Minor Catastrophe.

In July 1923 the treaty of Lausanne defined the borders of the Turkish state and Greece lost all territories over which it was given control in the treaty of Sèvres. A population exchange between Greece and Turkey was agreed. About 1,100,000 Greeks, classified as 'Greek' by their Orthodox religion, came to Greece and about 380,000 Turks, that is, Muslims, were transferred to Turkey (Clogg 1992: 101). The Greeks of Istanbul and the Muslims of Thrace were exempted from the population exchange agreement. In Salonika the population exchange brought about a radical change in the make-up of its inhabitants. More than 100,000 refugees came to the city, increasing its population by half. After the Balkan Wars, Greeks were a minority in the territories of 'New Greece'; they became a majority after the population exchange and Greece became 'one of the most ethnically homogenous countries in the Balkans' (Clogg 1992: 106).

After 1922 and the population exchange, the authorities adopted a clear 'Hellenisation' policy which discouraged separate ethnic identities. The new policy manifested itself, for example, in the ratification of a law in 1922 which forbade work on Sundays, a blow to all Jewish enterprises. Greek was made the compulsory first language in all schools.

The massive influx of Asia Minor refugees, who came to be seen as a catalyst for a homogenous Greek state, created an atmosphere of fierce economic competition between the Jewish and Greek working classes. The fascist party *Tria Epsilon* (*Ethiki Enosis Ellas*, National Union of Greece), founded in 1927, found ample support among the deprived refugees who were willing to blame communists and Jews for their misfortune. The tense situation led to the first large-scale anti-Semitic incident in the history of Salonika: the looting of Campbell, a poor Jewish neighbourhood. The incident was triggered by news that a member of the Maccabee society had participated in a meeting in Sofia which adopted a resolution for an independent Macedonia. *Tria Epsilon* thus launched a campaign against the 'foreign and communist Jews' who had 'betrayed' Greece. The quarter of Campbell was set on fire after an earlier attempt in the neighbourhood of Toumba had failed. The Campbell event was accompanied by anti-Semitic campaigns in various newspapers, *Macedonia* in particular, in which Jews were portrayed as foreign elements who were harmful to 'Greek interests'.

The Campbell incident caused another wave of Jewish emigration. Between 1932 and 1934 Salonikan Jews left for Palestine, France, the United States and South America.[9] This is a very important event in the history of the Jews of Salonika because it demonstrates that a certain political and economic climate can make an ethnic group appear 'suspicious' to the majority population of a nation-state. In the public eye the 'foreign' element of the actually 'indigenous' Jews was fuelled by the fact that they spoke Ladino and 'stuck to themselves'. The accusation of non-Greek, unpatriotic behaviour and treason which surrounded the Campbell events (and the Tobacco Strike in 1914) created an insecurity among the Jewish community which still exists today.

The question of nationalism and 'national minorities' (Turks, Slavo-Macedonians, Chams, Sephardic Jews and Armenians) was of vital importance to the three major political forces in the inter-war period: Venizelism, Anti-Venizelism, and communism (Mavrogordatos 1983: 230). With the exception of the Jews and the Armenians, the other three national minority groups could be easily identified with neighbouring states (Turkey, Bulgaria and Albania) and their presence in border areas was thus perceived as a potential threat to Greece's territorial integrity. Venizelism stood for nationalism and assimilation. It was seen as an agent for the irredentism which had been responsible for the annexation of the new territories in which the minorities lived. Venizelos' state policies, especially after the population exchange, were aimed at 'neutralising' the minorities.

Anti-Venizelism, on the other hand, served in the inter-war period as a protector of minorities against the policies of the Greek state. In some areas of 'New Greece' the conflict between Greek refugees and non-Greek natives was a conflict between rural and urban populations. In Salonika it was a conflict over the control of economic life between urban refugees and the urban Jewish population. The 'Greekness' of minorities became an important issue in this period and Venizelists often accused Anti-Venizelists of having relied on the vote of the Turks, the Bulgarians and the Jews, that is to say on the vote of non-Greeks. In defence some Anti-Venizelists argued that the Jews were more Greek than the refugees (Mavrogordatos 1983: 231).

The Communist Party adopted until 1935 a much more radical anti-national stance, in so far as it demanded 'a united and independent Macedonia and Thrace' and viewed Greece as an imperialist colonial power which conquered regions inhabited by other nationalities and oppressed them. After 1935, this policy, which had alienated many Greeks, was substituted by the demand for 'complete equality for the minorities'. In all the elections between 1915 and 1935 the minority question was of significance and the fear of 'alien minorities determining the outcome of Greek elections' was a recurrent theme. In the elections of 1915 and 1920 Anti-Venizelists succeeded in gaining 69 out of 74 Macedonian seats. In the elections of 1920 the Macedonian seats could have turned the nationwide vote to a Venizelist majority. The minority vote was blamed for the Venizelist defeat. In October 1923 separate electoral colleges were introduced for the remaining Moslems in Western Thrace and the Jews in Salonika. These were abolished in 1933 when a court ruled that the electoral segregation of Salonikan Jews was unconstitutional.

In 1936 General Metaxas established a military dictatorship in Greece, with the backing of the king. Metaxas prohibited the publication of francophone newspapers and made it difficult for Jews and Armenians to become officers in the Greek army. However, he insisted that the Greek state would continue 'to nourish the same feeling of sympathy for Jewish citizens which had previously existed' (Papacosma 1978: 14). In spite of a decreasing Jewish population, due to the emigration after the fire of 1917 and the Campbell incident, there was a vibrant Jewish community in Salonika on the eve of the Second World War. When the Italian–Greek War broke out in 1940 many thousands of Jewish soldiers fought in Albania. Seven thousand were from Salonika.

Germany came to the rescue of her Italian ally and launched an invasion of Greece through Yugoslavia and Bulgaria, on 6 April 1941

(*Unternehmen Marita*). Greek and British forces (a British expeditionary force had been sent to Greece in 1941) were overcome and by May 1941 the whole of Greece was occupied. While Germany kept strategically important zones, such as the area of Salonika, Western Macedonia and Eastern Thrace, Bulgaria occupied Eastern Macedonia and Western Thrace, and Italy was in charge of the rest of Greece. The occupation caused famine, food shortages and massive inflation in Greece. Following the occupation, the communist EAM (National Liberation Front) with its military wing ELAS and the non-communist EDES (National Republican Greek League) were formed and fought a guerrilla struggle against the German forces.[10]

The policies adopted towards Jews differed considerably in the German, Bulgarian and Italian occupied zones. The Jews of the Bulgarian zone were the first to be deported in March 1943. The Jews of Eastern Thrace were taken and deported to Auschwitz with all the Salonikan Jews. The Jews under Italian occupation were relatively safe because the Italian authorities did not comply with German deportation demands (Mazower 1993: 250). This changed after the surrender of Italian troops in September 1943 and the subsequent German occupation of the south of Greece. At the beginning of April 1944 the Jews from Athens, Larissa, Ioanina and Trikkala were deported to Auschwitz. By the summer the same happened to the 'island Jews' of Crete, Corfu, Kos and Rhodes. Soon after these deportations German forces were forced to withdraw from Greece because of the successful advances by the Red Army in Romania (Mazower 1993: 355). By October 1944 the whole of Greece was liberated.

After the withdrawal of the German troops in 1944, control of Greece was given to Britain in the famous 'percentage agreement' of 1944 between Stalin and Churchill. Control over Romania was assigned to the Soviets (Clogg 1992: 133). The clash between the communist ELAS/ELAM and EDES, supported by the British, subsequently turned into the Civil War, lasting from 1946 to 1949, which deeply divided Greek society into two sides, communists and anti-communists, the left and the right.

There is no clear periodisation in terms of communal Jewish history in post-war Greece. The immediate post-war years were characterised by the process of individual health recovery, the reclaiming of property, many weddings, some of them group weddings, a subsequent baby boom (between 1945 and 1951 402 births were registered in the Jewish community of Salonika), and several waves of emigration. From the early 1950s onwards the focus shifted from individual to communal

reconstruction and after 1956, the year in which the last wave of emigration took place, the demographic and economic situation of the
community started to stabilise.

In 1967 a group of colonels seized power and Greece was ruled by
the Junta until 1974. The Junta presented themselves as the defender
of the 'Helleno-Christian civilisation' (*Ellas, Ellinon, Christianon*) and
intensely persecuted any left-wing sympathisers. The colonels dis-
missed the Jewish community assembly and council and appointed a
new council, a process which all organisations which functioned as a
'legal entity under public law' had to undergo. It is surprising, however, that despite the Junta's stress of mono-religious nationalism, the
Junta years were not perceived as a threat by most of my informants.
In fact, many people stressed that the leadership change in the Jewish
community was very positive. The new council undertook significant
changes: the size of the assembly was reduced from 50 members to 20
(this measure was put into effect in 1975, the first elections after the
dictatorship), the rabbinical council was abolished, the official language of the council (in which the minutes were taken) was changed
from Ladino to Greek, and, most importantly, the new council re-eval-
uated the communal properties which led to a drastic increase of communal revenues (Jewish Community of Salonika 1978: 40). In the
decades to follow the by now financially independent community
opened a Jewish school and a Home for the Elderly, and provided welfare, social and religious services to its members.

In 1981 PASOK (Panhellenic Socialist Movement) won the general elections, Andreas Papandreou became Prime Minister, and Greece
became a member of the European Union. The new government
implemented a number of important reforms: the resistance to the Axis
was officially recognised, Greek communists were allowed to return
from the eastern countries they fled to after the Civil War, civil marriage and divorce by consent was introduced. When PASOK came to
power in 1981 the political change had a clear impact on the Jews of
Greece due to the Lebanon War and the increased criticism of Israel
(and thus indirectly of the Jewish community). Pro-socialist newspapers and television compared Israel to the German Nazis and raised
questions about the loyalty of Greek Jews. There was also talk of a
'Zionist conspiracy which aimed at turning Greece into a new
Lebanon' and of 'Jewish circles who have a great hatred for the Prime
Minister' (see Perdurant 1995: 9). Conspiracy theories (in which Jews
together with the Freemasons and the CIA are suspected of having
been responsible for the military coup in 1967 and Jews in general are

seen as 'agents of foreign interests') became popular in the political climate of 1982 and the following years (see Perdurant 1995: 11). Not sur-
prisingly, attendance figures of community assemblies peaked during
this time. When PASOK came to power again after a short interval
(1989–93),[11] the general tone of its policies regarding Israel, the United
States and Europe became much more moderate.

In the 1990s Greece maintained a troubled relationship with her
Turkish, Albanian and Macedonian (FYROM) neighbours, and this put
the minority issue back on the agenda. While there is only a tiny Greek
minority in Istanbul (around 3,000) and on the islands of Imvros and
Tenedos, there is a large Muslim minority in Northern Thrace (about
120,000) and a large number of Greeks in Albania. A further interesting
development in the nineties is the 'resettling' of thousands of Soviet
Greeks, known as Russo-Pontics, who have come to Greece after the collapse of the Soviet Union.

CONTEMPORARY ISSUES: CITIZENSHIP, NATIONALISM, RELIGION AND MINORITIES IN GREECE

Memories and identities are never formulated in a vacuum. The
accounts of the interviewees in this study are time-bound, which
means that they are formulated at a specific point of the individual's
life cycle and within a certain political and social arena. The following
section will discuss issues of the Greek political and social arena.

In her article 'Ethnicity, Nationalism, and State Making' Verdery
argues that 'identity choice varies with different kind of states' (1994:
39). In this understanding the state provides the context in which national, ethnic, religious and social identities are produced and negotiated. As
indicated in Chapter 2, I would like to extend this argument by suggesting that identity choice varies with different kinds of nationalism.

Two types of nationalism (one should bear in mind that these are
simplified ideal types) have been distinguished in the literature on
nationalism: ethnic nationalism and civic nationalism (see Chapter 2).
One can juxtapose these concepts as follows: ethnic nationalism is a
concept of the 'same people in many places', civic nationalism one of
'different people in one place'.

Greece displays the first type of nationalism. Someone's
'Greekness' is not determined by his or her place of birth but by religion (Christian Orthodoxy), language and 'culture'. Of these compo-
nents, religion is certainly the most important factor. This can easily be

explained if we look back at the Ottoman Empire and the emergence of the Greek state. In the multi-ethnic Ottoman Empire religion divided people into different *millets*. With the disintegration of the Ottoman Empire and the rise of nationalist movements in the Balkans, the Church became an important vehicle in spreading the Greek vernacular and Greek culture. It should also be pointed out that in the nineteenth century Balkan intellectuals were actively involved in defining and shaping the notion of a Greek national identity (Kitromelides 1994). Since the kingdom of Greece, which came to existence in 1830, only covered one-third of the total Greek population in the Ottoman Empire, Greek national identity could not have been defined by territory. In the years following Greece's independence, the idea of a Greek 'ethnos' (which refers both to a nation and a state) needed to be consolidated. Herzfeld illustrates that the discipline of folklore played an active part in asserting the historical continuity of the Greeks with their 'glorious past' (Herzfeld 1982).

The central themes of Greece's nationalism were (and continue to be) the historical continuity of the Hellenism of 'classic Greece', the Orthodoxy of the Byzantine Empire, cultural homogeneity (closely linked to the argument of continuity) and the stress on unity (illustrated, for example, in the liberation struggle against the Ottomans to free the Greek people from '400 years of slavery'). Stewart illustrates the interesting conflict between Greek nationalists of the nineteenth century, who focused on the survival of cultural remnants from Ancient Greece, and the Church, which opposed religious practices identified as pagan (Stewart 1994: 138). Through a discourse of syncretism, set out to prove the reality of the Helleno-Christian symbiosis, Hellenism and Byzantine Christian Orthodoxy have become the pillars of Greek nationalism (Stewart 1994: 140).

In his essay 'Continuity and Change in Contemporary Greek Historiography' Kitroeff argues that the work of the most famous exponent of the theory of continuity, Constantine Paparigopoulos, *Istoria Tou Ellinikou Ethnous* (The History of the Greek People), published between 1850 and 1874, has provided the unquestioned framework for Greek historiography until very recently (Kitroeff 1990: 145). Research on the teaching of history in Greek schools has also shown that the centralised school system has been of crucial importance in the process of disseminating 'a certain idea of Greece' (Varouxakis 1995) stressing continuity, homogeneity and unity, and dividing the outer world into two groups: *Philhellines* (Friends of Greece) and *Mishellines* (Enemies of Greece).

The notion of ethnic and cultural homogeneity has had serious implications: a) it led to a forceful Hellenisation policy in areas which were ethnically and linguistically diverse, particularly in the regions of Macedonia and Thrace which became Greek only in the twentieth century and which had large non-Greek populations; b) it created a problematic relationship between the Greek state and minorities. Minority populations who display signs of 'otherness' (such as speaking another language) can become suspected of expressing disloyalty towards Greece.

It is because of this specific understanding of 'Greekness' that the question of minorities in Greece has become a very sensitive, politicised issue. The Greek state recognises the Muslims in Thrace as a 'minority' and to a lesser extent the Jews (Stavros 1995: 9), but displays great reluctance to acknowledge other minority groups such as the Slavo-Macedonians, the Pomaks (who are Muslims), and other non-Christian Orthodox groups (Catholics, Protestants, Jehovah's Witnesses and so forth). As part of the Hellenisation of Macedonia, Slavo-Macedonians changed their names, villages were given new Greek names and Slavo-Macedonian was discouraged as a language (Karakasidou 1991).[12] The ethnic identity of both the Slavo-Macedonians and the Muslims (as Turks) is seen as problematic because it is closely intermingled with the fear of territorial claims made by FYROM (the former Republic of Macedonia) and Turkey.

It is due to this fear that Greece refused to accept the name of the new Republic of Macedonia (an ongoing diplomatic debate since 1991). From the Greek point of view FYROM has wrongly appropriated Greek historical symbols (like the star of Vergina, found on the tombstone of Philip) and names. The reaction to this contestation was an extensive emphasis that 'Macedonia is and always has been Greek' (written on signposts and as graffiti to be found all over Greece in 1994), an increasing usage of the star of Vergina in various forms (jewellery, advertisements, general decoration and so on), and a number of huge protest demonstrations throughout Greece. Stewart notes that the Church was at the forefront in the organisation of these demonstrations. By presenting itself as 'the guardian of the national interest' the Church strengthened its position (Stewart 1998: 7).

This situation, in which non-Greek ethnicity is seen as a potential threat, has created a complicated position for minorities. From a legalistic point of view members of minorities are Greek citizens with a different religion. From a popular perspective, however, they cannot be 'really' Greek because they are not Christian Orthodox. The following episode illustrates the close association of Orthodoxy and 'Greekness' in a day-to-day context. I was invited to a Jewish wedding and went to look for a present in a shop. The shop assistant offered to help me and asked: 'are you going to a Greek wedding?'. When I answered positively, he handed me a cross.

Since the state is seen as the organic extension of the *ethnos*, that is, as the embodiment of the nation, in which Christian Orthodoxy is central (Pollis 1992: 174), religious minorities remain in an difficult position. This point is underlined by the fact that Christian Orthodoxy is Greece's official religion, expressed in Article 3 of the constitution (adopted in 1975), which states that 'the prevailing religion in Greece is that of the Eastern Orthodox Church of Christ'. A further complication for the status of religious minorities arises from Article 13 of the constitution which guarantees the 'freedom of religious conscience' but also clearly states that 'proselytism is prohibited'. The group most affected by this law has been the group of the Jehovah's Witnesses who have been arrested (for actively seeking to convert Christian Orthodox) and imprisoned (for not serving in the army on religious grounds). Catholic, Jews and Muslims are not affected by the law against proselytism because they are considered to be 'historic religious minorities'. The religious rights of the Muslims are specially protected by the treaty of Lausanne, adopted in 1923 after the population exchange between Turkey and Greece. In his review on the legal status of minorities in contemporary Greece, Stavros argues that the special rules for the protection of minorities established under the treaty of Lausanne appear inadequate and unfair (Stavros 1995: 1). In contrast to the 'historic religious minorities', Protestants (Evangelists) and Jehovah's Witnesses are classified as heretic movements because they make Christian Orthodox Greeks abandon their faith and convert. Stavros points to the discriminatory nature of a number of laws introduced by the Metaxas government which are still in force, such as the law on the establishment of non-Orthodox churches which subjects these churches to ministerial approval (Stavros 1995: 11).

The law against proselytism exemplifies the symbiotic relationship between the state and the Church, in which the state attempts to secure the position of the Church and in which the Church legitimises the state. The existence of a Ministry of Education and Religion also makes the strong interdependence between state and Church apparent (Pollis 1992: 181). This is not to say that there is no conflict of interest between the institution of the state and the institution of the Church. Stewart demonstrates in his article on the controversy about the secular or religious usage of the Rotunda (built by the Roman Emperor Galerius in the fourth century), that the state and the Church also compete for the 'better' representation of the *ethnos* (Stewart 1998: 8).

The dominant role of religion in education is further underlined by the fact that for many years it was almost impossible for a non-Christian Orthodox person to become a primary school teacher in Greece. The debate about the category 'religion' on the Greek European Identity Cards also sheds light on the relationship between the state and the Church. Following pressure from Greece's EU partners, the Greek government decided in 2001 to issue identity cards without the mention of religious affiliation. This decision caused strong criticism and protest from the Orthodox Church. For many people it seems inconceivable that a Greek identity card should not have 'Christian Orthodox' written on it.[13]

The last legal aspect we should consider here is citizenship. Citizenship laws in general reflect a state's self-perception and perception of 'the Other' since it legally defines who is eligible, who could be eligible, and who is not eligible to obtain the passport of a specific country. Greek citizenship laws are based on *jus sanguinis* (the law of blood), a 'descent'-oriented law, which clearly favours individuals with 'Greek origins'. Under these laws Russo-Pontic Greeks from the former Soviet Union have been repatriated in recent years. Other countries which have recently repatriated populations, such as Germany and Israel, also use *jus sanguinis* citizenship laws. As in Greece, this specific notion of citizenship goes hand in hand with the 'ethnic nationalism' described above.

These legalistic aspects concerning the state, the Church, the *ethnos*, and minorities have been outlined here because I think they are relevant for the general socio-political arena in which individuals act. Of course one needs to bear in mind, however, that the day-to-day reality, in which people interact and formulate what they think, is very complex. Value and belief systems do not correspond in a straightforward way to institutionalised rules and laws. However, I am suggesting that the Greek state and its centralised education system (with its uniform curriculum) has had a severe impact on ideas and perceptions about 'us' and 'them'. Scholars of nationalism have repeatedly stressed the importance of a centralised education system for the formation of a national identity (Gellner 1983, Anderson 1991), to be more precise for the formation of a more homogeneous national identity. I suggest that in the case of Greece, nationalist historiography and state education have greatly contributed to the formation of a relatively homogeneous

Greek national identity which emphasises ethnic purity, Christian Orthodoxy, an unbroken bond with the past, and in which there is very little place for the multi-religious and multicultural history of Greece.

This is not only a matter of silence on 'other' pasts but a matter of articulated protest against 'multicultural history', seen as a threat to the continuity of Hellenism or Orthodoxy. Stewart quotes a representative of the Church who, together with other people, forced his way into the Rotunda and destroyed the piano which was going to be used for a concert: 'The people of God have triumphed. They tell us that Thessaloniki is a multi-historical city. If they mean that many conquerors passed through here, then I agree. But the Orthodox character of the city was never altered' (Stewart 1998:7). The building had been used as a church, a mosque, and a museum and became a 'national monument' in 1913. For the people who protested against the secular use of the Rotunda, its function as a church was the only one which 'counted'. In one of the protests people shouted: *'Oute havra, oute tzami, ekklisia elliniki'* (not a synagogue,[14] not a mosque, but a Greek church) (Stewart 1998: 5).

As a final point in this section, anti-Semitism should be considered. It is not being suggested that anti-Semitism is inherent in Greek nationalism but that Greece's stress on homogeneity can provide a fertile soil for a variety of discriminatory sentiments towards religious and other minorities. As not much has been published on Greek antiSemitism, I will refer to the paper by Perdurant (1995) and some of my own observations. The theme dominating anti-Semitic discourse in Greece is the notion of the 'Jewish and Zionist conspiracy to take over the world'. Variations of this theme can be found in various contexts. Among some elements of the Orthodox Church, Jews, often associated with Jehovah's Witnesses and the Freemasons, have been portrayed as 'anti-Greek, anti-Christ Zionists dreaming of the achievement of World Jewish domination' (quoted in Perdurant 1995: 3). The introduction of new European Union Identity Cards with an eight-digit identification number led to loud protests among some ultra-religious groups. It was claimed that the 'new IDs of the Jews and the Masons' are part of the conspiracy, as they will contain the number 666, the sign of the anti-Christ (quoted in Perdurant 1995: 4). At the time of my main fieldwork trip in 1994, books which published such views could be found on the display of most bookshops, sometimes next to Megas' *Souvenir* (1993) on the Jews of Salonika (see Figure 32). I interviewed a man who publishes and sells this kind of literature. He told me that of the 55 books he had published, 15 were written by Greek writers, others are translations (of the 'Protocols of

the Elders of Zion',[15] for example). He estimated that each year he publishes about 200,000 copies of books of this particular 'genre'. He was
himself a clear believer of the 'conspiracy theory' and tried to explain
to me the history of the 'secret societies of the Jews and the Zionists'.
When asked whether he believed that the Salonikan Jews are also part
of this conspiracy, he said that they were victims because like all the
Jews in the world they have 'to give a tenth of their property to the
Zionists in New York'. During the course of my research I came across
the 'Jewish conspiracy theory' a number of times. One such instance
was in an interview with a communist (non-Jewish) Salonikan in his
forties who insisted that his Jewish classmate ran for the office of class
president because the community had instructed him to do so. One of
the reasons why variations of the conspiracy theory can be found
among a wide circle of people is that it can function as both an outlet
for left-wing anti-American and anti-Israeli sentiments and for right-
wing anti-heterodoxy views. The most virulent anti-Semitism in
Greece is propagated by a small number of extreme right organisations, such as *Ethniki Metopo* (National Front) and *Chrissi Avgi* (Golden
Dawn). In their publications the Jews are portrayed as 'the eternal
enemy of our people who have the audacity to speak of persecution and
anti-Semitism' (quoted in Perdurant 1995: 14). The most notorious
weekly newspaper which is associated with the ideas of the above
organisations is *Stochos* which can be bought in most *periptera* (kiosks)
and which serialised the 'Protocols of the Elders of Zion'. Supporters
of these organisations are held responsible for spraying anti-Semitic
propaganda on walls of houses and shops (such as 'Greeks kill the Jews'
or 'Death to the Jews') and committing serious acts of vandalism. In
1987 swastikas and anti-Semitic slogans were painted on the synagogue and a number of Jewish shops in Volos. In 1994 I visited the van-
dalised Jewish cemetery in Trikkala. Some tombstones were smashed,
others had swastikas and 'Stochos' sprayed over the names. The cemetery was in a very bad state. This major incident was not publicised, an
example of the reluctance of the Jewish leadership to acknowledge the
existence of anti-Semitism in Greece, partly because of the fear that by
publicising such incidents one might incite more anti-Semitism.

CONCLUSION

Having outlined the historical and political developments which continue to play an important role in the formulation of Jewish collective and individual identities, the radical changes the Jewish community underwent cannot be overstated. At the beginning of the twentieth century Salonika was part of a multi-cultural empire and its population consisted in majority of Jews. Today, Jews represent 0.001 per cent of the total population of Salonika, the second-largest city of the Greek nation-state.

NOTES

1. This overview is based on secondary sources, that is, historiographical accounts of Greek, Salonikan and Jewish history.
2. A common anecdote recounts that Sultan Bayazid II exclaimed: 'How could the Catholic monarchs be considered wise, when by expelling their Jews they impoverished Spain while enriching Turkey?' (quoted in Molho 1991: 105).
3. Romaniot communities maintained their traditions in the regions west of the Pindos mountains, in Epirus, the Ionian islands and the Peloponnese.
4. This phrase was coined by the Spanish-born poet Samuel Ushque, who had settled in northern Italy.
5. As Muslims the Donme had to leave Salonika in the population exchange between Greece and Turkey in 1923.
6. Since Salonika was a port-city large numbers of Jews worked in the port. Molho estimates that 9,000 Jews worked as *Hamals* (porters and dockers), boatmen and fishermen (Molho 1998: 15).
7. Incidents of anti-Semitism during the Greek independence struggle had been reported. Rumours that the Jews had killed the Patriarch Gregory VI prompted anti-Semitic outbursts against the Jews in Patras, Tripoli and other cities. Consequently, many Jews fled to areas which were still under Ottoman or Italian rule (Corfu).
8. Eleftherios Venizelos (1864–1936) was repeatedly Prime Minister of Greece between 1910 and 1933.
9. The total number of Jews who emigrated from Salonika between 1908 and 1932 is estimated to be about 40,000 (Nehama 1989: 247).
10. Mazower estimates that about 40,000 people starved to death during the famine and 25,000 people died as a result of the guerrilla struggle between the resistance groups and the Wehrmacht (Mazower 1993: xiii).
11. After Papandreou's death in 1996 Simitis became the new Prime Minister and PASOK was re-elected on 23 September 1996.
12. The sensitivity of this issue was illustrated by the reaction to Karakasidou's research. When she came to Greece in 1994, during the period of my research, the far-right journal *Stochos* branded her a 'traitor' and published a death threat. She also faced tremendous difficulties in getting her book published (see Mazower 1996).
13. The Council of State, the highest Greek administrative court, decided in 2001 that the notation of religious beliefs on identity cards violates religious freedom.
14. The term '*havra*' is a pejorative term for synagogue.
15. The 'Protocols' is an anti-Semitic publication about an alleged conference of the leaders of World Jewry who plan to take control of the whole world. The first edition of the 'Protocols' appeared in Russia in 1905.

4

The Contemporary Jewish Community: Organization, Activities and Demography

It is important to understand how the institution of the community operates because the Jewish community as an institution plays two important roles: it links individual Jews in Salonika by providing services such as education, welfare, social activities, religious ceremonies and so forth; and it determines who is a member of the community and has a right to participate in its activities. The institution of the Jewish community is an important context through which individual identities are formed in negotiations and opposition with the community. It represents the Jews of Salonika on a collective level, and through its policies it articulates identities and boundaries. The Jewish community as an institution is also of vital importance for this research because it provided the 'main fieldwork site' for this study. Most of the interviewees participated in one way or another in the religious and social life of the community.[1]

The first part of this chapter will describe the contemporary community and some of the activities I participated in. The second part will present some statistical data on membership numbers, marriage patterns, births and deaths. These figures will give the reader an idea of the demographic development of the community after the war. As we will see later, membership numbers and marriages are of crucial importance to such a small community because they justify the overall concern for 'the survival of the community' in which the 'problem of mixed marriages' is seen as an immense threat.

THE JEWISH COMMUNITY AND ITS INSTITUTIONS

The Jewish community in Salonika is a 'legal entity under public law'. It falls under the jurisdiction of the Ministry of Education and Religion. This particular status of the community dates back to Law No. 2456 from 1920 which gave all Jewish communities in Greece this special status. The community thus functions as a 'public body' and –

unlike US or British Jewish communities – it is not a congregation which individuals join voluntarily. If one is born to two Jewish parents one automatically becomes a member of the community and remains a member until the end of one's life, unless one converts. As a remnant of the *millet* system of the Ottoman Empire, the institution of the community performs various functions during the life-cycle of an individual: it registers births, marriages and deaths, it provides elementary school education, it gives loans and grants to its members, and it provides social and medical assistance. The actual list of services is longer but the services listed above suffice to illustrate that the community does not only function as a religious congregation. The community consists of a wide spectrum of members who choose to be or not be involved in the community's life and who make use of the community in very different ways.[2]

The structure of the community is like a 'small parliament'. Apart from the administrative staff, most people work on a voluntary basis for the community. One of my informants noted on this point: 'It is a very wise organisation, the Jewish community, because it is the only organisation I have seen which has more than 100 volunteers who work like crazy and want to contribute something free of charge' (Am19). The entire community elects 20 members every four years (reduced from the original number of 50) to the community assembly. The assembly then elects the community council, which consists of five permanent members and two 'apprentices'. Finally, members of the council elect the president, the vice-president, the general secretary, the treasurer and the controller among themselves. The two apprentices vote, but they are not full members of the council.

At the time of my 1994 visit, community elections had taken place a year earlier and resulted in a leadership change, the first change after 25 years. The fact that the new government had not appointed any members of the 'old government' or the other parties to any of the committees created some bitterness and criticism. The number of committees varies, depending on actual events which need to be planned. There are about 20 committees, each usually consisting of five members. To list a few: the school committee, the school care committee, the cemetery committee, the synagogue committee, the summer camp committee, the youth club committee, the welfare committee, the medical care committee, the loan committee, the international public relations committee (this is a new one), the Greek public relations committee, the management of real estate committee, the Centre for the History of the Jewish Community of Salonika committee, and so on. At the time of this study there were three parties represented in the community assembly: *Enosi* (Union) with seven seats, *Ananeosi* (Renewal) with 12 seats, and *Proothos* (Progress) with one seat. When asked about the differences between the various parties one informant (who was an assembly member) gave me the following answer: 'I don't think they stand for different ideas. The only thing they can do is to serve the community's interests in a better or worse way. The possibilities of a different policy are very limited' (Bm37). One of the previous leaders reinforced this statement by saying: 'We don't have that many differences. The new government continues the same policy we laid out. They have not done anything new. Perhaps they can do something better, that is possible. But they cannot do anything new' (Am20).

Despite the fact that both statements stress the similarity of the various parties, people who were active in the community always knew who belonged to which party, or more precisely which family was associated with which party. The leadership change in the community was often perceived in terms of a 'generation change'. Members of the *Enosi* party were associated with more old-fashioned ideas than their colleagues from the other parties. The central issue in this 'generation gap' is the question of boundaries, in terms of the community's policy towards mixed marriages and its general openness. While the older leaders seem to have propagated a more closed notion of community which goes hand in hand with a stricter non-acceptance of mixed marriages, the new leaders are viewed as more open (to the general public) and more willing to look for new solutions regarding the 'mixed marriage problem'. One informant doubted that the change of council would make any difference. She said: 'Nothing changed and can change. It is only a small community of 250 families. So what do you expect to change?' (Bf33).

The new council had in 1994 not changed the membership policy which allows only children of parents who had a Jewish wedding to become members of the community. The problem arose after the introduction of civil weddings in 1982, when Jews could marry Christians without their converting. Although the Jewish spouses officially remain members, their children cannot be part of the community. If the non-Jewish spouse converts, the children are automatically community members. This policy has been relaxed in recent years. Within a declining Jewish community, the issue of mixed marriage is the most prominent and most contested issue. Some people feel that the community needs to embrace children of mixed marriages, others feel that if the community does so it will result in the 'end of the community' (for a detailed discussion of the mixed marriage issue see Chapter 9).

The Kinotita (*Community*)

The administrative centre of the Jewish community is located in the centre of Salonika on Tsimiski Street. This building is usually referred to as *Kinotita*, the community (see Figure 1). As a community centre it is unrecognisable from the outside. One cannot enter the building from the main street, but only through a door which is located in a small shopping mall. Inside the shopping mall there is no sign indicating the Jewish community, apart from the fact that there is usually a Greek policeman in front of the entrance. Next to the entrance a number of books on Jewish themes are displayed in a glass showcase. There is no indication of where one could purchase the books, nor does it say who is actually displaying these books. It is clear that only if one knows where to find the Jewish community can one actually find it. On a number of occasions I encountered desperate American tourists who were literally standing in front of the entrance and could not figure out how to find the community. Only after some months did I notice that on the building facing Tsimiski there were three big letters, IKΘ, the abbreviation for *Israelitiki Kinotita Thessalonikis.*

After passing the policeman, one can either walk or take the lift to the first floor of the community's building. Here we finally find a sign which reads as follows: *Elliniki Demokratia, Israelitiki Kinotita Thessalonikis, NPDD (Nomiko Prosopo Demosiou Dikaiou)*, which translates as 'Republic of Greece, The Jewish Community of Thessaloniki, Legal Entity under Public Law'. The first and latter part of the sign reveal the special status of the community with regard to the Greek state. Behind this door are the central administrative offices of the community. On the right we find the offices of the director, his secretary and the accountancy and property department; on the left we find the general assembly room, which consists of the president's desk (with Greek flags on both sides) and an assembly area, the rabbinate, the office of the secretary and the legal department. The other floors of the building are 'social spaces' divided by age groups. The second floor hosts the elderly in the 'Brotherhood Club', the third the very young, the fourth the teenagers and the adults. Various social activities take place throughout the year on all these floors. The 'Brotherhood Club' and the youth club are open during the week and provide a space to meet, chat, play cards (for the elderly), play table tennis (in the youth club),

or watch television. The meetings of the various women's organisations (there are three, catering to three age groups) also take place in
the *Kinotita*. A recent addition to the community's calendar is the
establishment of the monthly 'Kavedjiko', where community members
meet and speak Judeo-Spanish together.

The busiest time in the community is Friday night, when *Oneg
Shabbat* (the welcoming of the Sabbath) activities take place on each
floor for each age group (see Figures 6, 7 and 8). This ceremony consists of the recital of the Kiddush (a prayer recited over a cup of wine
to consecrate the Sabbath) followed by a meal.[3] The different floors
represent the different generational experience of Salonikan Jews:
while the elder generation sings and speaks Judeo-Spanish and the
prayers are recited in Ladino and Hebrew, the language on the other
floors is clearly Greek (the prayers are recited in Hebrew). During the
period of my fieldwork the community had recently introduced a special celebration for the 30- to 60-year-olds which meant that every
Friday four different Shabbat celebrations took place. The celebrations
for the elderly and for the very young start earlier than the others, following the religious service in the synagogue.[4] One of the issues particularly relevant for the *Leschi*, the youth club, is the question of
whether the youngsters who normally 'go out' after coming to the club,
can bring their Christian friends. Although the youth club has organised special 'open days' when people may bring their friends, it is generally understood that this should not be done on a regular basis. The
argument for this policy is that the *Leschi* is the only place for Jewish
youngsters to meet. In a community which is very concerned with the
high number of mixed marriages (see below) it seems important to
maintain such a space.[5]

The Synagogues and the Jewish Cemetery

Today there are two synagogues in Salonika, the small Yad Lezikaron
Synagogue (translated from Hebrew as 'Remembrance Memorial') in
Vassilis Herakliou Street and the big Monasterioton Synagogue on
Syngrou Street which serves as the principal synagogue. The
Monasterioton Synagogue was founded in 1927 by Jews from
Monastir and is the only synagogue to have survived the war because
it was used as a warehouse by the Red Cross.

The Yad Lezikaron Synagogue was built in 1984 on the site of the
former 'Bourla' prayer house on the ground floor of a modern office
block (Messinas 1997: 103). The daily services and Shabbat services
usually take place in the small synagogue (see Figures 11 and 12). They

are mostly attended by the subsidised *Minyan* (the required number of ten men). The Friday evening and Saturday morning services are frequented by mostly elderly people.[6] Memorial prayers for the dead (*Haskavot*)[7] are an important part of Sephardi services. Many community members come to services at the time of a family *Haskavah*, the anniversary of a death of a family member, when the men must recite the Kaddish in memory of the deceased person. The family who holds the *Haskavah* (in Ladino referred to as *Notchada*) sometimes offer food (such as biscuits) in the subsequent Kiddush ceremony to the other congregants. This is an important ceremony, and it brings people to the synagogue who do not attend any other community activities, such as women who are married to Christians.

Another kind of memorial is very prominent in this synagogue. These are the marble wall-plaques which list all the synagogues that ever existed in Thessaloniki (see Figure 13). Two pieces in the synagogue, the *heikal* (the ark in which the Torah scrolls[8] are kept) and the *tevah*[9] (the reading desk from which the Torah scrolls are read during the service) come from other Salonikan synagogues (Messinas 1997: 103).[10]

The main Monasterioton Synagogue is used for the holidays, and for the celebration of weddings and Bar/Bat Mitzvahs (see Figures 14, 15 and 16).[11] The celebration of weddings and Bar/Bat Mitzvahs[12] are big communal events and the whole community is usually invited. The inside of the synagogue is arranged in the Sephardi style: the *tevah* is in the middle of the prayer room and the 'important people' sit underneath the *heikal*. The womens' gallery is located on the second floor.

The only Jewish cemetery in Salonika is located on the industrialised outskirts of the city in Stavropoli (see Figure 30). As mentioned earlier, this cemetery hosts a Holocaust monument which for many years was the only place to commemorate the death of the Salonikan Jews. Near the entrance to the cemetery is a hall where the prayers are recited before the coffin is brought to the grave. It is a Salonikan custom that women do not accompany the coffin to the grave. This rule is generally adhered to although I was present at the funeral of a very young man at which the women did go to the site of the grave. This theme is also interesting in the context of conversion. I heard several times that it is very difficult for converted women to accept not going to the grave because in Greek Christian cultural terms this makes them a 'bad' mother or wife.[13]

The Jewish Primary School and Nursery

The school is housed in the building of a former Jewish charity organisation called *Matanot LaEvionim* (which translates from Hebrew as
'presents to the poor') which served free meals to poor students until
1943. It is located on Flemming Street which used to be called
Mizrachi Street before the war (see Figure 4).[14] Since 1979 the Jewish
community has been running a private primary school and a nursery
in this building. Until 1979 the community had made special arrangements with two private Greek schools to allow Hebrew teachers to
teach Hebrew and Jewish religion. Jewish children were encouraged to
attend these schools and most did. Due to the small number of Jewish
children, the community hesitated to open a Jewish school. But after
the school's first successful year with only two classes in 1979 the
school started to expand, and has about 55 pupils today. Table 1 illustrates the demographic development of the school.

The Jewish school operates like any other Greek private primary
school.[15] In addition to the usual subjects, two Jewish teachers teach
Hebrew, Jewish history, and religion classes. The director of the school
and most teachers are Christians.[16] Their children also attend the
school because they are entitled to do so according to Greek law. This
means that not all children listed in Table 1 are Jewish. The same
building also houses the Jewish kindergarten which in 1994 was
attended by 14 children.

TABLE 1
NUMBER OF PUPILS IN THE JEWISH SCHOOL, 1979–95

	Boys	Girls	Total	Number of Classes
1979–80	8	4	12	2
1980–81	10	15	25	3
1981–82	13	17	30	4
1982–83	19	20	39	5
1983–84	25	25	50	6
1984–85	33	26	59	6
1985–86	32	21	53	6
1986–87	33	21	54	6
1987–88	35	23	58	6
1988–89	31	27	58	6
1989–90	31	24	55	6
1990–91	25	27	52	6
1991–92	28	28	56	6
1992–93	23	25	48	6
1993–94	26	27	53	6
1994–95	28	24	52	6

TABLE 2
NUMBER OF CHILDREN IN THE JEWISH KINDERGARTEN, 1987–95

	Boys	Girls	Total
1987–88	9	8	17
1988–89	8	7	15
1989–90	7	7	14
1990–91	7	6	13
1991–92	6	14	20
1992–93	14	8	22
1993–94	8	6	14
1994–95	6	8	14

Today the kindergarten and the school are a central pillar in the activities of the community. They bring children and parents together and thus form an important platform for social contact. When I was discussing the Jewish school with Viktor V., who himself was involved in the creation of the school, he said:

A Jewish school is like other Greek schools just a bit better and you learn Jewish culture. But we knew that we, as a community, could not live and exist if there is not one synagogue, one school, and one community, *una comunidad*. These are the necessary things for every Jewish community. (Am28)

Although it seems so clear to the speaker what he means by 'Jewish culture' that he does not elaborate this notion further, this is a clear area of debate in the community.

The Kataskinosi *(Summer Youth Camp)*

The summer youth camp must be included in the 'sites' of the Jewish community because it forms a focus of communal activity and a central meeting point for community members in the summer, for both children and parents. It takes place at Lithohoro, about an hour's drive from Salonika. Jewish children and youth leaders from all over Greece attend this camp. The camp is also attended by Jewish educators from Israel. The programme for the children consists mainly of sports, but there is also a 'Jewish team' which organises discussions and events to do with Judaism and Israel. When I attended the *Kataskinosi*, I got the impression that it is very important as a social space for interaction, as well as providing the platform for struggles and debates about the meaning of Jewish identity in Greece. During my first visit in 1989 a major point of discussion was whether the children should carry

around the Torah scrolls outside the boundaries of the camp. Most of
the Greek Jewish educators felt this was inappropriate, while the others encouraged this practice (see Lewkowicz 1994).

During my second period of fieldwork in 1994, a major point of dispute erupted over the issue of the Israeli flag. The Jewish team had
organised an 'Israel Day'. At the end of the day the camp assembled for
the daily practice of singing the Greek anthem and taking down the
Greek flag (see Figure 9). The American-Israeli rabbi attached the
Israeli flag on the other end of the string of the Greek flag.
Consequently, when the Greek flag was lowered, the Israeli flag went
up. This caused a wave of uproar. The second leader of the camp tried
to get the Israeli flag down and some of the children left the ceremony
in protest. They did not think that they, as Greeks, should stand in
front of an Israeli flag. This event was widely discussed in the weeks
to follow. Some people felt that the American rabbi had acted completely out of order in imposing the Israeli flag, while others were very
upset about the strong reaction against the Israeli flag and saw this as
an indication of a 'weak' Jewish identity. The discussions around this
event encapsulate some of the dilemmas of contemporary Greek Jewry
in defining their Jewish identity.

The Saul Modiano Home for the Elderly

The 'Saul Modiano Home for the Elderly' was founded in 1932 with a
donation from Saul Modiano, a Jew from Salonika who died in Trieste
in 1924. It operated throughout the German occupation until 1943,
when its inhabitants were deported. In the 1970s the council of the
Jewish Community of Salonika decided that the Home for the Elderly
should be re-opened and undertook to erect a new modern building on
the site of the old institution on Vassilis Olgas Street (see Figure 5). So
in 1981 the new Home for the Elderly opened its gates to men and
women who are aged over 65 and members of a Greek Jewish community. It is the only Jewish Home for the Elderly in Greece, and
therefore not everyone who lives in the Home is from Salonika. In
1994, among the 36 men and women who were residents of the Home,
20 came from Salonika and 16 from other places. The Home for the
Elderly, mostly referred to as the *Yerokomiou*, was an important 'fieldwork site'. I often conducted interviews there, met with people for a
chat, and talked to the director.[17] As wonderfully illustrated in Barbara
Meyerhoff's book *Number Our Days* (1978), studying the elderly is
quite a challenging task, in particular when it comes to giving attention
to people who are often not on good terms with each other.

The *Yerokomiou* has six floors, each with a common sitting room. It seemed that some floors were more 'social' than others due to the willingness and physical ability of the individuals to mix with others. The most important communal activity in which most inhabitants of the Home participate is lunch and dinner, which is served in the restaurant on the first floor. Some Jewish festivals are also celebrated communally, and an annual Seder celebration for the first night of Passover usually takes place at the Home. The Yoshua Avraham Salem Synagogue, which is constituted by one prayer room on the ground floor, is used on these special occasions.

In 1997 a *mikveh*[18] was opened in the basement of the *Yerokomiou*. Its main use in the Salonikan context is the bathing of the bride before a wedding and the immersion into water which marks the end of the conversion process to Judaism. The bride's bath is followed by a special celebration for the bride organised and attended only by women. When I attended the first pre-wedding *mikveh* celebration in 1997 there was great excitement at the re-introduction of this tradition.

DEMOGRAPHIC DEVELOPMENTS

As mentioned above, community membership numbers are important not only because they actually reveal demographic developments, but also because they have a 'symbolic value' attached to them. Competing figures, especially on the number of pre-war Jewish inhabitants of Salonika, vary considerably. Some statistics seem to underestimate the Jewish presence in order to stress the strong Greek element of the city. Most authors, however, estimate the number of Jews in Salonika at the beginning of the German occupation at between 52,350 (Grand 1994) and 56,500 (Molho 1988), and the total Jewish population of Greece at between 71,611 (Fleischer 1991) and 79,950 (Molho 1988). During 1943 and 1944, between 54,533 (Mazower 1993: 256) and 62,573 (Molho 1988) Jews from all over Greece were deported to Auschwitz and Bergen-Belsen; between 46,061 (based on records of the Greek Railway) and 48,774 (based on the remaining records of Auschwitz-Birkenau) from Salonika alone (Fleischer 1991: 273). Fleischer estimates that 8,500 Jews survived the German occupation in Greece. In December 1945, after fewer than 2,000 survivors had returned to Greece, the Central Board of Jews in Greece registered 10,266 Jews (Fleischer 1991: 273). The number of Jews who were registered in Salonika in 1945 was 1,950. After waves of emigration to the United

States and Israel between 1945 and the late 1950s, the community's membership fell to less than 1,300 (Molho 1981).

Tables 3, 4, 5, 6 and 7 are based on community records to which I was kindly allowed access.

Age Structure

One could analyse the figures below in many ways. For the purpose of my study it suffices to underline two important trends. The first is the strong presence of the over-60 generation which characterises the general profile of the community. Second, one can clearly realise the impact of the war if one looks at the years of birth among the members (Table 6), bearing in mind that many survivors emigrated and thus do not appear on the list. There is a marked drop after 1927 and a sharp rise in 1951. The drop is due to the fact that hardly any youth or children survived the camps, and the few people who were born between 1927 and 1943 mostly survived in hiding. The rise of population in 1951 is due to the high number of marriages between 1945 and 1949 (see Table 7). The 'baby boom' generation constitutes the second largest group in the community today.

Weddings

As marriage is of such concern to the Jewish community, and is a topic which features prominently in many interviews, I thought it might

TABLE 3
BIRTHS, 1945–94

1945–51: 402
1951–71: 234
1971–94: 205

TABLE 4
MEMBERSHIP FIGURES, 1970–96

1970:	–	1980:	1,084	1990:	1,073
1971:	1,113	1981:	1,009	1991:	1,093
1972:	1,092	1982:	1,109	1992:	1,092
1973:	1,061	1983:	1,008	1993:	1,101
1974:	1,065	1984:	–	1994:	1,094
1975:	1,095	1985:	1,197	1995:	1,088
1976:	1,072	1986:	1,097	1996:	1,074
1977:	1,092	1987:	1,090		
1978:	1,060	1988:	1,092		
1979:	1,090	1989:	1,081		

TABLE 5
MEMBERSHIP STATISTICS, 1991–93

1991:

Age	Male	Female	Total		
0–6	37	23	60	Marriages	4
7–18	81	59	140	Births	9
19–30	53	55	108	New Inscriptions	23
31–59	198	204	402	De–Inscriptions	1
60+	174	216	390	Deaths	11
	543	557	1,100		

1992:

Age	Male	Female	Total		
0–6	33	23	56	Marriages	1
7–18	78	62	140	Births	9
19–30	49	64	113	New Inscriptions	5
31–59	228	198	426	De–Inscriptions	2
60+	142	215	357	Deaths	13
	530	562	1,092		

1993:

Age	Male	Female	Total		
0–6	39	26	65	Marriages	2
7–18	73	58	131	Births	4
19–30	53	56	109	New Inscriptions	26
31–59	214	210	424	De–Inscriptions	4
60+	145	227	372	Deaths	17
	524	577	1,101		

offer some useful insights to look at the entries in the 'marriage books' held by the community. I thus compiled the lists below which tell us about the number of weddings per year, the ages of the spouses, and the number of converted spouses. Since conversion is not explicitly registered in the 'marriage books', the figures should be treated as an indication only. It was possible to gather whether a person had converted due to the father's name and the new Jewish name given to them, usually Bat Avraham (daughter of Abraham). All cases of conversions which I noted were women. This corresponds with my general impression that in Salonika only women convert (either to Judaism or to Christianity).

The main result of the analysis of the marriage figures shows that, as in the age structure of the Jewish community, the effects of the war can clearly be seen. The fact that many survivors had lost their families and were on their own led to the very high number of weddings in

TABLE 6
MEMBERS BY YEAR OF BIRTH AND GENDER, 1993

Year of Birth	Male	Female	Year of Birth	Male	Female
1901	1	–	1926	7	16
1902	1	2	1927	5	6
1903	2	–	1928	1	6
1904	–	1	1929	4	8
1905	2	2	1930	2	6
1906	1	3	1931	2	5
1907	5	2	1932	2	7
1908	6	5	1933	4	3
1909	3	4	1934	4	2
1910	9	4	1935	3	6
1911	3	2	1936	4	5
1912	7	1	1937	–	2
1913	7	5	1938	4	2
1914	5	5	1939	3	4
1915	9	11	1940	3	–
1916	7	10	1941	1	3
1917	8	9	1942	2	5
1918	2	17	1943	3	2
1919	4	5	1944	3	5
1920	5	14	1945	5	3
1921	4	10	1946	7	6
1922	7	13	1947	2	5
1923	7	18	1948	5	5
1924	2	8	1949	4	8
1925	6	19	1950	1	2
1951	18	12	1973	7	4
1952	10	15	1974	5	4
1953	12	13	1975	4	5
1954	9	8	1976	10	2
1955	11	6	1977	10	7
1956	8	12	1978	5	7
1957	12	19	1979	8	4
1958	6	11	1980	4	7
1959	4	11	1981	7	6
1960	6	2	1982	7	4
1961	5	11	1983	7	4
1962	3	5	1984	7	4
1963	5	3	1985	3	5
1964	7	6	1986	1	3
1965	2	5	1987	7	6
1966	5	5	1988	73	
1967	4	8	1989	6	3
1968	1	2	1990	5	2
1969	9	5	1991	5	5
1970	1	3	1992	7	3
1971	3	3	1993	2	2
1972	4	8			

1 Jewish Community Centre on Tsimiski Street

2 Entrance to the Jewish
Museum of Thessaloniki

3 Ground Floor of the Jewish Museum of Thessaloniki

4 Jewish Primary School

5 Saul Modiano Home for the Elderly

6, 7, 8 Friday Evening Celebrations (*Oneg Shabbat*) of Different Age Groups at the Community Centre

9 Raising of the Greek Flag at the Jewish Youth Summer
Camp (*Kataskinosi*) (1989)

10 'Macedonia Evening' Organised by the Jewish School (1994)

11, 12 Interior of Yad Lezikaron Synagogue

13 One of the Marble Wall Plaques inside Yad Lezikaron Synagogue, Listing all the Synagogues that have ever Existed in Salonika

14 *Bar Mitzvah* Ceremony at Monasterioton Synagogue

15 Wedding at Monasterioton Synagogue

16 *Bat Mitzvah* Ceremony at Monasterioton Synagogue

17 Boy Outside Monasterioton Synagogue,
Holocaust Memorial Day (1994)

18 Obituary Notice for the 50,000 Salonikan Jews
Who Perished in the Holocaust

TABLE 7
NUMBER OF WEDDINGS AND NUMBER OF WOMEN CONVERTED TO JUDAISM PRIOR TO
WEDDING,[1] 1946–94

Year	Total Number Weddings	Number of Coversions	Year	Total Number of Weddings	Number of Conversions
1945	45	not known			
1946	151	13	1981	5	2
1947	74	11	1986	4	1
1948	25	2	1987	4	2
1949	30	7	1988	6	2
1950	16	3	1990	4	2
1951	19	10	1991	3	1
1952	8	6	1992		2
1953	18	3	1993	2	1
1954	15	5	1994	3	1
1955	13	9			
1959	5	1			
1962	4	2			
1970	5	1			
1972	8	2			
1974	9	2			
1976	6	1			
1980	8	1			

Note: Some years are not listed in this table because no marriages were registered in these years.

the immediate post-war years, some of which were conducted as group weddings. In 1946 alone 151 weddings were registered. It is also interesting to note that the average marriage age in 1945, when 45 weddings were registered, was relatively young, especially for men. The average male age was 26 and the average female age was 23. By 1949 the average male age went up to 36.6 years and the average female age to 26.1. The most likely explanation for this age gap is the fact that many of the weddings between 1946 and 1949 were second marriages and that most people who got married in 1945 were not camp survivors but young people who had survived in the mountains or in hiding. The high number of conversions in 1946 (13) and 1947 (11) suggests that quite a few men got married to women who hid them during the war. Table 7 gives us an idea about the number of weddings and the general number of conversions.

We can see that throughout the 1960s, 1970s and 1980s the number of conversions was quite low and there are many years in which we cannot find any conversions. Considering that from 1982 civil weddings which are not listed in the community files were introduced in

Greece, the number of converted women from 1990 to 1994 indicates a clear rise in the number of mixed marriages. Among the 12 couples who got married during this time, seven spouses had converted. The average marriage age for this period is 34.7 years for men and 28 years for women.[19]

CONCLUSION

As can be seen from this outline of the infrastructure of the Jewish community, many factors determine the degree of individual involvement in communal life: age, marriage status, family involvement, religiosity, professional commitments and so forth. The nature of involvement varies over time and with the changing needs of individuals and families. An individual is more likely to frequent the community if other family members are also involved. In terms of educational and social services, the community seems to offer most to children, youth, and the elderly. For the survival of the community it is crucial to ensure that the younger generation will remain active after leaving the youth group. Young people are expected to 'come back' to the community as parents who send their children to the Jewish nursery and school. This process can no longer be taken for granted due to the rising number of mixed marriages, seen as a serious threat to the survival of the community (see Chapter 9). In light of the unfavourable age pyramid, it is likely that the community might be forced to change its policy regarding civil marriages and open its doors to children of Jewish–Christian Orthodox parents.

NOTES

1. I also interviewed a few people who do not come to the community at all. Since I preferred to interview people whom I have met more than once and who have seen me in the community, it was more complicated to arrange interviews with Jews who never attended any communal functions.
2. I was present at a discussion when a woman reproached her nephew for not being involved in the community. She said to him: 'The Germans did not make a difference either. You cannot choose to be Jewish or not to be Jewish but you can choose to be involved or not to be involved in the community.'
3. The usual food served when I visited the community was eggs, sometimes pizza for the youngsters, but most importantly *Spanakopites* and *Tiropites*. These are savoury pies, also called *Borekas* or *Borekitas*, and they are considered the 'culinary representatives of Turkish, Greek and Balkan Jewry' (Roden 1997: 240). They are eaten as festive food during celebrations.
4. This makes sense because it is this age group which attends the synagogue services. The elderly choose to attend the service and the children are brought by a teacher from the Jewish school.

5. I once came to the Friday night celebrations accompanied by somebody non-Jewish who was interested in Ladino music. Downstairs with the older generation this was not a problem but when we went upstairs I felt quite uncomfortable.
6. On my more recent visits attendance at the Friday night and Saturday morning services seemed to have increased considerably. This has to do with the arrival of the new rabbi (shortly after my departure from Thessaloniki) who attracted people to the synagogue who had previously not attended the services.
7. *Hashkavah* is the designation of memorial prayer in the Sephardi ritual. This prayer is recited every Sabbath, on festivals, and on Monday and Thursday at the request of the mourner (see *Encyclopaedia Judaica*: 711).
8. Torah in Hebrew means 'teaching' and is the written form of the Pentateuch.
9. The terms *heikal* and *tevah* are Sephardi terms. In Ashkenazi synagogues the ark is called *aron* and the reading desk is called *bema*.
10. Interestingly, nobody mentioned this to me during my period of study.
11. Bar/Bat Mitzvah literally means 'son or daughter of the commandment'. This term denotes the attainment of religious and legal maturity and the occasion at which this status is formally assumed, for boys at the age of 13, for girls at the age of 12 (*Encyclopaedia Judaica*: 243).
12. Bat Mitzvahs are celebrated as a group (five or six girls) while Bar Mitzahs are celebrated individually.
13. Apart from the ritual differences between Jewish and Orthodox burial and mourning customs, the lamenting way in which particularly the women mourn is considered to be very 'Greek'.
14. Some time after Mizrachi Street was renamed Flemming Street, the municipality of Thessaloniki renamed a small street in the same area Mizrachi Street.
15. Section 5 of Act 2456/1920 on the Jewish communities provides for the establishment of Jewish schools under the supervision of the state. Only the Jewish school in Larissa falls under this category. The Jewish schools in Athens and Thessaloniki operate as private schools (Stavros 1995: 28).
16. In Salonika people say that there is a very good relationship between the Christian teachers and the community. This situation is in contrast to the Jewish school in Athens. Two teachers of the Athenian Jewish school apparently complained to the Ministry of Education about 'Israeli propaganda'. As a result the Israeli anthem cannot be sung any more at the school. This illustrates how sensitive issues of Jewish education are in the Greek context.
17. The director herself is a child survivor. She feels very close to the old people and tells me she sees herself as the 'caretaker of their stories'.
18. A *mikveh* is a bath with natural water which is used for spiritual cleansing. Orthodox Jewish women need to use this bath after the end of menstruation. This is not practised in Salonika.
19. This figure reflects the cultural notion of gendered marriage suitability. Men are expected to marry after they have established themselves and can support a family, while women are expected to marry relatively young. When I told one of my interviewees that I was 29 and not married, she suggested I should not tell anyone about my age.

5

Narratives of 'Distant' and 'Recent' Pasts

The following chapters will discuss the historical memories of those interviewed for this study, that is to say it will present statements and narratives about specific time periods of their lives and specific periods in the history of Salonika. The aim is twofold: on the one hand to present lived memory as historical narratives of lived experiences (in terms of a reconstruction of the past), on the other hand to investigate the 'texture' of memories. Within the latter framework one needs to look at the context in which certain issues are remembered, the different ways in which people talk about the past, and the importance of specific statements in the context of the overall interview. Both 'experienced memories' and 'indirect memories', transmitted to the interviewees by their parents and grandparents, and therefore termed the 'distant past', will be dealt with.

THE GENERAL BACKGROUND OF THE INTERVIEWEES

Among the interviewees who grew up in Salonika, two attended the Talmud Torah School, one the Talmud Torah and the Alliance School, two the French Lycée, one the French Lycée and the American Anatolia College, two the Italian School, one the Italian School and the Alliance School, two attended Greek schools, one the German School, and six the Alliance schools. The Alliance and the Talmud Torah schools were community schools, the French Lycée and the Anatolia College private schools. Six interviewees received only primary education or did not finish secondary education (four at the Alliance schools, one at a Greek school, one at Talmud Torah) and went to work at a very young age. All six interviewees lived in Jewish working-class neighbourhoods: the quarter No. 151 and the Regie Vardar quarter. The other interviewees lived in the Jewish middle-class neighbourhoods, east of the White Tower, in the areas of Mizrachi, Agia Triada, Evsonon and further east in an area called Campagne.

The wartime experience of those interviewed can be summarised as follows. Among them, 16 stayed in Greece throughout the occupation. Three men and two women survived in Athens under various circumstances. Two men experienced the occupation in different villages in the Larissa region, two men and two women joined the *Andartes* in the mountains, one woman survived on the island of Skopelos (with her child), one man was hidden in Salonika (with his wife and child), and two men remained legally in the city, one had an 'Aryan' mother, the other was married to a Christian Orthodox woman. Eight men and two women were deported to Auschwitz, two women to Bergen-Belsen. Two women fled from Salonika to Athens (with their husbands), and from there they went to Turkey and subsequently to Palestine. One woman interviewed had not been directly affected by the occupation because she had left Salonika for Istanbul with her family many years before the war.

At the time of the interview, ten of the 12 women were widows, and five of the 18 men were widowers. Five women and six men lived in the Home for the Elderly.

A CHRONOLOGY OF THE PAST IN THE LIGHT OF THE PRESENT

Studying the history of the Jewish Community of Salonika it is easy to discern the historically important 'events' which took place in the twentieth century: the annexation of the city by the Greek state in 1912, the great fire in 1917, the settlement of the Asia Minor refugees in 1923–24, the Campbell riot in 1931, the German occupation in 1941, the deportation to Poland in 1943 or survival in Greece, return and reconstruction of the community in the post-war years, the Civil War, and perhaps the military dictatorship of 1967–74. What is relevant here is the significance attributed to the various historical events and periods in the different life histories, and how the events are narrated in the context of the interviewees' own lives. As Collard has shown in her study of social memory in a Greek village, historical proximity and social impact do not necessarily result in articulated discourse. She found that the discourse of the past during the Ottoman Empire possessed more significance than the period of the Civil War which the villagers had experienced themselves. Collard argues that talking about the Ottoman period provides a means by which aspects of the more recent and painful history in the 1940s can be discussed (Tonkin *et al.* 1989: 116).

Another aspect which deserves attention is the public or private nature of the life histories. Given the importance of gender divisions in the Mediterranean and the association of the female with the private and the male with the public sphere, one would expect different versions of lived history between the men and the women, 'gendered memory' so to speak. It is difficult to make conclusive statements about this since the interviewer's questions shape the narrated memory which means that the interviewer's bias comes into play. This means that a more intimate relationship with the women interviewees might have led me to ask more personal questions and to receive more answers about the person's private life. On the other hand I did try to follow up what the interviewees were interested in talking about and within this process I received the impression that some male interviewees were more reluctant to talk about their private life. They felt compelled to discuss 'the history of the Jews of Salonika', almost as if they represent the 'Salonikan Jews' and they therefore had to make sure that they imparted the right information.[1] In these interviews the interviewees start their recollection by talking about the expulsion from Spain, as if this was the 'official' or 'real' beginning of the history of the Salonikan Jews. Mois B., for example starts by saying: 'The Jews came here from Spain after 1490. The Queen of Spain expelled all the Jews. Here, it was the Ottoman Empire' (Am15).

In another interview Leon L. also starts by talking about the expulsion from Spain and the settlement of the different groups in Salonika:

> Five hundred years ago many groups came from Spain and formed their own community. We belonged to the *Kehila Gerush* [which translates from Hebrew as 'congregation of refugees'], others belonged to the *Kehila Italia* [congregation from Italy], others belonged to the *Kehila Aragona* [congregation from Aragona]. (Am20)

He then continues: 'That's how the history of the Jews in Salonika began.'

Both Leon L. and Mois B. weave the Jewish experience in Spain, the Ottoman Empire, and Greece into a Diasporic narrative of a good co-existence between the Jews and the changing political powers (Spain, the Ottoman Empire and Greece).

> In 1912 there was a war between the Turks and the Greeks and Greece occupied Salonika. We had a good relationship. They

gave us the same liberties as the Turks ... We started speaking Greek; like we had learnt Spanish in Spain, we now learnt Greek because we lived in Greece. (Am15)

Our parents lived well with the Turks, as well as we live with the Greeks. (Am20)

In other interviews the 'beginning' is not the historical 'distant past' but the total break brought by the Holocaust. Baruch S. started off by saying: 'I was born in 1917. My father was a butcher. We were my mother, my father, my two brothers who survived and four sisters who were all massacred by the Germans' (Am23). He mentions the Holocaust when talking about his family. When I asked my interviewees early in the interview: 'Can you tell me about your family background?' I was often immediately told about the death of parents, brothers, sisters, spouses and children who died in the 'concentration camp' in 'Auschwitz', in the 'crematorium', in 'Germany', or just 'there', a place in Poland: 'I had two brothers and two sisters. I got married last and I had a daughter called Graciella. They all went to Auschwitz' (Am22).

The other context in which the Holocaust, or the general war experience, appears very early on in the interview is in phrases like 'we worked like this until the Germans came' (Am18) or 'I worked in a factory. Then the Germans came and took us to Germany' (Am23). In these statements the war years stand in juxtaposition to the 'normality' of pre-war life and thus gain significance in the entire life history.

These examples, of which there are many more, illustrate the enormous importance of the war for this generation. The war divides time into a 'before' and 'after' and divides space into a 'Jewish city' and a 'non-Jewish city'. Individual memories of childhood and adolescence therefore become memories of a past which did not continue into the present, of a broken past so to speak. 'How does one remember a lost world?' asks one of the interviewees. She sighs and continues: 'It is all a ghost that you see' (Af8).

Pre-war Salonika with its pre-war inhabitants is a 'lost world' for many interviewees, a 'lost world' in two ways: firstly in terms of the past, in terms of the murder of its people and the destruction of the Jewish spaces, such as the cemetery (which in a way symbolised the long Jewish presence in the city), but secondly in terms of the present, in the sense of cultural discontinuity, in which an old world was not succeeded by a new world but in which an 'old world' became a 'lost world'. Boyarin speaks of the 'shortage' of cultural heirs in his study of Polish Jews in Paris (Boyarin 1991: 10). He refers to the loss of one's children to a different cultural world.[2] Although he is concerned with an immigrant community, a similar process applies to the Salonikan Jews. One could call this process 'from being Jewish to feeling Jewish'.[3] For the older generation 'being Jewish' was a lifestyle reality, of course with variations in different families. Being Jewish meant, among other things, speaking Ladino, going to synagogue, keeping the Jewish festivals, eating different food and knowing many languages. In the course of two generations 'being Jewish' is not defined by life-style but by an emotional tie, by 'feeling Jewish' in a number of different ways. For the most part the survivors' grandchildren do not know Ladino nor do they go to synagogue. Furthermore, the older generation is aware that they are part of a 'dying community', a community with an uncertain future, in light of the small number of members and the high percentage of mixed marriages. One man tells me very proudly that his grandson, who lives in the United States, knows Hebrew and was able to say the blessings for the Kiddush in the synagogue. He contrasts this to the young people in Salonika: 'The young people here, they do not even know how to say Amen. The men marry Greek women and the children at home they see only 'Greek things', they don't see anything Jewish' (Am20). The sense of loss, discontinuity, and ending was voiced on many different levels. I was asked by somebody to attend the synagogue services because 'one day this folklore will disappear. I advise you to listen to our folklore in the synagogue at the hour of praying because we are on the way to losing it' (Am21).

Salonikan folklore is on the way to being lost because there are no young people who can claim or take over 'their heritage' (seen from the older generation's perspective). This generates a feeling of being a 'last remnant' and a sense of 'futurelessness', in which the interviewees see no continuity for their children as Jews in Greece because the forces of assimilation seem overwhelming. Since death among this age group is a day-to-day reality the question of succession or the lack of succession is a burning issue. Both Sam P. and Mois H., two camp survivors who have been working in the community for the last 40 years, mirror this sentiment when they tell me that they are tired and that they cannot go on working for the community any longer. Mois H. said: 'I am already old. I am 77. I cannot go on. They need to find somebody new' (Am18). Another person on the synagogue committee stated that only old people come to the synagogue and that of the six *Hazanim*[4] only two remained. The others had died in the last year (Am23). Death is certainly present in the minds of this age group. When I was trying to arrange an interview appointment with Mois B. in the Home for the Elderly he answered: 'If you cannot find me here, I will be at the cemetery'. Almost all the interviewees whom I interviewed in 1989 (and some in 1994) have died since.

In any other group of this age, and certainly in any other Home for the Elderly, the theme of death would be expected to be a prevailing topic, in one way or an other. The difference in Salonika is that individual deaths are linked to the theme of cultural death. The loss of Ladino, the loss of a Jewish historical consciousness, the loss of religious observance among the young Jews (Am14), culminates in the loss of young Jews through mixed marriages. In this view a 'culture under threat' cannot sustain itself in marriages with partners from the majority culture (even if neither spouse converts to the other's religion). Mixed marriages, or rather, the threat of mixed marriages, then becomes almost a general metaphor for loss and discontinuity. As Leon B. puts it: 'We have no future here ... From the moment they allowed civil weddings, we lost ... The civil weddings opened the doors ... For a long time there have not been any weddings in the synagogue' (Am14). Although the content and significance of Judaism might have changed for the young ones, from the perspective of the older generation they 'remain Jewish' until they marry out. Mixed marriages thus seal the process of assimilation and make it irreversible, therefore it is a major issue within families and the community.

In contrast to Meyerhoff's East European Jewish immigrants to the United States (Meyerhoff 1978: 17) and Boyarin's Polish Jewish immigrants to France (Boyarin 1991: 17), the cultural distance between the 'Old World' parents and the 'New World' children and grandchildren is not seen as a successful integration into the host society (although they also feel ambivalent about their children not being 'more Jewish'), but as an end, perhaps even a failure to guarantee a future Jewish community in the once Jewish city. Another kind of discontinuity is caused by the emigration of the generation of post-war children to other countries, mostly to Israel and the United States. While mostly viewed in positive terms it leaves quite a number of elderly people without the day-to-day care of their children.

It should be emphasised that generalisations are problematic and that there were not only voices of discontinuity and loss but also those of reconstruction and revival (mostly among people who were actively involved in the community after the war). Each life history is different as each individual constructs a different past, present and future as he or she narrates their life. But listening to the different life stories, some versions and perceptions emerge which are more similar to each other than others, and some of the factors which account for the similarities and differences need to be considered here.

The chronological memory framework for most interviewees is not an expression of permanence, defined by Bergson as a linear structure in terms of an 'it was', 'it is', and 'it will be' (Abels 1995: 337), but an expression of rupture and discontinuities, of a past which has never quite ended and an uncertain future. Their traumatic experiences defy the notion of memory as a linear process expressing continuity in terms of a past, a present and a future (Abels 1995: 337). Because of the tragic nature of the past, the past continues to be of immanent meaning. How one survived the war in hiding, in the mountains, with the *Andartes* (partisans), or in the camp as *omiros* (which literally means hostages), is essential to every life history of that generation and makes them all 'survivors'.

That's how two women, one who had been in hiding and one who had escaped to Turkey, describe their 'past': 'We are carrying around the old history. Perhaps the young ones will not be so melancholic' (Af11). The notion of a 'haunting past' is more strongly expressed by Lili M.: 'After so many years it comes back, after so many years. You are asking yourself, will there never be any forgetting? Or, I don't know, a little bit of sweetness, softening the pain. No, there won't' (Af8).

Abels calls this fixation of the past *'Leitmotiv Erinnerung'* (leitmotiv memory) which he found among survivors of the Armenian genocide (Abels 1995: 337). The process of surviving did not end when the actual persecution came to an end. He argues that for the survivors life after the deportation and the massacre is a permanent attempt to escape death. With Lili M.'s question in mind, 'will there never be any forgetting?', one could add, surviving is about the attempt to escape the memory of death and the realisation (for some) that this is impossible.

The interviewees' memories will be presented in chronological order although, as I have tried to show, individual memory is not as linear as the narrative might suggest.

'WE ALL CAME FROM SPAIN'

In the interviews, the topic of Jewish life in Spain before the expulsion did not feature at all. In a computerised word search the word 'Spain' comes up in a total of only 11 interviews, two with women and nine with men. In these interviews Spain is either mentioned in the context of the expulsion in the fifteenth century, in the context of the Spanish language, or in the context of the occupation and war, when a small number of Jews with Spanish citizenship were excluded from the anti-Jewish measures, subsequently deported to Bergen-Belsen, but after half a year transferred to Spain.[5]

As already mentioned the expulsion from Spain serves in some life histories as a form of introduction to the collective 'we'. It explains how the Jews, as a group came to the Ottoman Empire, or 'came here to Macedonia' as Daniel B. (Am13) puts it. Interestingly, none of the interviewees who grew up in 'old Greece' mentions Spain. Since they were incorporated earlier into the Greek nation their notion of the 'we' shifted earlier towards a 'Greek Jewish we' rather than a 'Sephardi (Spanish) Jewish we'. This is expressed in the Greek language proficiency of Jews who grew up in 'old Greece'. Their knowledge of Greek was much better than among Salonikan Jews of the same generation and therefore Ladino, mostly referred to as Spanish or Spaniolit, was a language associated more with 'home' than with outside, which was not the case in Salonika.

Speaking, singing, and praying in Ladino manifested the connection to Spain and the fact that 'we are all descendants from the families who came from Spain' is often talked about in the context of language, as in the next three quotations:

> We are originally from Spain 500 years ago. All the family spoke Spanish. (Am26)

> We spoke always Spaniolit. We came from Spain, like many families four hundred years ago. I learnt Greek at school. My parents knew Greek very poorly. (Af1)

> I learnt French, Hebrew, Spanish, the language our grandparents brought when they came in 1492 from Spain because Queen Isabelle had expelled us. (Am23)

It is clearly the issue of language, a concrete part of the interviewees' lives, which connects the interviewee's narrative to the expulsion from Spain.

As discussed earlier, Assmann distinguishes two types of memory: 'cultural memory' (*kulturelles Gedächtnis*) and 'communicative memory' (*kommunikatives Gedächtnis*). Those memories which an individual shares with his contemporaries are part of the 'communicative memory', memory which is created and transmitted by social interaction. In contrast to 'communicative memory', which relies on communication, 'cultural memory' consists of memory content which was (at some point) solidified and objectified. Assmann argues that the 'fixation' of memory in terms of texts, rituals, monuments, museums or institutionalised recitals, folklore, celebrations, pilgrimages and so on enables the transmission of knowledge over time (Assmann 1997: 11). 'Cultural memory', however, is not static. It selects the themes which are important for the recent identity of a group. According to Assmann 'cultural memory' is often concerned with a 'fixed point in the past', such as founding myths and origins of a group (Assmann 1997: 52). Needless to say, the notions of 'cultural' and 'communicative memory' operate on different levels for different group formations. Therefore, they can be easily applied to the case of the Salonikan Jews, where we can look at 'cultural' communal memory (that is, of the ethnic group) and 'cultural memory' of the Greek nation state, and 'communicative memory', the one with which we are mostly concerned in the analysis of the interviews.

The memories quoted above about the expulsion from Spain clearly fall more into the category of 'cultural memory'. As already stated, the informants refer to Spain in an almost official way, 'that is where we came from' or they link it with their experience of speaking Ladino, something to which they can relate directly. The following opening to an interview illustrates the point about 'cultural memory'. Leon L. asked me:

> Where do you want me to start? Before the war? Or with the history of Salonika? Has Mr Nar told you the history when the Jews came from Spain? Did you go to the synagogue and see the marble tablets which show the names and dates of arrival of each group who came from Spain and formed a community? (Am20)

This interview took place in the community's board meeting room, which is a rather official space. Leon L., who was the head of the synagogue committee, talked to me for almost two hours. He wanted to tell me as much about the history of the community as he could. Why is the beginning and the end of this interview particularly interesting? In the beginning Leon L. asked me whether I had spoken to Mr Nar, who was the official archivist of the community. He expected him to have told me about the time when the Jews came from Spain. Then he asked me if I had seen the memorial tablets in the synagogue. Both these questions underline that the time when the Jews came from Spain is a distant, fixed past, expected to be presented by the official historian or seen on the tablets in the synagogue. It is a past which has become part of the 'cultural memory' of the community. It is the beginning of the history of the Jews of Salonika, 'that's how the history of the Jews in Saloniki began' (although Jews were living in Salonika before the arrival of the Spanish Jews). This kind of memory plays a bigger part in the interviews where the interviewee feels that he or she should speak primarily about 'the history of the Jews of Salonika' and only secondarily about their particular life. This is of course also affected by the relationship I had with the interviewee at the time of the interview. The more formal and official the interview relationship, the more likely it was that the interviewee presented 'cultural' rather than 'communicative memory' to me. The interview with Leon L. was quite a formal one, as his last sentence underlines, 'now you have learnt something about the history of the Jews from Salonika'.

There is one other interesting aspect connected to the mentioning of Spain. Rather than talking about 'escaping', 'fleeing' or being 'expelled' from Spain, the interviewees talk mostly about 'coming' from Spain. Only two people use the word refugee (they use the Hebrew word *gerush*). Robin Cohen suggests that we need to transcend the classic notion of 'Diaspora', which is associated commonly with collective trauma, banishment and exile, and examine carefully the various Diasporic conditions (Cohen 1997: ix). He quotes Clifford who writes 'among Sephardim after 1492, the longing for "home" could be focused on a city in Spain at the same time as the Holy Land' (Cohen 1997: 13).

I suggest that the Salonikan Jews, because of their historic prominence in the city, did not really understand themselves as a 'victim' Diaspora (until the Second World War) and therefore do not emphasise the negative aspects (the push factors) of their migration to Salonika. The fact that the Jewish community flourished for so many centuries in the city makes the arrival of Jews into the Ottoman Empire a 'positive beginning' rather than a 'negative end'. This aspect of 'cultural memory' is illustrated well by the visit, in May 1998, of the Spanish King Juan Carlos and Queen Sophia (who is the sister of the former Greek King) to Greece. During their visit they laid a wreath at the Holocaust Memorial (erected in 1997) in Salonika. The king promised to donate 1 million pounds to the International Sephardi Union in support of Sephardi Holocaust victims. The president of the community, Mr Andreas Sefiha, gave a speech and the king was given a plaque engraved with a key. In his speech Mr Sefiha referred to Ladino and the attachment of the Jews to their lost homes: 'The only original mark that our ancestors took with them is our language ... When the Sephardi Jews left Spain they took their house keys with them and those keys were handed down from generation to generation' (*Jewish Chronicle*, 5 June 1998: 2).

This quotation underlines the point made above, namely that the Spanish descent of the Salonikan Jews is part of the 'cultural memory' of the community which is recalled in official and festive settings, such as the visit of King Jaun Carlos. It reflects a sentiment expressed in some of the Sephardi folk songs and in a poem by Jorge Luis Borges entitled 'A Key in Salonika'. The first two verses go as follows:

> Abravanel, Farias, or Pinedo, exiled from Spain – unholy persecution – they still keep the key of the house they previously had in Toledo. Free now from hope or fear, they stare at the key, as the day slowly fades, the bronze contains the yesterdays that remained there, a tired gleam and a silent suffering. (quoted in brochure accompanying Savina Yannatou's CD 'Primavera En Salonika')

The attachment to Spain thus remains part of the 'cultural memory', as a founding myth so to speak, although it does not reflect today's Jewish reality. Or perhaps this attachment regained significance in the 'cultural memory' of the community during the last years when public acknowledgement has enabled the community to reconstruct and reclaim its 'cultural memory'.

The cultural link to Spain seems to be more significant than the memory of persecution, which is seen in the light of the more recent Nazi persecution. Mr Seficha expressed this sentiment at the ceremony with the Spanish king by saying: 'At least they (the Spanish kingdom) gave us alternatives – a choice to either change our religion or leave. Hitler did not give us an alternative' (*Jewish Chronicle*, 5 June 1998: 2).

THE PERIOD OF TRANSITION: FROM THE OTTOMAN EMPIRE TO THE GREEK NATION STATE

As we have seen, only seven of the interviewees were born in Salonika in the last decade of Ottoman rule, and since they were very young children they do not have clear memories of this period. Therefore, the topic of 'what it was like under the Turks' is not a theme which was normally brought up by the interviewees but was more usually instigated by my question. It was mostly discussed in context of what the parents and grandparents had told the interviewees about the Jews in the Ottoman Empire and whether it was better for the Jews to live under the Turks or under the Greeks. The time 'under the Ottomans' is always referred to as a single time unit. Nobody referred to specific events within the 400 years of Ottoman rule, or specific time periods of rise and decline. The Ottoman period is generally associated with a 'Jewish Salonika', where 'all the shops were closed on Saturday' (Am22) and the Jews constituted the majority of the city. 'When we lived with the Turks, Salonika was called the "second Jerusalem" and we, the Jews, were the patrons of the city' (Am20).

The 'glorious past' of the community during the Ottoman Empire expressed in the above quotation is much more likely to be talked about in the private realm than in the public. It constitutes 'group memory' which is not shared, or is even in conflict with the 'cultural memory' of the majority culture, that is, the Greek nation-state, which mostly stresses the negative aspects of the 'Turkish occupation' and the 'Ottoman yoke'. Because of this 'memory conflict' some informants are very apprehensive about saying anything positive about the Ottomans and even more careful about saying anything negative about Greece, thus illustrating that memory is clearly influenced by the present in which the content of memory can easily be transformed into a political statement. Therefore many interviewees, even in the more private setting of the interview, were reluctant to make statements about the change from Turkish to Greek rule. Felix S., for example, when asked about the difference between the Turks and the Greeks, with regard to the Jews, prefaces his statement by saying: 'I don't know. It is a question of politics and I don't want to be involved in politics' (Am24). Other interviewees stop their narrative and go silent, clearly indicating that they would rather not talk about these things: 'During the Ottoman Empire everything was good, also with the Turks. When the Greeks came ...' [Solomon S. stops in the middle of the sentence]

(Am22). In an informal conversation in the community office I spoke about the same subject with an older man. He also went very quiet and then said: 'Do you know the proverb which says that you should not spit into the well whose water you drink?'

The dilemma of making 'positive' statements about the Ottoman rulers springs from this 'stay out of politics' attitude which many of the older generation grew up with and from an apprehensiveness of being accused of 'being a disloyal Greek citizen'. By a 'stay out of politics' attitude, I refer to common admonition given to some interviewees by their parents and grandparents not to get involved in politics because 'you will only find trouble' (Af8). This anxiety causes sometimes a rather defensive tone when talking about the positive Jewish experience under the Ottomans. The following story illustrates rather well what is meant here by a defensive or explanatory tone. While driving back to Salonika from Larissa and discussing the history of the Jewish community Viktor V. tells me this episode:

> After Salonika became Greek, the king could not understand why the Jews were not happy about the arrival of the Greeks. So he asked a famous rabbi to come and see him in order to discuss this issue with him. The rabbi gave him the following answer: 'If you are happily married and you are satisfied with your wife you don't look for another wife, do you?' That is the same with the Jews and the Ottomans. They were happy together. That's why the Jews were not overjoyed about the arrival of the Greeks.

The marriage metaphor was used by the rabbi and the narrator of the story to explain why the Jews were cautious and insecure about their new state. The interesting point here is that the marriage analogy is needed in order to make the Jewish reaction more understandable.

The 'happy marriage' between the Jews and the Turks, that is, the Ottomans, is reiterated by most interviewees when they speak about the Turks mostly in a positive context. The specific points which characterise this 'transmitted memory' about the Turks were the lack of anti-Semitism and the degree of autonomy of the Jewish community. As one interviewee puts it: 'The Turks were not interested in what the Jews did. As long as they were good people they did not care' (Af10). She contrasts this attitude with the Greek attitude: 'The Greeks were interested in the Jews. Not immediately, but little by little. They wanted the Jews to learn Greek so that they could live in the Greek way.'

This quotation encapsulates the basic difference between the Ottoman Empire and the Greek nation state, in fact the general difference between empires and nation-states. Within the *millet* system (see Chapter 3) the Jews had their own educational and legal systems. As *dhimmis* they had to pay a certain tax. Being a religious minority in the Ottoman Empire is therefore often perceived thus: 'The Jews enjoyed a great deal of liberty among the Turks, fear and anti-Semitism did not exist, it was all a matter of paying tax' (Am23). Some interviewees remember how well their parents spoke about the relationship between Turks and Jews: 'It was much better with the Turks. We lived very well. They always loved the Jews. My parents always said that one lived very well with the Turks' (Af1). Another woman uses the language to underline the good relationships between the Jews and the Turks: 'The Jews and the Turks lived very well together and that's why in our Ladino we have got so many Turkish words (Af7). Michael B. confirms that the Jews really liked the Turks. 'They used to call them *Yoyas del Dios* which means the jewels of God. This shows that they were good to the Jews' (Am16).

With the Greeks it was a 'different story' (Am16). In contrast to the Turks, the Greeks were interested in the Jews, as Lili S. specified above they wanted the Jews to learn Greek and to adapt to the Greek way of life. Language in the context of this narrative becomes a legitimate demand by the new state. It is seen as a premise for acquiring a new national identity, that is, a Greek identity. Being a subject of the Ottoman Empire did not require the knowledge of one particular language, since multilingualism was the norm.

The new Greek state had a different attitude, expressed in a law in the early 1920s which made Greek the obligatory language of instruction in all primary schools. Since nationalism can be defined as 'the principle which holds that the political and national unit should be congruent' (Gellner 1983: 1), it is not surprising that the Greek state was interested in spreading the usage of the Greek language among a population group which spoke many other languages (such as Ladino, French and Italian) but very little Greek. As in other cases of nation-building, education played an important part in this process. While Judeo-Spanish and French were still the most commonly used languages among the Jews, the younger generation started learning Greek. Within families the ability to communicate in Greek varied greatly among the various generations, as Lili M. recalls:

> Our parents, they did not know any Greek, they had to readjust.
> Our grandparents, they were completely lost in the new world.
> We spoke Ladino with our grandparents, French at home and
> then when the Greeks started sending girls as maids we started
> learning Greek. It was much later that there was a law obliging
> compulsory Greek education for the children, for primary school.
> That's where the younger generation started learning Greek. You
> see, here [in the community] some of the older ladies don't speak
> Greek correctly. (Af8)

The issue of Greek language acquisition is a relevant theme which features in different contexts: a) in the context of Jewishness and
Greekness, in which the knowledge of the Greek language is seen as a
necessary requirement for living in the Greek state and lack of Greek
as an indicator of a strong Jewish/Sephardi identity; and b) in the context of the Second World War in which the knowledge of Greek is seen
as a crucial asset for survival (see Chapter 7). Some interviewees feel
very strongly that Jews should have tried harder to learn Greek.

    The language abilities differentiated Jews from old Greece and
Jews from Salonika. Jews from old Greece were much more likely to
speak Greek (and less likely to know French and Italian) than Jews
from Salonika, where Ladino was in effect the lingua franca which
everyone had to know to some extent (including non-Jews). Not only
were the communities much smaller in places like Larissa and Volos
but they had also been part of the Greek state for much longer. The
Jewish experiences in the provinces were altogether very different (see
Fromm 1992 and Plaut 1996) as becomes very clear in the accounts of
the four interviewees who had moved at a later stage in their lives to
Salonika.

    Because of the multilingual reality where different languages were
spoken at home, in the market and at school, the acquisition of the
Greek language does seem very 'natural' in the interviewees' narratives. Since the language of the family, the house and the synagogue
remained Judeo-Spanish, Greek is viewed as an additional language
which had to be acquired. This view corresponds to a general notion of
transition. Although politically and historically the incorporation of
Salonika into the Greek nation-state in 1912 had a great impact on the
development of the community, in most narratives it is presented as a
transition rather than a radical break.

> First it was difficult for the Jews to readjust. But slowly, slowly we got accustomed [to the new situation]. (Am14)

> The Jews were more connected to the Turks than to the Greeks. When the Turks left and the Greeks stayed there was no choice. We were to be with the Greeks. There was no anti-Semitism. People lived a normal life. They respected us. I had many Greek friends. (Am17)

The political change is seen as a transition and is assessed in varying degrees of difficulty. Some interviewees say that the Jews were afraid of the Greeks and 'not happy about the arrival of the Greek army', others describe the process as a very swift change, as in the statement already quoted earlier, and here:

> In 1912 there was a war between the Turks and the Greeks and Greece occupied Salonika. We lived in a good relationship. They gave us the same liberties as the Turks ... We started speaking Greek, like we had learnt Spanish in Spain we now learnt Greek because we lived in Greece. (Am15)

It is interesting that the interviewee uses the word 'occupied' in this context which stands in sharp contrast to the official Greek discourse about the 'liberation' (*apeleftherosi*) of the city by the Greek army and points to a different memory. The choice of words – 'liberation' or 'occupation' – expresses a value judgement which stems from historical experience on the one hand and is influenced by dominant historical discourses on the other.[6] In the case of the events in 1912 the 'Greek' and 'Jewish' experiences were different and therefore the interviewee speaks of the Greek troops occupying Salonika. It is an expression of 'communicative memory'. This is a rare exception though. Most interviewees speak about the 'liberation' of the city in 1912. So do all the official leaflets of the community. This shows that their 'communicative memory' and the 'cultural memory' of the community has moved towards, or adopted, the Greek discourse, that is to say the Greek 'cultural memory'. Here again we understand that historical memory is shaped by current political concerns and becomes highly politicised. Since Greek 'cultural memory' and Greek nationalism stresses historical continuity and homogeneity, minorities cannot sustain 'their' different memories and different identity attachments without being suspected of disloyalty to the nation-state. The effect of this is the homogenisation of memory. In cases of memory conflicts (such as the one about the events of 1912), the minority group adopts the 'cultural memory' of the majority group. This can happen both in the 'communicative', more private, and the 'cultural', more public, memory of the minority group. An extreme example of the adaptation of Jewish 'cultural memory' is the following list of questions, taken from the brochure published by the community. Although there is no direct mention of the political changes in Salonika itself, these questions aim to underline the Jewish contribution to the Greek independence struggle and thus follow the discourse of Greek patriotism, stressing struggle and heroism for a united Greece (Collard 1989: 96).

> Did you know that during the Greek revolution of 1821 a) the reporter Lafitte, a French Jew, with his moving articles in the newspaper *France Libre* roused French public opinion in support of fighting Greece; b) the Chief Rabbi of Westphalia, Germany, made collections in the synagogues for the Greek liberation fighters; c) Moses Gaster, a Jew, diplomatic agent of Holland in Bucharest, helped Alexandros Hypsilantis escape the Turks who were after him after they had lost the battle of Draghatsani; d) Jews of international renown, such as Max Nordau and Salamon Reinach, supported in every possible way Greek national aspirations in Crete and Macedonia; e) David Skiacky, a Jewish physician, took an active part in the fighting during the Macedonian Struggle, helping sick and wounded Greek fighters in the lake of Yannitsa area? (Jewish Community of Salonika 1992: 27)

This quotation illustrates the need to participate in Greek memory strategies by stressing the active Jewish participation in the Greek struggle for independence, even though this point does not stem from transmitted Jewish memory and does not find any mention in the interviews. The time which is singled out in the quotation falls for most interviewees into the broad category of the 'Ottoman Empire'.

THE RECENT PAST: BEFORE THE WAR

The 1920s and 1930s constitute 'lived memory' for most of the interviewees. In contrast to the more static and general memory of previous time periods, which draws from 'cultural memory' (of written sources for example) the interviewees remember the 'recent past' through their own experiences of growing up, going to school, working and/or getting married, and having children. The political events of the time do not acquire much significance in most life histories (which they do of course with the beginning of the war), unless the person had been involved in some political activity before the war (only two of all the interviewees were). However, there are two political events which stand out in the narratives about this period: the settlement of the Asia Minor refugees after 1923 and the burning down of the Campbell neighbourhood in 1931.

What does come across as significant is the experience of a 'Jewish Salonika', with Jewish neighbourhoods, schools, shops, synagogues and social clubs; a 'Jewish Salonika' which was on the one hand westernised, modern and cosmopolitan, on the other traditional, religious and parochial; a city full of life: 'Saloniki was a charming city. In the 1930s it was a city of commerce. It was the *Chrissi Epochi* [Golden Age] until the war began with Poland and Germany' (Am23). The time before the war thus constitutes the 'real', experienced 'golden age' (in contrast to the 'historical golden age' of the community under the Ottomans). Despite the economic hardship and poverty experienced by many, the pre-war time acquires this status because of the war and the genocide which was to follow. 'Golden Age' can therefore be interpreted as a general metaphor describing both the 'golden age' of the community and the 'golden age' of the family, perceived as intact and complete.

Within the framework of the 'intact' pre-war world the interviewees talk about their families, their neighbourhoods and their schools. What emerges is a picture of a multicultural city, in which the Jews lived side by side with the Greeks and the Armenians, a city in which both ethnicity and class determined where you lived, which school you were sent to, and who you were supposed to marry.

MEMORY SPACES: NEIGHBOURHOODS AND SCHOOLS

Until the great fires of 1890 and 1917 most Jewish neighbourhoods were in the centre of the city and around the port area. The majority of the 17 Jewish neighbourhoods which are mentioned in the Ottoman records had Judeo-Spanish names, such as Pulia and Etz Haim (Molho 1993b: 66). While these Jewish areas were located in today's western part of the city, the Turkish neighbourhoods were located in the Ano Poli (upper town), and the Greek ones in the eastern part of the city. After the fire of 1890 the Jewish community had developed two new areas at Vardari and Kalamaria for the victims of the fire and for Russian Jews who had fled the pogroms. The next fire, the devastating fire of 1917, not only caused a massive resettlement of about 50,000 Jews but also destroyed much of the city centre which led to its neo-classical re-planning, still visible today at the Aristotelus Square (Volkgenannt and Rottger 1995: 100). In 1918 the Jewish community bought three areas which had been used as military camps by the entente powers in the First World War and which subsequently became Jewish working-class neighbourhoods, the neighbourhoods No. 6, No. 151, and Campbell. The arrival of the Asia Minor refugees in the twenties created an acute housing shortage and changed the urban landscape. The refugees moved into the houses which were left behind by the Turks in the Ano Poli and new neighbourhoods developed at the outskirts of the city, such as Charilao and Kato Toumba (Kokot 1995: 23). While most quarters in Salonika in the 1920s maintained their distinct 'ethnic' character, that is, Greek, Greek refugee, and Jewish, there were also some mixed wealthier neighbourhoods in the east of the city, such as Campagne or Campos, in which the biggest synagogue Beit Shaul was located (Molho 1993b: 68).

Lili M. grew up in a 'good' middle-class Jewish neighbourhood close to the White Tower called Evsonon. She recalls it the following way:

> I remember as a little girl we were a completely Jewish community in the area where I lived which was Evsonon, right across from the French School, the Mission Laïque Française and it was the centre of cultural life among the Jews. There were very, very few Greeks in that area. The only Greeks were the family Christidis, a very nice family. There also was to the left of our house a very nice Armenian family, the Pezimansians. (Af8)

Although Lili M. talks about the friendship between herself and an Armenian brother and sister she went to school with, she stresses that 'they were in their own world and we were in our own world. Our interests were different' (Af8). Lili M. does not only refer to different culture in this context but to the fact that the Armenians were 'new immigrants' who needed to establish themselves while the Jews had been settled in Saloniki for a long time.

Alici P., who lived very close to Evsonon in Agia Triada, remembers that all the Jewish neighbours would meet in the *Sukkah*[7] and that she and her mother used to go to a 'grand café' called 'Bekchinar' where they would meet Jewish friends, except on Saturdays. It is significant that most interviewees stress the Jewishness of their neighbourhoods whether they came from a working-class or middle-class area. Palomba A., who grew up on the other side of town, tells me at the beginning of the interview: 'There were only Jews. It was a Jewish quarter called Regie Vardar. There were not many Greeks. All our friends were Jewish' (Af1).

The picture which thus emerges is of distinct ethnic neighbourhoods in which Jews, Greeks and Armenians inhabited separate spaces in the urban landscape of Salonika and in which contact was mostly limited to the public realm (that is, business and commerce) and not extended to the private realm (friendships, marriages and so on). Having said that, one needs to point out that boundaries were not as rigid as they may seem in statements like: 'We did not have any relations with the Greeks' (Af1). Five minutes later the interviewee talks about her friendship with a Greek woman with whom she worked. Indeed, the perception (and experience) of inter-ethnic contact between Jews, Greeks and Armenians varies greatly among the interviewees. The neighbourhood provided one possible space for this kind of contact. But there are others which are equally or even more important: the school, the work place and social clubs, for example. The topic of Greek–Jewish relationships will be dealt with in Chapter 9.

Most interviewees do not describe their neighbourhoods in great detail. Among the 30 interviewees, four lived in the poorer neighbourhoods, in Regie Vardar and the neighbourhood of 151, the others lived in the middle-class neighbourhoods, either in the area around Evsonon, Agia Triada, and Mizrachi or further east in the area of Campagne. Moshe B., describes where he grew up: 'We lived in a quarter called 151, which was where the Baron Hirsch Hospital is. On the back of the hospital there were many big barracks where many families lived. They were not rich. Near there, there was a Jewish school' (Am17).

When I was taken on a tour through the former 'Jewish Salonika' (and the only remnant in most areas was my guide's memory) my guide pointed out that what seems nearby today was 'very far' before the war.

Now it takes us less than an hour to drive through all the areas
but you should not forget that transport was not as developed and
that people stayed largely in the area they lived in. That's where
they went to school, visited social clubs, went to their synagogues
and did their shopping. The ones who lived in the middle-class
areas hardly ever visited the poor neighbourhoods. If they did, it
was to recruit servants and maids or for charity purposes.
(Am12)

The neighbourhood one lived in was a clear indicator of one's economic status. While there were ethnically 'mixed' neighbourhoods
(especially in the middle-class areas), there were hardly any socially
'mixed' neighbourhoods. The social distance between the classes was
very significant and it was clearly expressed in the spatial distance of
neighbourhoods.

An episode from my fieldwork illustrates this notion of distance
very well. I interviewed Jean L. in the Home for the Elderly; she grew
up in a middle-class francophile family who lived on Evsonon. She
turned to Moshe B., now living on the same floor as her, and asked him
something related to the interview. When he told us that he lived in the
151 neighbourhood she was very surprised. 'So your father was not so
rich?' she asked him carefully. After he had left she whispered to me: 'We
took our servants from 151. But I did not know that he is from that area'
(Af6). It seemed very hard for her to imagine that her contemporary
neighbour came from an area which was worlds apart from hers, before
the war. These worlds, defined by economic status, were clearly delin-
eated. Lili M. describes the world of the Jewish middle class as follows:

If you were among the middle class, the parents were merchants
and had their stores downtown and their sons were sent to study
in Paris or elsewhere, to raise their status. Until the Germans came
usually the son would continue the business of the father, on
Ermou Street or Venizelou Street which were all Jewish. There
were all Jewish shops and stalls, nice and beautiful stalls. (Af8)

This world is juxtaposed to the world of the poor:

Our poor people lived in Las Colibas, east of Radio City. The
Colibas was an area set on a kind of little hill, all huts and bar-
racks. We used to go there because the maids came from this area.
We had two maids and a woman who came to clean. (Af8)

The usage of the word 'our' shows that the different worlds had some kind of connection, a connection that was also expressed in the numerous Jewish philanthropic organisations and institutions which existed at the time (such as the Baron Hirsch Hospital, the Alatini Orphanage, the Saul Modiano Home for the Elderly, and so forth). It was pointed out to me that the Salonikan philanthropic tradition was unique and could not be equalled by any other Diaspora community (Am14). An interviewee who came from a poor family and had started working from the age of seven attests to a similar notion of 'connectedness' between the rich and the poor: 'The Jews were together, we were together. If somebody had a lot of money he would not necessarily mix with somebody poor. But they would still try to help' (Am24).

The need for charity and philanthropy stemmed from the enormous poverty among many Jews in pre-war Salonika. Interestingly, a detailed description of the living conditions among the poor is not given by any of the indigenous Salonikan interviewees but by Hella K. who moved from Karlsbad to Salonika in 1925. As an outsider she was shocked by what she saw:

> I came to Salonika in 1925. Then it was still a Jewish city, there were about 60,000 Jews … There was an enormous class difference among the Jews. There were the very poor Jews in 151, Regie Vardar and there were the rich Jews who lived in Campagne, from the White Tower upwards. There were areas where only Jews lived, in a kind of ghetto without gates. There was a lot of poverty in these areas … The area near the railway station was called Regie Vardar, the hygiene conditions were horrific there. People were poor and worked very hard. They were *hamals* [porters and dockers] and manual workers. There was a lot of misery. (Af5)

This very non-nostalgic, realistic description stands out among the interviews. The poor living conditions receive a great deal of attention in Hella K.'s narrative because they were so different from what she was used to and because she gained first-hand impressions of the poor areas by accompanying doctors who treated patients in Regie Vardar.

Another indicator of status and the expression of social and economic difference were the schools. There were four kinds of schools: the community schools (Talmud Torah – more religious – and Alliance Israelite

Universelle schools – more secular), private Jewish schools, Greek
schools and the foreign schools (the French Lycée, the Italian School, the
American Anatolia College). The majority of my interviewees attended
the Alliance school or the French Lycee. Only two interviewees went
to Greek schools.

Rebecca V., who attended the French Lycée, remembers her
schooling:

> The French Lycée was very expensive. I remember that my
> grandfather gave me and my sister one golden pound each month
> and said, 'you should shine as this golden pound coin'. All chil-
> dren in school came from the best families. Most of them were
> Jewish … The Alliance school was also good but the rich wanted
> to send their children to a better school. (Af11)

The two interviewees who went to the Italian School also remember that most of the children were Jewish. Once a week a teacher came
from the community to teach religion to the Jewish children. Most
interviewees do not recount any details about their schools, nor do
they describe the physical look of the schools. However, they all point
out which languages they learnt, namely French, English, and Greek (a
minimum of three hours per week became compulsory) at the Lycee;
French, Greek, and Hebrew at the Alliance; Italian, French and Greek
at the Italian School. Since the Greek government realised the importance of schools in the nation-building process, a law was passed which
made it compulsory for Greek citizens to attend Greek primary
schools. Some Jewish parents decided that their children should attend
Greek schools in order to adapt better to the Greek environment. Hella
K. sent her children to Greek schools. 'We wanted our children to learn
Greek and go to Greek schools. If we lived in Germany we would have
put them in a German school, in England in an English school. We live
in Greece and the children have to know the official language' (Af5).
But we need to bear in mind that Hella K.'s children went to school in
the 1930s when Salonika had belonged to Greece for almost 20 years.
The childhood and school years of most interviewees took place at a
time when Salonika had only recently been incorporated into the
Greek state.

In the provinces, which had become Greek earlier,[8] where the
Jews were a small minority and often attended Greek schools, similar 'language policies' to that of Hella K. had been adopted much earlier. Lili S., who grew up in Larissa and went to a 'very good' Greek

school from 1909 until 1918, recalls that her father wanted the children to speak Greek in the house because 'we were going to live in Greece and therefore we should know Greek' (Af10). Her brothers, however, spoke more Judeo-Spanish because they attended the Jewish school. At the Jewish school there were 'many children from not high families who spoke Spanish' (Af10). The last statement illustrates the double significance of language: on the one hand it was an identity marker (if you spoke Judeo-Spanish you were clearly Jewish, if you spoke Greek you or your family made a conscious effort to become part of Greek society) and on the other it was an indicator of class (in the provinces the educated classes would speak better Greek than the 'common' Jews, in Salonika the educated classes conversed and read in French or other European languages, such as Italian or German). Despite the language orientation of the Salonikan Jewish middle classes, being Jewish was mostly associated with speaking Judeo-Spanish. One interviewee recalls that when he came back from a long stay in Switzerland he could not easily mix with the other Jewish children because he did not know Spanish and therefore the other children 'did not accept him as a Jewish guy' (Am24). Since both Felix S.'s parents had come from 'old Greece' their knowledge of Greek was better than their knowledge of Judeo-Spanish. In a sense, Greek had started to replace Spanish in the provinces without diminishing or threatening the Jewish identity. Greek or Spanish in this transition became languages of the Diaspora, the 'country we live in' (Af10) and hence are replaceable, while the language which carries Jewish identity in this understanding is Hebrew. The situation was different in Salonika because the Jews constituted the majority population and therefore Spanish was the language of the 'city we live in'. The pressure and the willingness to learn the language of the 'country we live in' came about in the late 1920s and early 1930s.

MEMORY OF LOVE: FAMILY LIFE

Greece has been described as a society largely based on kinship (Loizos and Papataxiarchis 1991: 3). In both Jewish and Greek traditions kinship has functioned as a fundamental principle of relatedness and a powerful idiom of action. In both traditions marriage which leads to the reproduction of kinship is of enormous significance. A sense of personhood is developed, maintained and formulated within the boundaries of kinship (Solomon 1994: 95). For most of the interviewees the world of kinship, which was inhabited by grandparents, aunts, uncles, sisters, brothers and cousins, came to an end with, or was radically altered by, the Holocaust.

As Halbwachs argues, memory is always linked to group membership, particularly kinship, religious and class affiliations (Halbwachs 1925). This argument is quite complex because it refers both to the content of memory and the process of remembering. This means that:

a) memory is transmitted by these groups (parents tell their children for example why they should be proud to belong to group x);
b) the actual memory is structured by various group references, that is, references to the family, circle of friends, work colleagues, political comrades or, in the case of the Salonikan Jews, concentration camp inmates, and partisans; and
c) remembering is often part of a group activity or a communicative situation.

The experience of genocide has a great impact on the memory process. While individuals could and can remember their families and their 'family memory', they often could not recall these memories in exchanges with other family members. This increases the importance of other survivors and community members in the memory process. The generation who can remember a pre-war Jewish Salonika thus becomes a 'community of memory'.

Memory of family in the interviewees' narratives is thus of triple relevance: firstly, as memory of the earliest group membership of an individual which had a lasting impact on the individual's identity, for example with regard to language ability, religious and political orientation; secondly as memory of family and family members who mostly did not survive; and thirdly as reference to kinship which used to be and still is a meaningful principle of relatedness and a basis for action in pre-war Salonika and contemporary Greek society.

References to family background fulfil a similar function in the narratives as do references to Spain: family is the beginning of a story about the individual self, just as 'we all came from Spain' is the beginning of the 'collective self'. Both beginnings place the individual within a historical and personal continuity, as expressed by Michael B. in his opening remarks: 'I come from a rabbinical family. My grandfather was the Chief Rabbi of Salonika' (Am16). Other quite common opening lines were the date of birth, followed by a description of the father's business:

I was born in Salonika in 1924. My parents were not rich, but were well off. My father was in the wood business. (Af2)

My father owned a building with his brother. He was an exporter, a merchant. He was in good shape. He was very well known here in Salonika. (Am24)

I was born in 1917. My father was a butcher. (Am23)

The continuity introduced by these narratives is often immediately followed by a reference to the Holocaust. Continuity (of the Jewish community and the family) thus stands side by side with interruption and discontinuity. Baruch S., who made the last statement, says at another point in the interview:

Salonika was the biggest Jewish community in the whole world. There were many religious schools. My grandfather was a very learned man, he went with me to the concentration camp, he was over 80. He was an outstanding man, his name was Aaron, my father was called Avram. My son is called Avram. He has his grandfather's name. (Am23)

The fact that Baruch S.'s son has his grandfather's name is seen as a proof of continuity despite the historical discontinuity marked by the concentration camp. It also becomes apparent in Baruch S.'s statement that the notions of 'community' and 'family' are closely intertwined and talked about in the same context. Both the 'family' and the 'community' are portrayed with a certain nostalgia (in which negative aspects have no place) for a lost world. The 'family' is seen as happy and intact, the 'community' as lively, large and flourishing. One important area where the two worlds of the family and the community meet is the realm of religion and religious practice, expressed by Alici P. in her opening statement in the interview: 'We were 55,000 Jews. We had houses and everything. We celebrated each festival the way they do it in Israel. We were happy' (Af9).

I found that very often interviewees would preface any concrete childhood memories with a statement about happiness and love. Because of the traumatic experiences of the interviewees in later years their childhood took place in a world in which things were 'still normal' (within the family and the community) and thus gains important significance in their narrative as a contrast to what happened later. A preface about love and closeness of the family seems to underline this contrast. Palomba A. starts the interview by saying:

> I was born in 1924. We were a family of seven. We were very, very *agapimenoi* [loving]. There was a lot of love in our family. We were five brothers and sisters, two sons and three daughters. We were a family and we lived well, until the war began, *otan archise o polemos.* (Af1)

'Living well' is of course a relative notion, in this case relative to the war and the war experiences. Palomba A.'s father was a blacksmith. The family was not rich and she started working in a shop at the age of 11. Life was certainly not easy but Palomba A.'s narrative does not focus on the pre-war day-to-day difficulties of economic hardship. In the retrospective life history, these aspects of her life do not seem relevant.

As mentioned above, religion and the celebration of religious festivals at home and outside is an important locus of the childhood memories of the survivors. Alici P. recalls the preparation for the Shabbat (the Hebrew word for the Sabbath):

> When I was young my mother used to call me and say: 'come Alici. Let us make some *pita* or some *borekita*.[9] Do it like this'. She used to make jam for two or three days but on the Shabbat she would not do anything, anything at all. On Friday night we got dressed and sat down at the table to say the Kiddush. It was something wonderful. (Af9)

Alici P. also stresses the communal aspects of religious festivals. She recounts that on Sukkot they built a *Sukkah* outside their house. Her father, who owned a beer factory, provided the wine and the Grand Rabbi, who was their neighbour, would say the Kiddush (blessing of the wine). Every year in the *Sukkah* 'one would meet all the Jews' (Af9). Rebecca V. also recounts that during the 'time before the war … there was a *Sukkah* on the balconies of all houses' (Af11).[10]

It is interesting that Alici P. does not say that 'one would meet the Jewish neighbours' but that she says 'all the Jews' and that Rebecca V. also talks about 'all houses'. Phrases like 'all the shops were Jewish', 'all the neighbourhood was Jewish', 'all our friends were Jewish' appear very frequently. I argue that these phrases are used because they evoke best the image of a lost world and underline the contrast to today's reality (the Jews are a tiny minority). Statements about the closeness of the family are as strong in evoking an image of pre-war intactness and they also stand in contrast to the post-war reality of having no, or a very small, family: 'In the family we had a very close relationship. People who passed our house always said what a happy family we were. We were very close and loved each other very much' (Am17).

The description of the closeness and love in the families can be found in most interviews, irrespective of class and family background. This testifies to a) the importance of the family as a social unit in the 1920s and 1930s and b) the powerful metaphoric usage of the family discourse as a narrative strategy for describing a pre-catastrophic world. The notion of family closeness emerges also in the narrative about marriage, that is, arranged marriage. Among the women interviewees four got married before the war. Lili M. discusses in great detail the process of getting engaged and married in a traditional way:

> I had an arranged marriage. I did not know my future husband. I had graduated from Anatolia but at the same time I had received a degree in Piano at the Conservatoire. I had modern ideas, I wanted to go to Salzburg. My father did not have the same ideas. He did not think that young ladies should go and study in Salzburg so he decided I should marry without telling me anything. One day I went, it is so clear in my mind, my mother said to me: 'Lili we are invited tonight to Mr Nar. They are inviting us and we will have a lovely evening.' So I go there, there was a big salon, you know a wealthy Jewish family. And you know where they lived? Just over there, the corner of Diagonios. They had a lovely apartment. There, I see a number of young men and we spent a couple of hours together. It was nice. Two days later my brother comes. He was older than I by four years and we loved each other, we were very close, the family. 'You know Lili you are engaged.' 'To whom?' I asked. 'Don't you remember the young man who was sitting in the corner?' I did not remember anything. There were two young men who were brothers, my husband and his younger brother. 'Which one? The one on the left or the one on the right?' Do you know what? I did not resist a moment. I adored my father and I had a deep respect for his judgement. If he has chosen someone for me it means he must be very good. (Af8)

In this narrative the clash between tradition (girls got married at a young age) and modernity (girls also attended schools, colleges and universities) is avoided (or solved) by the notion of 'family closeness' and 'family love' which enabled the interviewee to accept her father's decision regarding her marriage.

It is striking that we do not find descriptions of friction and tension in the family very often although we do find descriptions about generational change in the family, which hint at the change and the modernisation which had been taking place in Salonika at the time. In these descriptions the interviewees talk mostly about their grandparents who did not speak any Greek or feel Greek, but more importantly were much more religious (in the observance of Jewish laws). When asked about the religious observance in the family, Moshe B. answered:

> No we were not religious. My grandfather was religious. He wanted everything to be done proper. We kept the Shabbat. But after he died we did not continue. He tried to make me a *Hazan* [a singer in the synagogue]. He wanted me to sit and study, but I did not do it. (Am17)

In the light of the later radical developments, the changes caused by Westernisation and modernisation are not seen as a disruption but as a natural generational development and therefore do not receive that much attention. Changes in religious observance receive more attention when they are linked to Greek legislation which forbade shops to be open on Sundays (the law came out in 1922) which in effect meant that many Jews had to open their shops on Saturday. Lili M. describes this change like this:

> I remember another thing. Every Saturday morning, until the Greeks forbade it, all stores were closed during the Shabbat. It was the habit to go visiting on Saturday mornings. The sons would go to visit their mother's or uncle's home and they would give you eggs, hard-boiled eggs. We, the children might go with the father and would collect a basket full of eggs and presents. Then there was the law that it was forbidden and then it stopped. (Af8)

Since Lili M. was born in 1922 and she remembers these visits on the Sabbath, it could not have been the immediate impact of the law which changed the Shabbat activities of her family (which she generalises by saying 'it was the habit') but the long-term effect of the

Hellenisation of the city which gradually changed the observance of the Sabbath.

Both 'cultural' and 'communicative memory' single out specific events or specific years to structure time and to demarcate change. In Lili M.'s narrative it is 'the law' which brought about the change she describes. The two events in the pre-war period which are singled out in many narratives are the arrival of the Asia Minor refugees after 1923 and the Campbell event in 1931. Both these dates are not part of the official 'cultural memory' of the city, which focuses mostly on three dates: 315 BCE, the date when Salonika was founded, 1430, the date when Salonika was occupied by the Ottomans, and 1912, the date when Salonika was 'liberated'.[11]

MEMORIES OF ANTAGONISM: THE ARRIVAL OF THE ASIA MINOR REFUGEES AND THE CAMPBELL RIOT

The word antagonism here is an etic category rather than an emic category used by the interviewees. Both the arrival of the Asia Minor refugees and the Campbell riot are mostly talked about in the context of pre-war anti-Semitism. However, the significance given to both events varies from interview to interview. Despite the different evaluation of these events, one does get the impression that both the arrival of the refugees in 1923 and the Campbell riot in 1931 are seen as turning points, even more so than 1912 (although of course of lesser magnitude than the time between 1941 and 1943). The arrival of the Asia Minor refugees became a turning point because it marked the beginning of the consolidation of the nation-state, in which the Jews were no longer an 'indigenous' population but became a 'foreign' minority. The Campbell riot became a turning point (in some life histories) because it took this process even further and marked the point at which the Jews became the victims of Greek nationalists. Furthermore, the Campbell riot is also viewed in the light of what happened to the Jews later in the 1940s.

As above, most interviewees describe the change after 1912 as a swift transition in which the Jews 'got used' to the new Greek state and accepted Greece. But the arrival of 100,000 Greek Asia Minor refugees in Salonika disturbed this normalisation:

It was difficult for the Jews to readjust [after 1912]. But slowly, slowly we got accustomed to the new situation. There was something else which created a certain tension, the arrival of the Asia

Minor refugees. Without work, without anything, they slept on the streets and all they saw were the rich Jews and naturally that created tension. (Af8)

When the Greeks came things changed. But things became worse when Greece lost the Balkan Wars and the Asia Minor refugees arrived. (Am12)

The Jews accepted Greece. But then came the Greek refugees. (Am24)

When I asked Felix S., who made the last statement, whether the Greek refugees were anti-Semitic he said that he did not want to talk about it (implying that he did not want to say anything bad about the Greeks) but then he continued: 'They came without homes and they were poor and they saw people with homes and big buildings' (Am24).

The arrival of the Asia Minor refugees thus changed two major aspects of Jewish life in Salonika: firstly the Jews became a minority and secondly Jews became exposed to anti-Semitism through the arrival of the refugees. Most interviewees do not think (or say) that the refugees were genuinely anti-Semitic but that 'they made them anti-Semitic'. The interviewee may refer by 'they' to the politicians or to the political and economic situation. In any case, the anti-Semitism of the 'Greeks from other places, the Greeks from outside' (Am15) is often contrasted to the good relationship between the Salonikan Jews and the Salonikan Greeks. In this contrast the Asia Minor refugees are seen as villagers and the 'old Salonikans' as urban Greeks who often were able to speak Spanish. This is another variation of the language metaphor as an indicator for social relations or ethnic and national sentiment. While knowledge of Greek (by Jews) is often perceived as an indicator of integration and assimilation, knowledge of Spanish (by Greeks) becomes an indicator for the good relationships between the Jews and Greeks. When asked about the relationship between Jews and Greeks, Solomon S. replies:

> The relations with the old Salonikans who lived here during the Ottoman Empire were very good. All the refugees who came here were from small villages. The old Salonikans spoke our language, Spanish. During the Ottoman Empire the Greeks spoke Spanish, like us, do you understand? (Am22)

On the whole, the interviewees were very careful about what they said concerning anti-Semitism and it is difficult to make generalisations. Some said there was never any anti-Semitism, some say there was a bit of anti-Semitism, and some say there has always been anti-Semitism.

What is of particular interest in this context, is that the question of anti-Semitism cannot be discussed within specific historical time frames. The interviewees always link the different time periods and want to make general statements, like 'we have always been like brothers' and 'there was no anti-Semitism' (Af9), or 'there has always been anti-Semitism'. Depending on this general outlook the Campbell riot is interpreted differently. For the first speaker it was a riot by a small group of nationalists (the *Ethniki Enosi Ellas*, National Union of Greece), similar to the Neo-Nazis in contemporary Germany (Af9); for the second speaker Campbell was an anti-Semitic pogrom which caused many Jews to leave for Palestine (Am22). It can be argued that the memory of anti-Semitism is mostly shaped by the different experiences of later years, mainly during the war, rather than the different experiences at the time. Anti-Semitism and the question of Greek–Jewish relationships are not recounted in different historical periods but in a 'general' time frame. Therefore, individuals who were helped by Orthodox Greeks during the war or were with the partisans in the mountains are much less likely to talk about Greek anti-Semitism (in the pre-war period) than individuals who suffered the severe consequences of German anti-Semitism in the concentration camps. It is also striking that some of the concentration camp survivors are much more reluctant to discuss the subject of Jewish–Greek relationships in order not to say anything 'negative' about the Greeks. When asked about the relationship between Jews and Greeks in the pre-war time Mois H. replied: '**It is** better not to talk about it because sometimes **it was** not good. But I don't want to say ... We respect them [the Greeks], we like them [the Greeks], but it is better not to talk about this. Otherwise **they will** say: the Jews are not grateful' (Am18).

This response illustrates the aspect of the 'timelessness' in the question of anti-Semitism. The speaker uses the past, present and future tenses in the same context. A statement about 'then' is followed by an expression of 'now' which is followed by a fearful statement of the future. Similarly, Jean L. jumps from one time period to the other. She starts off by discussing the Jewish reaction to the Greeks after 1912 and then talks immediately about her own war experience:

At the beginning we were a bit scared as it is with every occupation. But we got used to the new situation. Also the Greeks were
scared. They thought that the Jews kill children to make the
matzah for Pesach. On the other hand, I was saved by Greeks.
Thanks to the Greeks I am alive. If the Greeks had not protected
me from the Germans and showed me how to escape I would
have died. (Af6)

The collapse of the chronological time frame can happen in different variations. Lili M., for example, links the Campbell riot directly to
the war events. For her the Campbell riot symbolises what was to
come ten years later. She describes the day of the riot in July 1931 as
follows:

I remember it very well. I remember one morning, we lived on
Evsonon, and we had a balcony on the street and suddenly we see
a long line of carriages. The old people sitting in the carriages, the
younger people walking, with babies crying. They had burned
their homes at Campbell … It was a terrible day, we were all very
scared. It was something that you did not expect although the
EEE [*Ethniki Enosi Ellas*] had been very active. When they burnt
[homes], it was a sign that we should have taken our shoes and
left. I remember it so very clearly. (Af8)

To my next question: 'What was the public feeling about Campbell?'
she replied:

I remember only much later the newspaper which came under
German control, the New Order, the New Europe. Every day, it
was terrible. Death to the Jews. They were very difficult times,
very difficult. Many people emigrated to Israel [then Palestine]
and France … My father's sister also went to France with her husband. We lost them, they had three sons. (Af8)

In the last statement the mixing of the two time periods is very obvious. The newspaper under German control was published in the
1940s while the emigration to France and Palestine took place in the
1930s, following the Campbell riot, but she 'lost them' again in
the1940s. Lili M.'s most traumatic past, the time when she lost her
whole family, overshadows the other past, the past around the
Campbell riot.

Having said that the Campbell riot is regarded as a turning point or a departure, it also needs to be pointed out that in other interviews the event does not receive much attention, despite my specific questions. This is surprising if we consider that the Campbell riot was the first violent anti-Semitic pogrom in Salonika, partly incited by a virulent anti-Semitic press which later blamed the riot on the communists (Vassilikou 1993: 22). This caused the formation of young bands of armed Jews to protect Jewish neighbourhoods. One explanation has been given here, namely the significance of later historical developments, but it should be added that the memory of Campbell as a clear and violent antagonism between Jews and Greeks is not cultivated because it challenges the narrative of a peaceful Greek–Jewish co-existence, which emerges from the contemporary context of the interviewees. In the brochure of the community the Campbell riot is only briefly referred to as 'the sad incident of arson that destroyed the Campbell neighbourhood' (Jewish Community of Salonika 1992: 18). Due to the breakdown of time (with a separate past, present and future), illustrated above, a description of the past could imply a criticism of the present. A description of violence between Jews and Greeks could be read as a statement about the relationship between Jews and Greeks in the present.

It is suggested here that this process can only be understood if we relate it to the general meaning of 'the past' and of 'history' in the contemporary Greek context which is characterised by an emphasis on continuity and a past that legitimises the present. At the time of my fieldwork, for example, at the height of the crisis with the neighbouring Former Yugoslav Republic of Macedonia, there were signposts everywhere saying 'Macedonia has been Hellenic for 3,000 years' (in different variations). Another example for the notion of continuity with a slightly different nuance is taken from the text of one of the many publications by the Organisation for the Cultural Capital of Europe, published in 1994: 'Salonika **has always** been the place where ideas flourish, where people meet, where religions co-exist. All this **is** the work of the spirit of Hellenism which dwells in the city' (Salonika: 8). The text goes on to talk about the spirit of Hellenism which awakens collective memory. Interestingly this collective memory is not 'a selective recall of events from the past, but a universal experience of history, where everything has its place and its value, where everything is consequent [*sic*] and coherent' (Salonika: 8). Needless to say, this text is a contradiction in terms and does exactly the opposite of what it claims, namely it operates with the idea of a 'normative' past which of course is selective and in which Hellenism is portrayed as the main agent of history.

The individual's memory is as selective as the kind of 'cultural memory' we have just encountered. If the memory of certain events is not institutionalised (that is, it does not become part of a codified 'cultural memory') and the events are not regularly remembered within a certain group (for example in the family and in the community), they will lose their meaning and perhaps even eventually be forgotten (Halbwachs 1985: 3). Looking at the interviewees' memories of the arrival of the Asia Minor refugees and the Campbell riot, this process becomes apparent. On the one hand, it is difficult to combine memories of antagonism between Greeks and Jews with the official narrative of Hellenism and on the other hand, the memories of these events have not become essential in the transmission of 'family memory'. Compared to later historical events both the arrival of the Asia Minor refugees and the Campbell riot took place within a world which perhaps was changing (from a multicultural entity into a homogenising nation-state) but which still 'made sense'. The anti-Semitism of the Asia Minor refugees can be understood ('the refugees came from Turkey and asked themselves: "Why do the Jews have everything and we have nothing?"' Am19) and is therefore less traumatic than later experiences.

A quotation, taken from an interview with a Salonikan woman who was born in 1906 and moved to Paris in the 1920s, gives a very clear account of the arrival and the impact of the Asia Minor refugees. Although she probably had very little personal experience of the time, she states:

> We were living harmoniously, Greeks, Jews, Turks. In Salonika we lived very, very, very, very, very, very well … When Venizelos came to power in 1922, there was an exchange of population in 1922 … After that exchange anti-Semitism started in Greece, you understand? We were living well until anti-Semitism started. Anti-Semitism started in Greece with the arrival of the people from Asia Minor, not with the Greeks, but with the sub-Greeks. (Valensi and Wachtel: 1991: 222)

This memory stayed with her because it was part of transmitted family memory. In her case, the arrival of the Asia Minor refugees is directly linked to the emigration of her family to France and thus linked to a family narrative in which the beginning of anti-Semitism brought by the Asia Minor refugees constituted a 'push factor' for the emigration. In contrast to my interviewees, as a Parisian Salonikan, she is not under the constraint of the Greek notion of a continuing past, in which statements about the past have ramifications for the present and the present thus shapes the memory of the past.

CONCLUSION

In an article on 'generational memory' Hareven describes an encounter between Claude Cookburn and three Ladino-speaking Jews shortly after the war in Sofia. They told him about their family history: 'Our family used to live in Spain before they moved to Turkey and now we are moving to Bulgaria' (quoted in Hareven 1984: 249). When Cookburn asked how long ago their family had moved from Spain, he found out that this had happened 500 years ago. It startled him that the three Jews spoke of these events as if they had occurred just a couple of years ago. Based on this episode, Hareven points to the relativity of historical memory and to the different nature of 'generational memory' in different cultures.

This chapter attests to a similar notion of 'generational memory' as described by Hareven. The interviewees say 'we came from Spain' as if this had happened recently. The sense of 'connectedness' with the past is also expressed in the link made between the migration from Spain and recent migration experiences ('they moved to Turkey ... we are moving to Bulgaria' or 'we started speaking Greek, like we had learnt Spanish in Spain, we now learnt Greek because we lived in Greece', Am15). This sense of continuity with the 'distant' past of the 'generational' or 'cultural memory' exists parallel to the sense of discontinuity of the 'communicative' family memory of the 'recent' pre-war past.

NOTES

1. Kokot reports the same 'gender bias' for her interviewees in Kato Toumba. While the men often talked about the history of the quarter in very general terms, the women narrated the history of the quarter within the context of their own lives (Kokot 1995: 82).
2. There is of course a certain 'feeling of loss' in every generation since the world of the young has certainly changed in some aspects from the world of the old. However, I would argue that there is also a feeling of continuity in most cases which is not there among different generations of immigrant groups or generations which have grown up under different political systems.
3. I have adapted this phrase from Anny Bakalian's study on Armenian Americans (Pattie 1997: 144).
4. A *Hazan* is a trained religious reader who conducts the prayers in the synagogue.

5. Reilly writes that 367 Jews who held Spanish citizenship were brought to Bergen-Belsen in the summer of 1944 where they were put in the *Neutralenlager*. They were not subjected to hard labour and left the camp in February 1944 for Spain and Palestine (Reilly 1998: 13).

6. Most times the words 'occupation' and 'liberation' are used in the context of the German occupation (*Katochi*) and the liberation in 1944. In this case they express a shared historical experience (of Jews and Greeks) and are therefore not contested.

7. A *Sukkah* is a hut built with plants and branches during the festival of *Sukkot*, also known as the Feast of Tabernacles, which is a harvest festival.

8. Most interviewees who are not from Salonika come from Larissa and the surrounding area which became Greek in 1896.

9. *Borekas* or *borekitas* are savoury pies. The word comes from the Turkish word *borek* for pies. They are the 'culinary representatives of Turkish, Greek and Balkan Jewry' (Roden 1997: 240). They were considered festive food for celebrations. At communal Shabbat ceremonies *borekitas* (made and delivered by a restaurant) are still eaten today (see chapter four).

10. She contrasts this to today, when only the community puts up a *Sukkah* and people visit it for memory's sake (Af11).

11. The official leaflet about Salonika as the 'Cultural Capital' of Europe points out: 'Few cities are granted as long a life as Thessaloniki which recently celebrated 2,300 years of history' (p.12). 'Having remained in the limelight of history ever since (its foundation) the city had known great moments of glory' (p. 8). In this understanding 'history' did not end, it legitimises and gives meaning to the present.

6

Narratives of War and Occupation (1940–43)

This chapter will present the memories of those difficult years which made all the interviewees into survivors. Whether the interviewees were in the concentration camps, in hiding, or with the partisans in the mountains, they survived the war, whereas many of their family members and friends did not.

Consequently, remembering these years can be a very painful process, especially when it follows years of silence. The notion of 'silence' does not imply that the Holocaust was not given any 'memory space' but that the 'memory space' was ritualised (in the form of the yearly Holocaust commemoration, for example), not specific, and was often private. Only recently the community and other organisations (Yale University and The Shoah Visual History Foundation) have started recording detailed testimonies of Salonikan survivors, and a public monument for the victims of the Holocaust was erected (see Figure 23 and 24). Niethammer argues that this kind of public recognition and 'memory work' is a necessary prerequisite which enables individuals to voice their own experiences which often have not been communicated and were 'tucked away' for many years as part of the individual's search for 'normalisation' (Niethammer 1995: 38). It is important to note that, during the main period of study, the process of recognition, 'bearing witness', and socially shared remembering had just begun, namely with the 50th anniversary in 1993 of the deportations in 1943.

Being acutely aware of the painful and traumatic nature of the memories of the interviewees, I did not want to 'make them remember' and evoke those memories unless I felt that the interviewees wanted to talk about their experiences. Consequently, only three of the ten concentration camp survivors spoke in detail about their experience in the camp, while most interviewees who had been in hiding or with the partisans described their experiences in more detail. This reflects the interviewees' and my own narrative strategies. Experiences of escaping, hiding and fighting can be integrated more easily into the narrative form (on the side of the interviewee) and more easily asked about (by the interviewer) than the experiences of the concentration camp. The experience of death and destruction can be 'narrated' but defies the notion of meaning and understanding which characterises other narrative sequences within a life history. This experience also defies the notion of 'generational knowledge' which can act as a model for the next generation (Abels 1995: 315), and through which the next generation can learn something about the 'right responses' and the 'right choices' of the older generation. Thus the memory of traumatic experiences forms a very distinct form of memory, a memory characterised by rupture rather than continuity, and 'meaninglessness' rather than 'meaning'. In his study of Holocaust testimonies Langer underlines this point:

> Oral Holocaust testimonies are doomed on one level to remain disrupted narratives, not only by the vicissitudes of technology but by the quintessence of the experiences they record ... They do not function like other narratives, since the losses they record raise few expectations of renewal or hopes of reconciliation. This does not mean that the witnesses have no future ... but they are hostages to a humiliating and painful past that their happier future does little to curtail. (Langer 1991: xi)

Since the act of remembering has been given social significance in the Jewish community in recent years (for example, the motto: *'Pote Pia! Never again!'* appeared in many official community publications), this traumatic memory gains new relevance which makes it easier and encourages individuals to share their painful experiences.[1] In recent years the Shoah Visual History Foundation has also collected more than 250 interviews throughout Greece. This chapter will describe the different experiences and perceptions of 'the war' among the interviewees.

NARRATIVES OF CONCENTRATION CAMP AND OTHER SURVIVORS

In the epilogue of *The Truce* Primo Levi talks about two categories of concentration camp survivors: the ones who want to forget and the ones who see the act of remembering as their duty. The first group consists of people who came to the concentration camp through 'bad luck and not because of political commitment' (Levi 1994: 390), which brought the second group of survivors to the camps. Levi argues that for the first group the suffering was more traumatic because it was devoid of meaning, like a misfortune or an illness, whereas the second group of political prisoners embedded their suffering into a larger map of political and historical developments (Levi 1994: 390). Without discussing in detail Levi's hypothesis, the argument can be taken up and adapted to this case study. First of all, the argument illustrates that while we need to make general statements about survivors, we also have to take into account individual differences. It certainly holds true that there is a significant difference between the Jewish non-political concentration camp inmates and the political prisoners in the camp, and that in general terms Levi captures this difference. However, this difference does not fully explain the very different ways people have been dealing with and remembering their experience within these groups. Here, other factors come into play, for example: age at the time of survival; survival of other family members; and the perceived success or failure of post-war life. This is similar for the three groups of survivors interviewed. While it will be argued here that the different experience of the war years has deeply affected their general sense of identity, we need to bear in mind that there are variations within each group.

Just as Levi argued that political prisoners can more easily 'make sense' of their experience, it is suggested here that individuals who were with the partisans or in the mountains, that is, had experience of Greek help and/or of a common fight against the Germans, can more easily 'make sense' of their experience and integrate it into their life history than the concentration camp survivors (none of whom were 'political' in this study). It seems to me that the war experiences are extremely significant because they have shaped and continue to shape perceptions and notions of 'self' and 'other' in later life (such as, for example, views on anti-Semitism and Jewish–Greek relations).

Individual narratives and memories are formulated in dialogue with other discourses, such as narratives produced by the Jewish community and the Greek state, which try to make sense of historical processes. The community has emphasised the rebuilding aspect, which exemplifies the strength and the vitality of the community: 'Despite its tragic ordeal the Jews of Thessaloniki managed to rise from their ashes and offer a tangible example of vitality and strength' (Jewish Community of Salonika 992: 19). An earlier version of the same notion read:

> In spite of the devastating hurricane brought about by the Nazi persecutions and the annihilation of a glorious community sever-

al centuries old ... the surviving deportees of the death camps and those who managed to survive in the guerrilla forces in the mountains and villages with the assistance of their non-Jewish fellow citizens, aimed at reviving this community. Thanks to the dedication of the good-willed men who have been guiding the community since the liberation of the country, the once glorious Jewish Community of Salonika has managed to survive, thus setting an example of [the] vitality, the strength and the spirit of the Jewish people. (Jewish Community of Salonika 1978: 49)

The Greek state has largely ignored the Jewish experience, although the Jewish partisans have been acknowledged together with the other partisans shortly after PASOK came to power in 1981. When the Holocaust monument was erected in 1997, it was the first time that a number of Greek politicians, including the Prime Minister Simitis, made public comments about the Jewish experience in a very publicised event. In the speeches, the memory of the destruction of the Jewish community was seen as a reminder of totalitarianism and fascism which should never occur again ('Never again totalitarianism and atrocity! In Thessaloniki of today, in Greece of today, and in Greece and Thessaloniki of tomorrow, fascism will not have its way', *Chronika* January/February 1998: 32). Furthermore the Jewish experience was woven into the narrative of the Greek resistance and the fight against the Germans, characterised by the 'great struggle' and the common 'sacrifice':

> In the struggle of humanity against fascism and racism, Jews fought with all other Greeks for freedom, basic values of civilisation, human rights and the dignity and honour of peoples. The price they paid was heavy and inhumane ... This monument will remind all of us ... of the sacrifice of the Jews. (Mr Petsalnikos, Minister of Macedonia-Thrace, *Chronika* January/February 1998: 31)

> Those whom we have lost were not simply victims. They were fighters. They were involved in the great struggle of the Greek people for freedom. (Mr Pangalos, Foreign Minister, *Chronika* January/February 1998: 33)

Both statements illustrate how an historical event is given meaning in official communal and national narratives. The communal narrative tells the story of catastrophe and reconstruction whereas the national narrative tells the story of heroic struggle, sacrifice and victory (commonly used for other historical time periods such as the Independence struggle).

Both narratives are attempts at building 'a monument of hope on the rubble of decay' (Langer 1991: 205). They use a vocabulary which is meant to take the reader or listener away from the event of destruction towards a consoling future. By talking about the death of Jews in terms of 'fight' and 'sacrifice', the official Greek narrative turns victims into active fighters whose death was meaningful because it brought about 'freedom'. The narrative thus renders death meaningful ('they died for something') and weaves, so to speak, the experience of the Holocaust into the 'master narrative' of the Greek nation state. In contrast to communal and state narratives, it is much more difficult to 'make sense' of survival, destruction and annihilation for individuals. As Langer notes: 'The raw material of oral Holocaust narratives, in content and matter of presentation, resists the organising impulse of moral theory' (Langer 1991: 204).

Coming back to the earlier argument about the different groups of survivors, it can be said that Jewish partisans and Jews who were in hiding can identify, to various extents, with the official Greek narrative because they have, again to various extents, experienced solidarity and support. The concentration camp survivors' experiences do not conform to either narrative: they did not take place in a 'heroic struggle' nor do they describe their post-war lives as a 'personal triumph' over what happened to them. In their post-war lives both groups had to cope with the death of family members and friends. But in contrast to the partisans, the concentration camp survivors' experience of the time between deportation and return is very different. It is a time many interviewees did not talk about. Perhaps because it was too painful for them, perhaps because they felt that they should or could not communicate their experience to a 'young girl', like myself. As Levi stated, often concentration camp survivors want to eliminate the specific memory of the camp experience, like a 'painful object which intruded into their lives' (Levi 1994: 390). Their narrative therefore often starts with the return from the camps or jumps from the time of the deportation to the time of return: 'We were all sent to the concentration camp. We were five days without food. That is our history. When we came back most people were dead' (Am20).

This statement not only illustrates the focus on the 'before', that is, before the deportation and the 'after', that is, the return from Poland, but also the usage of the collective 'us'. Despite the fact that Leon L. was the only surviving member of his family (he had lost his wife and two children) he speaks of 'our history' and says 'we came back'.² The question arises as to whom Leon L. refers to by 'we'. Is it all the surviving Jews in Salonika or is it the group of concentration camp survivors who share the memory of common suffering? This chapter and chapter 7 will attempt to illuminate how the different groups of survivors perceive and narrate the wartime past and what role group references play in this process.

Another way of looking at the different groups of survivors is to look at age, marital status, and geographical location of each interviewee at the time of the outbreak of the war. These factors determined the range of possibilities for every individual during the occupation and their fate in the concentration camps. The age distribution among my interviewees at the time of the deportations in 1943 was as follows: two were infants, three were between the ages of 8 and 10, three were between the ages of 16 and 18, six were between 19 and 23, nine were between 25 and 33, and seven between 34 and 42. The other important factor is that of geographical location, as the situation of Jews differed considerably in the three occupation zones (see Chapter 3).

A brief word needs to be said here about the terminology of 'the war'. The older interviewees who were born before 1914 actually experienced three wars in their life time: the First World War, the Balkan Wars, and the Second World War. However, when talking about 'the war' (*polemos, guerre, Krieg*) the speaker is usually referring to the Second World War. The term 'war' appears more frequently than any other word with regard to the experiences from 1940 to 1945. In a computerised word search, the word 'occupation' (*Katochi, Besetzung*) came up only 12 times in five different interviews, only one of which was with a concentration camp survivor. In contrast the term 'war' appears numerous times in every interview. The term 'war' is used as a broad term which encompasses the Greek–Italian War, the German Occupation, the deportation and experiences in the concentration camps in Poland and Germany, or the experiences of hiding and fighting in Greece.

A chronology of the war, in terms of distinct phases, varies of course with the distinct experiences of the interviewees but fits mostly into the following chronological order:

1) The war with Italy (1940–41)
2) The German/Italian occupation (1941–43)

3) Introduction of anti-Jewish measures (1942–43)
4) Escape or deportation (1943–44)
5) Experiences of 'there' – in the concentration camps, of hiding, or of being with the partisans (1943–45)
6) Liberation and return (1944–45)

Depending on the interviewee's experience and general narrative, he or she discusses certain periods in greater detail than others.

THE WAR WITH ITALY

On 28 October 1940, Germany's ally, Italy, delivered an ultimatum to Metaxas. After the rejection of the ultimatum (the famous '*ochi*'), Italian forces entered Greece. In the subsequent Greek–Italian War, the Italian troops were pushed back to Albania by December 1940. After a very severe winter Greek troops had to withdraw from Albania. The war with Italy thus lasted from October 1940 until the spring of 1941.

On the whole, the war with Italy does not feature very prominently in the interviews. As with the other historical events, it is overshadowed by the later more traumatic experiences. Out of the 15 male interviewees, 11 were old enough to be called to arms. Five men were drafted to war, two were exempted, one for health reasons, the other one because he was a *Hazan* in a synagogue, and the others did not talk about this period of their life (mostly because they started talking immediately about the other 'war', that is to say about the German occupation and the deportations).

It is very interesting that only Moshe B. tells me of his experiences at the Albanian Front in a detailed and chronological account. The other men talk about this war very briefly and mostly in two contexts: in the context of nationalism and sacrifice and in the context of Jewish–Greek relations. Let us first look at Moshe B.'s account:

> A year later the war broke out and Italy occupied Greece. At that time we were in the army. We received an order to move ... There were rivers and with the boats we made bridges. Another Jew and myself were responsible for putting together, loading and sending all the materials to Albania. We went to Albania and there were many difficulties on the way. I managed on the way to Albania to go through Salonika and to send a letter to my parents saying: 'I

cannot come to see you at the moment. Be healthy and pray that I will be alright'. So we went to the Front. The Italians were destroying the bridges. I got hurt by a bomb dropped from an airplane. The bomb fell not very far from me and I was very lucky that a boat was in front of me which was made from metal. So I was not badly hurt. I was taken to a hospital in the area. After they gave me first aid they sent me to Ioanina. The biggest problem of the Albanian War was the cold. It was very cold and we did not have warm clothes. The Greek soldiers were not used to the cold. Their feet were badly frost-bitten. In Ioanina in the hospital they wanted to amputate the toes of my left leg ... But one had to sign a consent form and I did not sign this. So with four others we escaped from the hospital. One of the patients told us to take a shower with snow every day. We did this all the way from Albania. That's how my legs survived. The Germans saw that the Italians could not beat the Greek army. The Italians suffered and the Greeks had many victories. When the Germans came and we lost the front we started to withdraw. On the way the Germans bombed us and we had to go through the mountains until we got to Athens. The Red Cross helped the soldiers who came from the Front. Slowly we were going back to our families. I went back to my family in Salonika in 1941. (Am17)

This very factual account tells us about the course of the war with Italy, about the initial Greek victory over the Italians and the eventual surrender to the Germans, but more importantly about the suffering of the ordinary soldiers due to the severe winter. The return of soldiers who had their toes and feet amputated is often mentioned in the context of this war. Two women interviewees speak about this topic. Lili S. remembers that she went to see her youngest brother in a hospital in Athens who 'came from the war with his feet amputated' (Af10). Lili M. also talks about her brother, but within the broader context of all the Jewish soldiers:

When the Greeks became serious they sent them all to Albania, including my brother, from where they came back with their legs amputated. How many came! There was a young man in their house, he left and he came back with both his legs cut. And they were sent to Auschwitz. There was no one to defend them. Another friend of mine, a young groom. I had gone to their wedding. He went to Albania and died there, died there, never found the body. So you see, these were the sacrifices. We gave our blood. (Af8)

The contrasts between Moshe B.'s narrative and Lili M.'s statement are striking. Moshe B. gives an account of his personal experience, with only a brief reference to another Jew, while Lili M. refers to her brother's experience in terms of a collective experience ('… **they** came back … **they** were sent to Auschwitz … **we** gave **our** blood'). As a collective Jewish experience Lili M. makes a clear link between the Jewish sacrifice and the deportations. Since 'there was no one to defend them' Jews seem to have sacrificed their lives in vain and were thus betrayed. Although they gave their life for Greece, Greece did not prevent them from being deported.[3]

As in the case of the Campbell riot discussed in Chapter 5, the speaker immediately relates the topic of the war with Italy to the experience of the Holocaust and to the theme of betrayal. This illustrates a point made by Ricoeur regarding the nature of historical and political 'events'. Firstly, an 'event' needs to be defined as an event in order to find mention in a narrative; and secondly, narratives are constructed around certain themes which determine the relevance, that is, the exclusion or inclusion, of certain events (quoted in Sutton 1998: 135). In Lili M.'s narrative, the 'event' of the Greek–Italian War is overshadowed by the later event of the Holocaust and by the general theme of betrayal which runs through her whole interview.

From this it would appear that there is a correlation between the detailed description of an event and the importance of an event for a narrative theme. It seems that the more important the theme which an event serves to demonstrate, the less important is the detailed account of this very event, and vice versa. Moshe B.'s description of his experiences in the Greek–Italian War are of a factual and detailed nature because in his narrative this event does not serve to demonstrate a wider point. His account is thus very exceptional because in most other cases the Greek–Italian War is referred to within a specific theme bracket. This theme can be called the 'good Greek citizen'. What is meant by that becomes clearer if we look at the following two statements:

I also fought in the Albanian War with the Italians. There was a General Frizis and the Jewish community made a monument for him, he was the first who died on the Albanian front, a Jewish officer. He could not speak Greek well but he died for his fatherland. (Am22)

> I have all the rights of a Greek because I was wounded as a Greek
> soldier in the war with Italy. [He shows his scars.] I was wound-
> ed quite badly. I stayed five months in Athens. I was wounded
> three days before the war ended. (Am23)

What is revealed in these statements is the sentiment that individual or
collective Jewish participation in the Greek–Italian War made Jews
into full Greek citizens. The willingness to 'die for the fatherland', to
'sacrifice Jewish blood' is conceived as the ultimate proof of having a
rightful claim to Greek citizenship. The emphasis here is on political
rather than ethnic belonging (to 'have all the rights of a Greek'). The
underlying assumption here is one of ethnic nationalism. The fact that
the Jews were different from Greeks, marked for example by difficulties in speaking Greek, makes their contribution to the Greek–Italian
War even more remarkable: 'He could not speak Greek well but he
died for his fatherland.'

   In this view the war becomes a test of loyalty to the state, which
when successfully passed, entitles the minority (that is, the non-major-
ity population of a given nation-state) to full citizenship and to participation in the imagined national community. In some cases, the actual
experience of being in the army also contributed to the feeling of being
an equal citizen. Leon B. recounts the following episode:

> But even when I was a soldier I had positive experiences. I got an
> exceptional job and I worked in an office because I could translate
> Italian into Greek. It was in 1940. We were in Koritza [a town in
> Albania] and one of the soldiers said: 'Hey Jew, come here.' The
> commander of the office got upset and said to that soldier: 'He
> has a name, his name is Leon. If I hear again that somebody will
> call him "Jew", I will send him to the front.' That was really
> something. (Am14)

   It would seem that the memory of the Greek–Italian War is highly
significant because it functions as a tangible proof of the loyalty of the
Jews to the Greek state, the integration of Jews within Greek society,
and the good relations between the Greeks and the Jews. The figures of
Jewish soldiers and officers who fought, were wounded and were killed
in the war are often used to underline these points. They are, for example, mentioned in the community brochure in the question section.

> Did you know that 12,898 Jews fought during WW2 in the Greek Army, defending their country? That 343 were officers? That they suffered 513 dead and 3,743 wounded? That among the first dead of the war was Colonel Mordechai Frizis of Chalkis? (Jewish Community of Salonika 1993: 27)

These points are often reiterated in public speeches. When the secretary of the community gave a lecture in England about the history of the Jews of Salonika, he underlined these very points. Immediately after talking about the harmony between the Jews and the Greeks he listed the above figures of Jewish participation in the Greek–Italian War, stating proudly 'that the Jews fulfilled their duty towards their country' (Limmud Conference in Manchester, 1997).

Another variation of this narrative emerged in the context of the Greek Foreign Minister's cancellation of his participation in the ceremony of the 50th anniversary ceremony of the liberation of Auschwitz in 1995. Following the Greek foreign policy at the time, the Foreign Minister cancelled his visit to Poland, as Greece boycotted all political and cultural events which acknowledged the newly formed state of Yugoslav Macedonia as 'Macedonia' (and not as FYROM, the Former Yugoslav Republic of Macedonia). In the days to follow this issue was discussed in the Greek media, and representatives of the Jewish community were asked for their opinion. On the whole, the decision not to participate in the ceremony was carefully criticised and marked as a 'sad event' but at the same time it was pointed out that as 'Greek citizens we respect the issues of Greek diplomacy' (*Elefterotipia*, 30 January 1995). The former president of the community, Leon Benmajor, criticised the absence of the Greek state at the celebrations. He is quoted as saying: 'Among the 56,000 Greek Jews who died in the concentration camps were 3,500 Jews who fought and were wounded in the Albanian War … Just for this reason, the Greek Foreign Minister should have gone to Auschwitz' (*Elefterotipia*, 30 January).

This is a good illustration of the 'claim to citizenship' argument. In order to enforce the Jewish right for state representation (in this case at the ceremony in Auschwitz) the speaker refers to the Jewish participation in the Greek–Italian War, as if it is not enough to say that all the Jews who died in Auschwitz were Greek citizens. Interestingly, Leon Benmajor also points out that 'anti-Semitism has never existed in Greece and even less so today', to make sure that his criticism of the Greek government is not misunderstood as an accusation of anti-Semitism.

As with the Campbell event, the memory of the Greek–Italian War is linked to later historical developments and the (for today's Jews very relevant) question of Greek–Jewish relations. Perceived as 'shared Jewish–Greek history', the Greek–Italian War, from the Jewish perspective, provides a legitimate resource for claiming membership and representation in the Greek nation-state. While later in the war the Jews suffered as Jews, in the Greek–Italian War they suffered as Greeks. Having suffered as Greeks for Greece seems to mark the transition to 'becoming national' (in the narratives of some informants). However, the need to stress one's own or the collective contribution to the Greek cause illustrates a deep sense of vulnerability and insecurity among the interviewees, who explicitly refer to the Greek–Italian War in order to defend their status as 'legitimate nationals'.

We can clearly see similarities here between individual and collective narratives. In order to participate in the 'Greek meta narrative', the community brochure stresses the Jewish participation in the Greek Independence struggle, while individuals stress their contribution to the efforts of the Greek state. One can interpret these strategies as typical positions of minorities who do not belong to the 'core' of the nation-state, which is defined by ethnic rather than civic categories, and thus have to constantly reassert their membership (and negotiate their difference). In several instances my question: 'do you feel Greek?' was answered with a statement about the participation in the Greek–Italian War, sometimes substituting a more detailed answer. The importance of the historical event of the Greek–Albanian War stems from the wish to assert the 'Greekness' of the Salonikan Jews. Criticising other Jews who are reluctant to speak Ladino in public, one informant told me: 'Why should I not speak Ladino? You can be a very good patriot and speak Ladino. I say: "look, I fought in Albania" … It was the Jews who fought in Albania' (Am14).

These 'we are good Greek citizens' narratives also reveal a specific understanding of the state which can be linked to the concept of reciprocity. The importance of the concept of reciprocity in Greek society has been stressed by Hirschon (1998), Herzfeld (1987), and Sutton (1998). The notion of reciprocity describes the nature of relationships in which exchange takes place. Linked to the notion of reciprocity are notions of debt and obligation based on past exchanges. Sutton describes very vividly how the notion of failed reciprocity is not only used in the context of the failure to fulfil social obligation by neighbours or other family members but also when talking about the 'betrayal of the Western powers' who criticise Greece over the Macedonia issue and do not acknowledge what Greece did in the Second World War.

When looking at the narratives of the Jewish contribution to Greek independence and the Greek–Italian War, we can detect a notion of the Greek state which is rooted in the concept of reciprocity. The underlying assumption is that one cannot expect anything from the state unless one gives something to it. The state is not just there in order to serve its citizens, as a civic entity so to speak, but the state has legitimate demands on its citizen, such as the demand to fight in a war. To have fought in a war proves the loyalty which might have been in doubt before (as members of a group perceived as non-Greeks) and thus one can expect a 'return gift', such as state protection and full citizenship.

In Lili M.'s statement it became very clear that the state failed to fulfil its duty, or better, its obligation (in reciprocity to the Jewish sacrifice in the Greek–Italian War), by not preventing the deportations, and hence it 'betrayed' the Jews. Despite the fact that the Jews fought in the war 'they were sent to Auschwitz and there was no one to defend them' (Af8). From Lili M.'s perspective there is a close link between the two distinct historical events of the Greek–Italian War and the deportations of the Jews by the Germans, although they are historically of a very different nature. Once again (as in the memory of the Campbell event), this illustrates that the historical narratives of the interviewees are governed by themes which determine the periodisation and the linking of historical events. They are remembered and described as 'proofs' of particular themes which often break down time chronologies in terms of a distinct past, present and future. (Sutton 1998: 141). In Lili M.'s narrative the theme is the 'betrayal by the Greeks'. In other narratives it is the 'good relations between the Jews and the Greeks'. The particular theme, or leitmotiv, almost always emerges from the historical experience of the war, from the time of the deportation or of going into hiding and returning home. Langer writes about the 'absence of an independent time', resulting from the 'past of the disaster [which] casts a net over a redeeming future' (Langer 1991: 74). The above perceptions of historical events before the Holocaust show that the absence of independent time relates both to the past and the future. The key to understanding these interviews lies therefore in the memories of war, which start in most interviews with the memories of occupation.

'WHEN THE GERMANS CAME'

The war memories and recollections of my interviewees are of a varied nature. They are either very lengthy and detailed or very brief and sketchy. It is difficult to do justice to all the material, and in the following I will try to arrive at an understanding of these war memories by focusing on a few selected life histories. The war is mostly perceived as an event which radically disrupted and shattered ordinary and happy lives. It is that contrast between 'before' and 'after' which runs through most interviews, clearly expressed in the following quotation, taken from the beginning of an interview: 'When I was young I went to the Alliance Israelite Universelle until the fourth class ... My father was not rich, he was a tinsmith. He had a shop. We were a family and we lived well, like me today *otan archisi to polemos* [until the war began]' (Af1).

The war began for Palomba A. in 1940–41. She recounts the beginning of the war as follows:

> It was war, in '41 the bombs were falling. There was no work. What were we supposed to do? We started to do business. I started taking stuff from people who did not have money, they gave me clothes and shoes and I sold them for bread and butter. Life was very hard and the whole family worked, nobody was married. My brother was a soldier. My father could not sell anything. I took many things and went to the villages to sell and they gave me flour. My brother and sister took the flour and we made bread. My sister and I went at four o'clock in the morning to the bakery, at seven we picked it up and went to Vardar to sell it. Like this we passed the time when there was a lot of hunger. We were walking in the street and we saw people on the street [with bellies] distended by hunger. Then the Germans came and we were scared of going to the villages. Like this we passed a year. I had a sewing machine and we gave things to the villagers. The Germans took our shop. We all lived together in the ghetto until 1943. Then we had to go to Baron Hirsch. My mother and father were sick. They took us at four o'clock. They gathered us and the wagons came. (Af1)

This condensed narrative covers the period 1940–43. In the first part Palomba A. switches from 'when the Germans came' to the time of the Albanian War and back. While her later narrative of her experiences in the concentration camp is chronologically very precise and very detailed, the beginning of the war and the time leading to the deportation is portrayed in a very general way, a time characterised by extreme economic hardship for the interviewee and her family. The

German occupation is 'just the beginning', pre-catastrophic so to speak, and therefore not that important in most survivors' narratives.

It should be added here that while this time, that is, the time of the German occupation, is not important in historic detail, it is important as a marker which sets apart life 'before' and 'after'. Often the interviewees describe day-to-day life, such as work, or describe the general atmosphere in Salonika which ended 'when the Germans came'. Mois H., for example, speaks about working with his father 'until the Germans came':

> We were selling vegetables, cheese and yoghurt. The shop was on Tsimiski, in the centre … He knew some things and I knew some things. His eyes were not so good anymore so I used to read to him and he would explain to me things I did not understand. We did this **until the Germans came**. (Am18)

The phrase 'until the Germans came' is used in this and other narratives to denote the end of an era. The arrival of the German occupying force denotes this end, although major changes for the Jewish population occurred only about one and a half years after the arrival of the Germans. The notion of an 'end' is also clearly expressed in the following: 'Salonika was a very charming city, in the 1930s it was a city of commerce. Until the war started with Poland and Germany. **Until then**, it was the *"Chrissi Epochi"*, the "Golden Age"' (Am21). Very early on in the interview the same speaker says: 'We worked in a metal factory from 5 a.m. in the morning. The pay was double the usual because it was so difficult … **Then** the Germans came and took us to Germany. **Before** that we were free here' (Am21).

Through the last passage, we understand that for the interviewees the references to the arrival of the Germans and the subsequent deportations were not only the end of a historical era but the end of their freedom. In terms of the interview, it denotes also the end or the disruption of a consistent life history in which individuals make sense of their choices and decisions. For some interviewees the German occupation marks the beginning of the disrupted narrative, for some the disruption starts with the deportations.

Since the period 'in between', that is, in between the German occupation, the deportations, the liberation and the return, evades an autobiographical, teleological narrative it is often summarised in a few sentences. This does not mean that the interviewees do not talk more extensively about the period 'in between' in other parts of the interview, when prompted by a specific question. However, it does illustrate an attempt to not talk about the experiences between departure and return, between 'being sent' and 'coming back'. 'Koretz sent all the *Hazanim*, all the families, and all the wounded to the concentration camp. We were five days without food. That is our history. When we came back most people were dead' (Am18).

When I asked Solomon S. when he was deported to Auschwitz he replied:

> In April 1943 and I was liberated in May 1945. Here almost everybody left for Auschwitz and Birkenau. When the Front came closer I was taken to Mauthausen and then to Besern in Austria. There, I was liberated by the Americans. (Am22)

The next segment of Solomon S.'s interview illustrates what Langer means by saying that Holocaust testimonies 'do not function like other narratives since the losses they record raise few expectations of renewal or hopes of reconciliation' (Langer 1991: xi). To my question 'what happened to your family?', he replies: 'I am the only survivor. My wife, the baby, a 3-year-old girl, they took them all. I will tell you one thing, they might have been luckier because they went to the gas chambers and that was the end' (Am22).

These last two passages illustrate the most important dilemma of interviews with Holocaust survivors: on the one hand they point to the utmost relevance of the 'past of the disaster' which certainly 'casts a net over a redeeming future' (Langer 1991: 74), on the other hand they point to the existence of a 'closed' or rather 'encapsulated' memory which leaps from 'before the war' to 'after the war'. This silence about the 'in between' can be explained in various ways: it can be a) a protection against the pain concrete memories of the war experiences could evoke, b) an effort not to expose me, that is the 'young interviewer' to these painful memories, or c) a narrative 'habit' not to talk in detail about brutal experiences. Niethammer argues that individual memory of a traumatic past is often only expressed after a general, sometimes institutionalised, interest has started to deal with these very memories, which can function as a 'protective cocoon' for the individual (Niethammer 1995: 38). In the case of this study, a collective memory process had not been fully developed and I did not see it as my function to receive as much information as possible. I therefore mostly accepted silences and proceeded with the interviewee to discuss the post-war situation. This process was enforced when interviewees explicitly stated that they did not feel good when talking about their experiences, as, for example, Sam P.:

> The Germans had come in April 1941. We went to the *Konzentrationslager* [concentration camp] in March 1943. Every week 3,000 people arrived in Auschwitz. Very few went to work and the others went to the crematorium. It is very difficult, I feel sick when I speak about the *Konzentrationslager*. (Am26)

Under such circumstances I found it difficult to ask more detailed questions, both regarding the German occupation of Salonika and the experience in Auschwitz. We thus need to understand that there are different reasons why the period of the German occupation in Salonika does not acquire much importance in individual narratives: either this period is part of a general silence about the war or it is considered negligible compared to the narrative of destruction which is to follow. Another factor is the degree of personal contact with the Germans; the more contact there was the more likely the interviewee will include this period in his/her narrative.

Most interviewees point out how 'normal' life was in the first year of occupation. 'It was not bad at the beginning', says Felix S., who had been captured by the Germans as a Greek soldier and made his way back to Thessaloniki on foot. Lili S., a schoolteacher, puts it in similar words: 'At the beginning they didn't do anything bad to us. They were living like everybody else' (Af10). These statements underline what Steven Bowman writes: 'The Jews suffered during the first months of occupation not as Jews but as Greeks' (Bowman 1989: 9). Bowman refers here in particular to the economic hardship which was brought about by the famine in 1941–42, exemplified in Palomba A.'s statement above. Rolli A., who was 18 in 1941 and stayed in Salonika throughout the occupation, also told me about the extreme hunger he and his family were experiencing: 'We were very hungry. The Germans used the premises next to our house as a stable. My mother used to beg for some peas which they were feeding the horses with. She cooked them and that's how we survived' (Am12).

In the first phase of the German occupation, for almost 15 months, no immediate measures were taken against Jews. Some Jews, like Chief Rabbi Koretz, were put under house arrest. After Koretz was arrested in May 1941, he was then sent to Vienna where he was imprisoned. He returned to Salonika eight months later and was appointed president of the community by the Gestapo. The arrival of the Wehrmacht was accompanied by the arrival of the Sonderkommando (special squad) Rosenberg. The mission of this Sonderkommando was to:

> document the anti-German activities of the Jews, the Freemasons and other political enemies of the Reich and to confiscate this material in order to remove the spiritual foundation of their work. (Sonderkommando Rosenberg, *Abschlussbericht* 4, transl., Mazower Archive, Wiener Library, London)

The Sonderkommando Rosenberg was instructed to collect scientific and archival material about the Jews of Europe in order to establish an institute of destroyed European Jewry in Frankfurt.[4] With the assistance of the Wehrmacht, the Sonderkommando ransacked Jewish libraries, synagogues and archives, interrogated individuals and searched Jewish houses all over Greece.

Interestingly, none of the interviewees talks about the activities of the Sonderkommando Rosenberg. The topic which was addressed by the interviewees who talked about this period was the personal contact between Jews and German officers. This contact was facilitated by the confiscation of rooms in Jewish houses: 'The first thing they did was to confiscate all the radios, all the big radios. Then the second thing was that they confiscated rooms in the Jewish houses for German officers' (Am24).

Five of my interviewees had a German officer staying in their house. In two cases the families had very strong connections to Germany and everybody in the household spoke German. All these interviewees come from well-to-do, middle-class families. It is striking that the German officers are generally described as well-behaved. Felix S. continues the above statement:

> The German officer used to come once in a while and the other guy who used to be there was a German soldier, Wehrmacht. He was very good, very educated. He spoke French and Italian. He knew that I was a Jew. He was very nice. They were very polite and they talked to me in German. (Am24)

Hella K., who had come from central Europe to Salonika in 1925, also had a German officer and his *Putzfleck* (the officer's batman) staying in her house. She recounts that within days of the German occupation a German armoured car with a swastika stopped in front of her house and a German officer told her that he was looking for a room for a German officer. Hella K. told him that she only wanted an older officer in her house since she had a 14-year-old daughter. After playing on Hella K.'s piano, the officer inspected the room and the bathroom and then put up a sign outside the house which said: 'Do not enter! Requisitioned by the Gestapo.' Some time later a Gestapo officer arrived. He was 60 years old and from Austria. The 'normality' or 'day-to-day' aspect of the interaction between Hella K., her family and the Gestapo is even more strongly emphasised by the way Hella K. talks about the following episode:

> The Gestapo officer was staying with us. Sometimes we sat together and my husband and he drank some whisky. Once it got very late and he asked me whether I could wake him up at four o'clock the next day. 'I will rather give you an alarm clock and you will let me sleep,' I replied. 'But why do you have to get up so early?' 'We have an *Aktion* (round-up) in a village where two German soldiers have been killed.' When he came back the next day he told me that they only found a dying grandmother and three chickens in the village. Apparently the village had been warned. 'At least you found something', I said. (Af5)

Rolli A. also remembers that they used to sit with the German offi-cer in the evening and have a chat. He recalls that the German officer told them that he suspected that the German owner of the building, who lived in the ground floor, was a communist because he said 'Heil Hitler' too often when they met on the staircase (Am12).

Lili M. recounts how the SS officer who was staying with her and her family chatted regularly with her sick father and even baby-sat her son when she had to attend a funeral. She still cannot understand why this officer did not try to warn them about what was going to happen: 'He didn't say a word to us, like "Watch out, try to save the child". My baby was in his arms sometimes or he would sit on his legs … and he didn't do anything to save him, he just disappeared' (Af8).

Because of the limited number of interviews it is not possible to ascertain whether the above cases were the exceptions or the rule. Lili S. gives quite a different account of the contact between the German officers and Jewish hosts. She and her family had left Salonika after the arrival of German troops but decided to return after ten months.

> They settled themselves in Jewish houses and high-ranking offi-cers requisitioned rooms with Jewish wealthy families living well

with their terrorised hosts. Gradually, even in their presence, they started packing 'presents', books, carpets, paintings, their hosts' most valuable belongings and sent them to Germany. (Af10)

In the light of the above experiences and the fact that no specifically anti-Jewish laws had been implemented for a period of 15 months (although all Jewish newspapers had been shut down), the events of July 1942 came as a dramatic shock.

PLATIA ELEFTHERIA AND AFTER

After a massive anti-Semitic campaign in the local press[5] the first collective action against the Jews was taken in July 1942. On the 11 July, male Jews between the ages of 18 and 45 were ordered to gather at the Platia Eleftheria (Freedom Square) to register for forced labour. About 10,000 men stood for hours in the hot sun, some being forced to do physical exercise. Subsequently they were sent to work for the Wehrmacht on the construction of roads and airfields. Jacques Stroumsa describes this day in his book:

> More than 9,000 men, among them my brother and I, had followed the German order. I heard screams and whip lashes. Young men had to perform degrading exercises, such as jumping like frogs, while lots of bystanders followed the spectacle. Many of us fainted, as a result of these tortures and the burning sun. The Germans poured jars of water over them in order to revitalise them for more tortures. (Stroumsa 1993: 33)

The events at the Platia Eleftheria mark the beginning of the anti-Jewish measures. Michael B. recounts the events as follows:

> The first thing the Germans did, I don't know if you were told that, was that they put an ad in the paper for the Jews to come to the Platia Eleftheria, where the bus stop is now. Jews from such an age to such an age should be there and, you know, we dumb-bells went there and I was there. I was there. And we were surrounded by Germans, on all the balconies around, you know, and they started picking up people. (Am16)

On that day the men were released, but about 3,500 men were later mobilised to work on airfields and roads under very harsh conditions. Michael B. was one of them:

> and after they listed our names and we had to go to work at the airport ... Do you know where it is? Not where it is now. There was and there still is a village called Thermi. Across the street from Thermi, there was the airport where German planes land-ed. So everybody was listed there to work. Either there or some other place. And I had to go to work there. They picked you up somewhere around here with a truck and took you down there and we tried to dig ditches and things like that ... At noon time they gave us a few minutes to rest. We used to go to the village and pick up green tomatoes and eat the green tomatoes and we are still alive today. (Am16)

In contrast to the other narratives, Michael B. connects the places of the past to the places of the present. Platia Eleftheria is 'where the bus stop is now' and he was taken to forced labour where 'there was and still is a village called Thermi'. This element of placing the past in the landscape of today is mostly not a mere explanatory narrative device, as in Michael B.'s case, but an indicator for the contemporary relevance of a certain issue to the speaker.

One of these themes is the old cemetery which was destroyed in December 1942,[6] which occurred after the community paid a ransom of 2.5 million drachmas to the German army for releasing the Jewish work-ers (about 400 men had died during this forced labour operation). The cemetery was destroyed and the marble was used for the construction of roads and buildings, partly still visible in contemporary Salonika (see Figures 27, 28 and 29. 'The Germans used the marble for pathways to their stables and the marble shops took all the marble to make crosses ... Here in Panorama [a suburb of Salonika] the pavement is full of Jewish stones' (Am12).

The existence of the scattered tombstones on pathways, in church-yards, and in houses makes the topic of the cemetery both a historical and contemporary topic. Leon L. was among the interviewees who was very eager to talk about the old cemetery:

> Let us talk about the Jewish cemetery. The cemetery we had cov-ered a big terrain where the university is located today. When the Germans came they asked to build a street through the cemetery.

This cemetery was an old cemetery, 500 years. Since we have come from Spain, very famous rabbis were buried there. We were told to take away the bones because the cemetery was going to be destroyed. There were many famous rabbis and family graves. People would go to the graves of these rabbis and pray. The tombstones were very valuable. They destroyed all the cemetery. At the new cemetery you can see some of the old tombstones. Until today the land of the university is owned by the community. But we don't talk about this. (Am20)

It becomes clear that the subject of the cemetery is very important to Leon L. In this statement the cemetery physically embodies the long and continuing history of the Sephardic Jews in Salonika. Bearing in mind that the cemetery had about 350,000 graves and that in Jewish tradition graves cannot be moved, we need to understand the importance of the cemetery, both historically and symbolically. It is a place which was not only destroyed in 1942 but also a place 'where the university is located today', that is to say a place which acquired a totally different meaning after the war. The cemetery does constitute a 'place of memory' for most older Jews. However, it is a 'place of memory' which is of a private nature because the pre-war history of the university site is nowhere acknowledged and because of the silence about this. The narrative about the destruction of the old cemetery is closely linked to the awareness of a missing memorial at the University or any other place (in 1994). Leon L. continues his statement about the cemetery by saying:

You know the monument in Larissa. Here, there should be a much bigger monument because there were 63,000 Jews here. The day when the Germans came here we were 63,000 Jews and now we are only 1,000 Jews ... We, the old Salonikans, know what the Jews did for the development of the city. (Am20)

The fact that the memory of the old Jewish cemetery has not become part of the 'cultural' Greek memory is very much present in the above statement, which thus links the individual memory of the past, that is, of a place, to the present situation. A former leader of the community attaches similar importance to a memorial at the university: 'The only cemetery in the world which was destroyed was the cemetery in Salonika ... The only place to put a memorial is the university because people who come to study there should see that Jews used to be here' (Am14).

Although he expressed his wish for a memorial at the university, he was not very optimistic about the realisation of such a project. Only one interviewee spoke in detail about the destruction of the old cemetery. Lili M. remembers that her grandmother's remains were taken from the old to the new cemetery where she was reburied with four others:

> My mother's mother had died at the end of 1936 and was buried in the old cemetery. And then during the occupation when the Germans destroyed it they called the members of our family and the younger son was obliged to go and witness the unburial ... I go to the cemetery now and there is a great grave with the names of four people whom I don't know. And the last name is my grandmother. There are quite a number of those graves. (Af8)

In Lili M.'s interview it becomes very clear that her sense of identity as a Salonikan Jew (who has emigrated to the States and now spends half the year in Salonika and half the year in Cleveland) is very much linked to having family members buried in the cemetery. She says:

> I feel *Thessalonikia*, I was born here, I have people in the old cemetery, where I used to go before I left. I went to cry on their graves, I am from Salonika. To whom Salonika belongs is another thing. What I am, I am. You see? (Af8)

It is precisely because the link to the past, symbolised by the 'old cemetery', has been destroyed and its existence has not been acknowledged, that a vision of the future is under severe strain. Lili M. gets very agitated when talking about the contemporary university site, where Jewish tombstones were visible as part of pathways until very recently.

> I go to the university and want to shout at them [the students] when I see these tombs, Hebrew marked, and all of these young students are jumping on them. Why? Why? Tell me! ... men and women? It is evident it is destruction, it is assimilation. (Af8)

Looking at the last statement we begin to understand fully Langer's notion of 'disrupted narratives'. The vocabulary Lili M. draws on is that of loss, destruction, injustice and meaninglessness. Since she cannot answer the question 'why?', which seems to refer to the fate of the Jews in Salonika in general, she cannot see a future for the Jews in

Salonika. The neglected and walked upon Jewish tombstones at the university become a symbol for destruction which, in the contemporary context, is not about the physical destruction of lives but the destruction of Jewish culture caused by assimilation.

Other statements from Lili M.'s interview make it evident that the past, that is, the past of the war, does not constitute a 'closed chapter' in her life history. This becomes apparent through her usage of time, in which she leaps from the past to the present and to the future; and through her consistent 'commentary' which accompanies the chronology of events she recounts (such as 'you see, these were our sacrifices', 'this is one sin that will remain always in my head', 'we were stupid, we lived in fear and ignorance').

Moshe B. narrates in a very different way. He stays very factual and tells the events in chronological order. He mostly remains in the past tense, hardly ever comments on the events he describes, and recounts the course of events 'from outside', without the presence of the 'I' narrator. Lehmann differentiates two forms of narrations in the genre of autobiographical interviews, *Erzählen* (telling) and *Berichten* (reporting) (Lehmann 1983: 64). In contrast to the form of *Berichten*, the speaker *erzählt* (tells or narrates) when including him or herself in the narration, as Lili M. constantly does. When Moshe B. summarises the time between the arrival of the Germans and the deportations, he narrates it in form of a *Bericht* (report).

> After the Germans came the life of the Jews was not especially hard. They did not give them such a hard time because they wanted to get to know the mentality of the Jews of Greece. After two years they started thinking of how to annihilate the Jews. This was in 1943. They started to build ghettos in Salonika. The first ghetto was near the railway station, the new one. There was a poor Jewish neighbourhood. They took the Jews there and closed it. They brought the Jews from the other ghettos there. When they closed No. 6 they brought them to Hirsch and from there they were taken to Germany by train. (Am17)

It is striking that in this short account Moshe B. speaks of 'the Jews' and 'them', as if 'they' had nothing to do with himself. One could suggest that this perception has to do with his later experiences. Although he was in one of the ghettos, he escaped and went to fight with the partisans. This experience differentiates him from 'them', that is to say the other Jews, who were ghettoised and deported. Apart from this inter-

19a Holocaust Day Commemoration Ceremony at
Monasterioton Synagogue. Banner reads: *Aonia I
Mnimni* (Eternal Memory) (1994)

19b Entrance to the Monasterioton Synagogue

20 Survivor Lights a Candle During the Holocaust Memorial Day Ceremony in Synagogue (1994)

21 Monument to Jewish Salonikan Victims of the Holocaust at the Jewish Cemetery (erected in 1962)

22 Holocaust Memorial Day Ceremony at the Jewish Cemetery (1994)

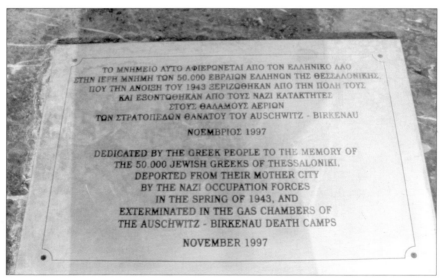

ΤΟ ΜΝΗΜΕΙΟ ΑΥΤΟ ΑΦΙΕΡΩΝΕΤΑΙ ΑΠΟ ΤΟΝ ΕΛΛΗΝΙΚΟ ΛΑΟ
ΣΤΗΝ ΙΕΡΗ ΜΝΗΜΗ ΤΩΝ 50.000 ΕΒΡΑΙΩΝ ΕΛΛΗΝΩΝ ΤΗΣ ΘΕΣΣΑΛΟΝΙΚΗΣ,
ΠΟΥ ΤΗΝ ΑΝΟΙΞΗ ΤΟΥ 1943 ΞΕΡΙΖΩΘΗΚΑΝ ΑΠΟ ΤΗΝ ΠΟΛΗ ΤΟΥΣ
ΚΑΙ ΕΞΟΝΤΩΘΗΚΑΝ ΑΠΟ ΤΟΥΣ ΝΑΖΙ ΚΑΤΑΚΤΗΤΕΣ
ΣΤΟΥΣ ΘΑΛΑΜΟΥΣ ΑΕΡΙΩΝ
ΤΩΝ ΣΤΡΑΤΟΠΕΔΩΝ ΘΑΝΑΤΟΥ ΤΟΥ AUSCHWITZ - BIRKENAU

ΝΟΕΜΒΡΙΟΣ 1997

DEDICATED BY THE GREEK PEOPLE TO THE MEMORY OF
THE 50.000 JEWISH GREEKS OF THESSALONIKI,
DEPORTED FROM THEIR MOTHER CITY
BY THE NAZI OCCUPATION FORCES
IN THE SPRING OF 1943, AND
EXTERMINATED IN THE GAS CHAMBERS OF
THE AUSCHWITZ - BIRKENAU DEATH CAMPS

NOVEMBER 1997

23, 24 Monument to Jewish Salonikan Victims of the Holocaust
at the Intersection of Nea Egnatia Street and Papanastasiou Street (erected in 1997)

25 Honorary Award Ceremony for the Saviours and Benefactors of the Jews of Salonika at Aristotle University in Salonika (1994)

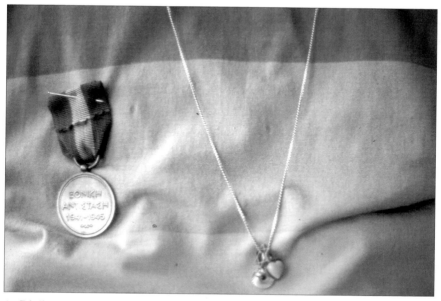

26 *Ethniki Antistasi* (Greek Resistance) Medal, Worn by a Jewish Woman Who Fought with the Partisans

27, 28 Fragments of Jewish Tombstones Scattered on the Campus of Aristotle University (1989)

29 Fragments of Jewish Tombstones in a Church Courtyard

30 New Jewish Cemetery at Stavropouli

31 Spray-Painted Signpost of the Platia Evreon Martyron (Jewish Martyr Square)

32 Display of Antisemitic Literature in the Window of a Bookshop in the Centre of Salonika

esting aspect of narration, the above account expresses a very important aspect of the German occupation, namely the fact that almost two
years passed between the arrival of the German troops and the systematic discrimination and segregation of the Jews in Salonika.

SEGREGATION AND DISCRIMINATION

At the beginning of 1943, with the arrival of Dieter Wisliceny and
Alois Brunner from the RSHA (the *Reichssicherheitshauptamt*, the Reich
Security Head Office, a subdivision of the SS), the first steps towards
the systematic segregation and deportation of Jews from Salonika were
taken. Wisliceny[7] was instructed by Adolf Eichmann to make Salonika
'judenfrei' within six to eight weeks (Mazower 1993: 240). From
February 1943, Jews were forced to wear the yellow star, were restricted in their movements, and had to leave certain areas of the city and
move to ghettos. These ghettos were created in three areas: one in the
neighbourhood of Campagne (east of the White Tower), one in the centre of the city, and one near the railway station, called Baron Hirsch
(which became a transit camp for the deportees) (Molho 1988: 80).

We have seen above that the arrival of the German occupation
forces in 1941 marks a kind of end in the interviews (we did this 'until
the Germans came'). The ghettoisation and segregation of the Jews,
interestingly, does not have such a function. Most interviewees did not
spend a long time talking about the situation in the ghettos. In the
interviews with concentration camp survivors, the stay in the ghetto is
clearly pushed back by the powerful memory of the deportation. In the
interviews with people who survived in hiding or in the mountains,
memories of the ghettos are mostly associated with saying goodbye to
other family members. When looking at the memories of the ghetto,
we must also bear in mind that the time spent in the ghetto could have
been quite short (depending on the time of the deportation or escape)
and that these ghettos were not as tightly secured and segregated as the
East European ghettos. Often the interviewees lived in areas which
later became 'the ghetto'; and especially for the poorer families the
quality of life did not change drastically with the ghettoisation.
Therefore, in Palomba A.'s statement, the ghetto is incorporated into
the narrative without any specific reference to the beginning of the
ghettoisation. She does, however, refer to the Baron Hirsch ghetto,
which did resemble a tightly secured East European ghetto after
March 1943, to which she and her family were taken just before being

deported. 'We all lived together in the ghetto until 1943. Then we had to go to Baron Hirsch. My mother and father were sick. They took us at four o'clock. They gathered us and the wagons came' (Af1).

The Baron Hirsch ghetto is important because it precedes the moment of deportation, which was very traumatic. This is similar in Hella K.'s narrative. Although she had to move from her house on Koromilas Street to the part of the city which was designated for the Jews, she mentions only the three days she, her husband and her two children had to spend in a derelict coffee house in the Baron Hirsch ghetto before they were sent on the first transport to Auschwitz on 13 March 1943. In contrast to the detailed description of the conditions in Baron Hirsch in her daughter's book (Kounio-Amariglio 2000: 54, 55), Hella K. does not describe the conditions in great detail. As in Palomba A.'s interview, the ghettoisation is only the preamble to the 'real' subject, the deportation and the camp survival.

This is also true for other processes which are not talked about in great detail, such as the registration of Jewish property ordered by Dr Merten, the head of the city's military administration, on 13 March. Michael B. is the only interviewee who mentions the registration of Jewish property at the building of the *Matanot LaEvionim*. He talks about this in the context of the deception of the Jews, with a certain sense of irony:

> You see, it was very well organised. They gave clear instructions to the rabbi how to do it. For instance, they were filling up the heads of people telling them that whatever they have here, they will be rewarded there. And they convinced them … There is a place *Matanot LaEvionim* on Misrachi, where they set up … a few desks and tell all the people of the ghetto: 'we are going to write names here and whatever you have at home, you know, we'll reward you with the same items'. And dumb people were going there and writing 'we have this, we have this' and some people thought they were cheating the guys there by telling them that they have more with the idea that they will get more stuff where they go. (Am16)

Michael B. portrays the process of the registration of Jewish property within the general theme of deception, in hindsight often seen as betrayal. In many interviews historical details are often neglected because of the importance of a certain theme for the interviewee. The themes of deception (by the Germans) and betrayal (by the Jewish leadership) appear in most interviews when discussing the time 'in the ghetto'. The theme of betrayal, which is more painful than the German deception, mostly focuses on Rabbi Koretz, who is seen as responsible for encouraging the Jews to follow the German orders. Jacov Handeli writes in his autobiographical novel: 'In Salonika, we were all taken in by Rabbi Koretz's reassurance.' He then adds what many interviewees feel: 'that is what hurts more than anything' (Handeli 1993: 48).

The judgement on Rabbi Koretz varies from calling him a 'collaborator' and 'traitor' who wanted to save his own life, to portraying him as a person who was gullible and misguided. Baruch S., who is the only survivor of his family, recalls:

> Unfortunately, the rabbi who came from Vienna did not tell us what was happening to the Jews in Germany. We did not know anything. So we went to Germany, all the eight of us ... Yes, some people went to the mountains but the majority went to the concentration camp because the Germans made them believe that they would work in Poland. They made them change money and they were saying all kinds of things. Like you should get married because you should live with your wife and a lot of other promises ... Rabbi Koretz assembled all of us in the big synagogue in Syngrou and told us these things. He had to say these things otherwise they would have killed him. We were sold to the Germans. (Am23)

Most interviewees believe that Koretz 'played the game of the Germans' (Am17) and 'that he sold us for a piece of bread' (Am17). Some interviewees are convinced that he made a deal with the Germans during his imprisonment in Vienna in 1941; some interviewees simply refer to him as a 'spy'; others think that he 'knew only the things the Nazis told him' (Am21). His behaviour is always contrasted to the behaviour of Rabbi Barzilai in Athens, who fled to the mountains. Palomba A. is very upset when she speaks about Rabbi Koretz:

> The rabbi was German, Rabbi Koretz ... He was not good, he was one of the *prodotes* (traitors). In order to survive he spied on us. If he was a good rabbi he should have said: *Figete* (leave). That's what the rabbi in Athens did. He did not say this because he wanted to save his own life. (Af1)

It is interesting that all interviewees explicitly point out that Koretz 'was German', 'from Vienna' or 'from Poland'. On the one hand this can be interpreted as a factual description about his background (he originated from Krakow and his wife was from Germany), on the other, this does point to a perception of difference among the interviewees, in which Koretz is clearly seen as an Ashkenazi, non-Sephardi and non-Salonikan Jew. His non-Salonikan origin is not explicitly used to explain his behaviour but does acquire some relevance in some of the accusations against him. Thinking of Koretz as a 'spy', for example, does put his 'natural loyalty' clearly in question. The fact that Rabbi Koretz and his family were deported on the last transport and that he died of typhus shortly after the liberation of Bergen-Belsen does not redeem him in the eyes of the interviewees. His death is hardly mentioned.[8] Hella K. is one of the few who talks about his death: 'Luckily he died in Bergen-Belsen. For me he was a traitor. Perhaps he was beaten so badly that he was made to become a traitor. He was scared of the Germans. I never liked him' (Af5). She also expresses what all interviewees think: 'Why did he not talk about what had happened to him in the Gestapo prison? Why did he not tell people to leave? Many more people could have survived in the mountains and in hiding' (Af5).

When talking about Koretz, memory does become specific. Several interviewees, such as Baruch S. above, recall the day they assembled in the Monasterioton Synagogue (17 March 1943), to listen to Rabbi Koretz.

> Once he gathered all Jews in the big synagogue to talk to them. He told us not to be afraid. 'We will build a new life. There is no danger.' He wanted to convince us. After his speech, ten Jews, among them was my father ... went to Koretz and told him that his task should be to fight for the Jews to stay and not to agree to be taken to Poland ... Then his policemen forced the group to leave. (Am17)

Lili M. remembers that Rabbi Koretz's wife gave a lecture about '*Le Devoir de la Femme Juive*' (the duty of the Jewish wife), in which she spoke about the duty of obeying the head of the family and the necessity of following German orders. Lili M. concludes: 'They were big traitors, big traitors. We had some other traitors around, but they were the worst. That's right ... It was the poorest leadership we could have. We were not organised, we were scared' (Af8).

Apart from the anger which is expressed against Koretz, the interviewees also refer to Koretz when justifying or explaining why they did not escape, and why they followed the ghettoisation and deportation orders. Erika Kounio-Amariglio talks in her book about making her grandson understand why almost 50,000 Jews 'let themselves be herded like sheep to the slaughter' (Kounio-Amariglio 2000: 47). I felt that many interviewees wanted to explain the same point to me. In hindsight this is, of course, a crucial question. Leon L. explains:

> He [Koretz] told us that we would go to Poland, we would work there, we would build houses. All the Jews believed him. What could one have done? I was 32 and I had my shop, my wife with two little children, my mother, my father, my brother. I could not have gone to the mountains and left the whole family behind. The Jewish family was very attached to each other. Only very few people went on their own to the mountains. (Am20)

The question 'what could one have done?' expresses the sense of powerlessness and lack of choice the narrator conveys when talking about the time before the deportations. This sentiment is also prevalent in other interviews. The closeness of the family is given as the most common explanation of why more young Jews did not go into hiding or to the mountains.

It was seen as a clear disadvantage to be young and unattached. Young men especially feared that they might be taken as forced labourers. Therefore, a 'marriage epidemic' broke out in the ghetto (Molho estimates that about 12 couples got married every day in the ghetto, Molho 1988: 105).[9] Three of my interviewees got married in the ghetto in 1943. Mois A. was one of them. He says: 'We wanted the family all to be together. We also wanted to encourage ourselves because we did not know where we were going' (Am21). Lili M.'s younger sister also got married in the ghetto. She recalls:

> In 1943, I remember, we went to a wedding, oh my God. I'll never forget that wedding. It was my younger sister's wedding. She was engaged and we were in the ghetto. She said: 'I don't want to be separated from Peppo, we want to be married, to go together, we go to Poland together.' My father used to say: 'Marcelika, watch out and listen, don't get married, who knows what will happen, don't tie yourself.' She said: 'no, no, no.' The marriage was in the apartment of our house and the rabbi came and we were celebrating. And that moment two German soldiers

knocked on the door ... 'What are you doing?' said the officer. Someone said: 'they are getting married.' He said: 'This is no time to get married.' ... That was my sister's wedding. This is one sin that will remain always in my head. (Af8)

Lili M.'s memory of the wedding is as much shaped by 'what happened after' as the memory of Koretz. In the light of the death of Lili M.'s sister and the death of thousands of people, the wedding in the ghetto, which prevented her younger sister from escaping with her to Athens (and surviving), and the encouragement of Rabbi Koretz to follow the deportation orders, become painful foci of the memory of the time in the ghetto. They are very painful because they are memories of events and behaviour which, had they been different, could have led to a different outcome. The survivors know **now** that had Koretz behaved differently, many more people could have survived; as Lili M. knows **now** that her sister could have survived if she had not got married in the ghetto.

At the time of the ghettoisation people did not know what was going to happen. Mois A. tells me: 'We believed what we were told, that we would work and that everything would be fine. We would work there as we did here' (Am21). The blatant contrast between the expectation of the above statement and the later experience and knowledge of extermination makes the memory of the pre-deportation time very difficult.

CONCLUSION

The interviewees remember the war period up to the moment of ghettoisation as a time when the Jewish leadership and, to some extent, the individual, could still make some choices. In contrast, after the deportation neither the leadership nor the individual could make choices, and were therefore not in control of their collective and individual destinies.

The beginning of the war is also a time which stands for the acceptance and integration of Jews in Greece, expressed by the active Jewish contribution to the war with Italy. While the detail with which the interviewees discuss the war with Italy varies, the Jewish contribution to the Greek–Italian War and the death of the Jewish Colonel Mordechai Frizis are of vital importance for the communal Jewish memory of this period. This was clearly expressed in the speeches of the Jewish–Greek week held at the Hellenic Centre in London in 1998. In almost all the speeches by Christian and Jewish Greeks, the death of Colonel Frizis received a great deal of attention. In these descriptions Colonel Frizis epitomises the patriotism of Greek Jews and their integration in Greek society.

To quote from one of the speeches:

> The highest-ranking Jewish officer at the time was Colonel Mordechai Frizis, who died honouring the Greek arms and his death sealed the struggle of Hellenism in the mountains of Epirus … King George II and Prime Minister Joannis Metaxas called him personally to commend him for his brilliant actions. On 5 December Italian planes flew over his squadron. Colonel Frizis ordered everybody to take cover, while he stood alone on his horse making sure that all his men had taken cover. He died through a shell which exploded next to him. He died on the spot and his last words were for Greece. (Speech by the President of the Jewish Community, delivered by another member of the community council)

NOTES

1. Anne Karpf talks about a similar process in Britain where the 50th anniversary of the liberation of Auschwitz has created a public space in which remembering has become a more social act than before, when remembering was done within families and personal networks (Karpf 1998: 10).

2. Kristin Platt refers to the usage of the 'collective we' in life histories as a means for the individual narrator to distance themself from the traumatic events, and as a means to transcend individual memory. She also states that it very common among Armenian survivors of the genocide to start off their life history as 'we' until the massacres and then continue as 'I' after the events of 1916 (Platt and Dabag 1995: 359).

3. One could draw an interesting parallel between the notion of betrayal in this particular narrative and other Greek personal narratives, collected for example by Herzfeld (1987) and Sutton (1998). Sutton suggests that narratives on Kalymnos often contain recounting of injustices and betrayals perpetrated, both on a personal and political level, because of a strong sense of reciprocity and historical debt. On a personal level betrayal is perpetrated when failing to repay and recognise past generosities; on a political level betrayal is perpetrated when not acknowledging Greece's historical efforts. 'The current Western criticisms of Greek positions on Macedonia and Yugoslavia are seen as a betrayal of the historical debt owed to Greece for its sacrifice for "Europe" in the Second World War' (Sutton 1998: 160).

4. A huge archive of the Jewish community in Thessaloniki, recently found in Moscow, had been gathered by the Rosenberg Kommando and was taken to Russia after the war.

5. The anti-Semitic campaign must have been of crucial importance to the Germans because as the commander of the Rosenberg Kommando noted, 'for the average Greek there is no Jewish question. He does not see the political danger of world Jewry' (Mazower 1993: 258).

6. The Greek government had already unsuccessfully attempted to move the Jewish cemetery from its central location in the city in the 1930s.

7. Dieter Wisliceny had organised the deportations of Slovak Jewry in 1942. In his affidavit at the International Military Tribunal at the Nuremberg War Trials, he states that he learnt

about the implementation of the 'Final Solution' in July/August 1942 (see affidavit of Dieter Wisliceny 1947). He thus was fully aware of the fate which awaited the deportees. After the war he was tried and executed in Czechoslovakia in 1947.

8. In an interview conducted by Yad Yashem (File 03/7093) Elvira F. also talks about Rabbi Koretz. She blames Koretz for the fact that the Jews 'went like sheep to the slaughter'. In her eyes he was a traitor who wanted to 'save himself and his family'. She apparently is not aware of his death in Belsen because she tells the interviewer that he survived the war, was convicted of war crimes and served a long prison sentence.

9. In *Documents on the History of the Greek Jews* (Ministry of Foreign Affairs of Greece and University of Athens) the number of these weddings is reported to have exceeded 100 per day (p. 267).

7

Narratives of War and Occupation (1943–45)

This chapter will continue to explore the different experiences and narratives of the war. In early March Chief Rabbi Koretz[1] was informed that the entire community was to be deported to Poland. Between March and August the majority of the Jewish population was deported in 19 transports to Auschwitz and Belsen. According to the records, 48,974 Jews from Northern Greece arrived in Auschwitz; 37,386 were immediately gassed (Mazower 1993: 244).[2] The destination of the last transport in August was Bergen-Belsen. Rabbi Koretz, other community officials and Jews with Spanish passports were among those deported to Bergen-Belsen.

The time after February 1943 is when the 'real' war started for most interviewees. It was the beginning of their physical displacement, either through deportation or through moving to the mountains or the Italian occupied zone. As it is not possible here to give an exhaustive historical account of this period, this account will be restricted to describing and analysing the different experiences of the interviewees. These experiences do represent the different modes of survival of Greek Jewry (some of the interviewees are from Athens or the provinces): in the concentration camps, under Italian occupation, with the *Andartes* in the mountains, hidden in villages or on islands, or having escaped to Turkey and eventually Palestine.

THE CAMP SURVIVORS

As mentioned earlier, some of the camp survivors did not want to talk about their deportation and their experiences in the camp. I did not see myself in a position to challenge their silence. Therefore, I only have four detailed accounts by camp survivors, who all clearly wanted to talk about the war. The following episode, briefly discussed in the introduction, illustrates the problems encountered.

During my first visit at the summer camp, I was introduced to Sam

P., who was aged about 75 at the time. I was told that he had dedicated his life to working with young people since he had come back from the concentration camp. When I interviewed him in *Kataskinosi* he was clearly ambivalent about talking to me. At the beginning he answered my specific personal questions with general statements, such as 'There were 70,000 Jews here. After the war there were only 2,000. Then many left, to Israel and the States' (Am26). When I asked him about his parents' origins he told me: 'My parents were born in Salonika. But when I came back from the *Konzentrationslager* I was alone. The whole family had died' (Am26). He paused and continued: 'It is very difficult for me to tell my story.' Some minutes later he said: 'I feel sick when I speak about the *Konzentrationslager*. I cannot speak much because this story makes me sick, do you understand?' (Am26).

The dilemma which presented itself in this difficult interview situation became clear: on the one hand Sam P. did not want to talk about his war experiences, on the other he felt that the camp experiences were the main legitimisation for him being interviewed. He assumed that the war years were the only period I wanted to talk about and therefore decided he could not continue the interview. This put me in a very difficult situation. I knew that it was important to acknowledge the history of the survivors but at the same time I did not want to inflict an act of painful remembering. Some interviewees could only talk about their individual experiences by elevating them to the collective, more general level. Abels calls this process 'structural memory'. Individuals recall their traumatic experiences by relating them to the collective experience in their narrative (Abels 1995: 321). This narrative technique underlines the importance of the experience of the individual because it interlinks individual and group experiences. It also functions as a distancing device between the narrator and the 'story', as at the beginning of Sam P.'s interview. Only after switching from the safe, general level to the individual level does Sam P. realise that it is too painful to tell me 'his' story ('my story'). Since I did not want the interviewees to feel uncomfortable I often chose to stay on the 'safe' level, that is to say I remained on the general level or discussed 'safer' time periods, such as the pre-war and post-war. This is the reason there are only four detailed camp survivor accounts. Niethammer reminds us that individual memory of traumatic events can often only be communicated after the emergence of 'cultural memory', in the form of historic research, documentation and commemorations.

When I first spoke to Sam P. this had not happened. In 1994, when I interviewed Sam P. again, he wanted to talk about the war time in greater depth. By then the cultural memory had begun to encompass the experience of the survivors and by then he knew me better. Both factors contributed to the fact that it felt now 'safer' to discuss the time in the concentration camp. Having said that, it should be pointed out that many interviewees chose to summarise their war experiences in a couple of sentences. When asked about Auschwitz, Solomon S., for example, told me:

> In April 1943 [I left Salonika] and I was liberated May 1945. Here almost everybody left for Auschwitz and Birkenau. When the Front came closer I was taken to Mauthausen and then to Besern in Austria. There I was liberated by the Americans. (Am22)

In the next few sentences he talked about the fate of his family:

> I am the only survivor. My wife, the baby, a 3-year-old girl, they took them all. I will tell you one thing. They might have been luckier because they went to the gas chambers and that was the end, some people wanted to die and they did not. (Am22)

There are a number of possible reactions by the interviewer when confronted with such a strong statement. I decided that silence was the most appropriate response, and then moved on to another topic. These examples of Sam P. and Solomon S. illustrate the difficulties faced in the interviews with the camp survivors, and there is another point which is linked to my non-inquisitorial style of interviewing. Steven Bowman writes in his introduction to the memoir of Marco Nahon that there are three distinct aspects of the Greek experience (Nahon 1989: 13): the bravery of about 400 young Greek Jews who refused to work in the crematorium *Sonderkommando;* the fact that Greek Jews were able to join forces with the beleaguered Polish forces when they were sent to the ruins of the Warsaw ghetto; and the involvement of the Greek Jews in the revolt of the crematorium *Sonderkommando.* Bowman also points to the fact that most of the 12,757 Greek Jews who were selected for labour could not communicate with the other Ashkenazi Jews.

Primo Levi (1994: 210) and Yaacov Handeli (1993: 68) write about two factors which distinguished the Greek Jews from the other prisoners: language capability and climate. Handeli explains the high mortality rate of Greek Jews as follows: 'We could not understand them [the Germans] and had trouble adapting to the climate. These two factors caused deaths among the Greek Jews from the beginning' (1993: 68).

In the accounts collected during this study, most of these points hardly find any mention. I did not probe or set out to challenge the interviewees' narratives, and the reader should bear this in mind.

Deportation and Arrival

The following section will concentrate on a number of testimonies, but in particular on those of Hella K. and Palomba A. since they talked about their experiences in great detail. Hella K. is an exceptional case because she and her family spoke German. Her life was very different from that of Palomba A. Hella K. comes from a German-speaking, middle-class family while Palomba A. comes from a working-class, Ladino-speaking Salonikan family. There is also a considerable age difference between Hella K. and Palomba A.; Hella K. is 18 years older than Palomba A. and was married with two children at the time of the deportations.

Having looked at other Holocaust testimonies (in Langer 1991 and at the Yad Vashem Archive), Hella K.'s testimony stands out. While in most interviews with camp survivors' feelings of total rupture, discontinuity, and inability to understand these horrific experiences are conveyed, Hella K. seems more able to incorporate her camp experiences into her general life history. In contrast to Palomba A. and other testimonies, Hella K. perceives of herself as an *acteur* rather than a helpless victim throughout her interview. This expresses itself at various points during the interview, for example in her description of the arrival in Auschwitz:

> I was never scared … I was neither scared in Auschwitz nor here. When we arrived in Auschwitz all four of us were standing in front of the wagons. My husband said to me: we will never survive this. I answered in German: *keine Angst Rosemarie* ['don't be scared Rosemary', a line from a German song]. A tall SS guard heard what I said and asked me why I speak German. I said to him I learnt it like him, from my mother and father … I told him that my children and my husband speak Greek, German, French, English and Spanish. He looked at us, you know my husband had one leg shorter than the other, and said: the two women go to the *Politische Abteilung* [political section], the two men to the *Häftlingsschneiderei* [tailoring workshop]. That was our salvation. We had a roof above our head, there were showers, and we did not have to work outside. (Af5)

Hella K. talks about her arrival in Auschwitz as if her behaviour influenced the situation, and in terms of a certain continuity: 'I was neither scared in Auschwitz nor here.' She thus imposes a 'layer of continuity over the discontinuous interval of the death camp experience' (Langer 1991: 43). This sets her testimony very much apart from other testimonies, as one can easily realise when looking at the description of Palomba A.'s deportation and arrival in Auschwitz:

> My mother and father were sick. They took us at 4 o clock, they gathered us, and the wagons came … When we arrived there, we were 75 people in a wagon. But some family members were in a different wagon. They had the food, while we had the clothes … There was no water. All the babies cried. Eight days. This was our journey … I cannot talk … I was in the *Schuhkommando*. I also was in the *Aussenkommando* with my sister. We had to work every day from 5 o'clock. My mother and little sister went to the crematorium. She wanted to come with me but I said you should stay with our parents, they are sick; she was 14. In our wagon two people died. Do you know what it means to have two dead people lying in the corner? You could go crazy in this, other life. (Af1)

This short narrative illustrates a number of features very common in survivors' testimonies. One is the categorisation of all experiences 'there' as something different from all previous experiences. They took place in a different life, in the 'other life', as Palomba A. calls it and constitute 'experiences on the limit of the possible and thus on the limit of the narratable' (Pollak 1988: 89). These experiences are difficult to talk about ('This was our journey … I cannot talk …') because of the pain involved for the speaker and because of the commonly held conviction that nobody can really understand the concentration camp experiences unless they had been 'there' themselves.

Hella K.'s daughter struggles with this dilemma when she tells of her experience of the deportation and arrival in Auschwitz:

> So we were in a train, in a wagon, a hundred people, maybe more. I remember that there was no room to sit down. We were like sardines. There were some biscuits and olives and that was all and of course there was a big bucket for our physical needs … There were sick people and there were babies crying, moaning. Terrible. It was indescribable and incomprehensible how it was. The *odours*

and seeing all the people so sick without air and people going on top of each other to snatch a little air from the window ... That was terrible. And then we arrived in Auschwitz Birkenau. There, it was again something you cannot describe ... (Yad Vashem Testimony 033C/1424 Erika Amariglio)

Individuals developed different strategies to deal with the dilemma of 'describing something indescribable'. One of them was silence. The other, often a later response, was 'to bear witness' and thus attempt to describe the indescribable. Survivors often feel an obligation to remember their friends and family members who did not survive and to remember on behalf of their friends and family members. In her introduction to her book Erika Kounio-Amariglio writes:

My remaining years are growing shorter all the time and soon my contemporaries and I will no longer be living. The last witnesses to the Holocaust will some day be gone. Fifty years later, I too feel the need to write down my own testimony, to memorialize my cousins, my relatives, my three beloved friends and classmates (Kounio-Amariglio 2000: i, ii).

The extremely long journey and the arrival at Auschwitz link the survivors' narratives to this 'other life', which in a way is not bound by space and time. It is not bound by time because it is so present to the survivor ('Fifty years later everything is still vivid in my memory', Kounio-Amariglio 2000: ii) and it is not bound by space because the reality of the camp was outside geographical boundaries. Baruch S. recalls that his whole family went 'to Germany', 'we did not know anything, so we went to Germany, all eight of us' (Am23). The fact that Auschwitz was in Poland is irrelevant in his memory.

The journey took about eight days. We arrived there at 12 o'clock at night. We could not take our luggage. We had to go to different sides, the people who could work here, the boys here, the women there, the pregnant women there. That's how I got to Auschwitz. There was a big sign which said: *Arbeit macht frei*. They rounded up all the people and made us undress. Only our shoes we could take with us. Then we washed and were given other clothes, with stripes. After 17 days they tattooed numbers on our arm. There were no names, 150 297 [he says his number in German]. That's what you were called. (Am23)

Another aspect of the transition from the 'normal' to the 'other' life becomes apparent in the above statement. The prisoners were stripped of their personhood by having a number tattooed on their arm, 'there were no names' in Auschwitz. The loss of names corresponds to the loss of family relationships caused by the separation of family members, normally immediately after the *Selektion* upon arrival in Auschwitz. As in some other interviews the silence about the fate of the other family members implies that they did not survive and that the arrival in Auschwitz was the last time Baruch S. saw his parents and sisters. In some cases the silence about the whole concentration camp experience implies the same, the death of all family members. Leon L. talks about his arrival in Auschwitz and his return to Salonika in three sentences:

> We arrived on 13 April. I was with my family [his wife and two children], my mother, my father and brother, all my family. When we came back, after six, seven months we made a special tombstone for the rabbis and *hahamin* [the learned men] at the new cemetery. (Am20)

By 'we' Leon L. does not refer to his family but to the other Salonikan survivors. The fate of his family is expressed by his silence. Only some time later in the interview does he explicitly say that all his family had died: 'I came back and looked for my family. But nobody of my family had survived so I took a wife from Larissa' (Am20).

In other accounts, such as in Palomba A.'s above, the fate of other family members is made explicit in the beginning of talking about the camp, 'they went to the crematorium'. In Sam P.'s narrative, the death of his family is embedded in a reflection on the meaning of death at Auschwitz and the meaning of his own survival.

> They all went to the concentration camp and they all died. On the first day we arrived in Birkenau they all went straight to the crematorium. They took me for work. At that time I did not know what had happened to my family. When we found out what happened we could not believe it. I remember one mother with one child in her arms and one child on her hand. The bigger child asked: 'Mama, where are we going?' She said: 'we are going to have a bath and later we will meet father and grandmother.' They did not know that they were going to the crematorium. I asked myself: 'Does God want to punish us? But that small boy

what could he have done?' Then I made an oath: If I will ever
leave this place I will give all my heart to the children. (Am26)

In this statement Sam P. gives positive meaning to his own survival (he
survived so that he could dedicate his life to the children) and thus creates a connection between his camp experience and his post-war life,
which becomes the leitmotiv of his life history. I follow Lehmann's definition of '*Leitlinien des lebensgeschichtlichen Erzählen*' (leitmotives of life
history narratives) which posits that every life history needs to put
events in a narrative sequence (Lehmann 1983: 19). Sam P.'s leitmotiv
is that he made a vow at Auschwitz and that he had worked with
Jewish children since his return to Salonika, a fact of which he is very
proud. Other interviewees also make a connection between Auschwitz
and their post-war life but this connection is mostly negative: they 'had
to start all over again'. Palomba A. presents her post-war marriage in
this light. In her own perception she did not marry out of choice, she
married because none of her family had survived ('What could I do? I
did not have anybody', Af1).

Life in the Concentration Camp(s)

The survivors spent about two years in imprisonment. As mentioned
above, most interviewees do not discuss this time at great length. The
ones who do, talk about the work and living conditions in various
camps and more importantly, their close encounters with death. The
closeness to death throughout the time in the concentration camp is a
pertinent topic which structures the narratives of the camp experience,
accompanied by the attribution of survival to luck and coincidence.

> There were three or more times when I was already dead. I don't
> know how I was so lucky to survive. Every time when I was sup-
> posed to go to the crematorium something happened … and I
> always started to work again … Some time later, when the Front
> came closer, the Germans started to move the prisoners from
> Poland to Germany and Austria. There was no crematorium there
> but we worked, worked and worked and got very little food. What
> could we do? Many people died. After some time the Americans
> came. I was lying in a place, almost dead. Somebody took my hand
> and saw that I am still alive. I weighed twenty-seven kilos. (Am26)

In this narrative the memory of death is very present, the closeness of
one's own death and the death of other people, siblings, friends, or

strangers. This is more the case in detailed testimonies in which the chronology of events is told as a chronology of 'chance' survival among the reality of death.

Let us look closer at Palomba A.'s testimony. Palomba A. spent the first four months working in an *Aussenkommando* at Birkenau. She worked together with her sister, who was pregnant. In her narrative she links the death of her sister to her own survival. After some time in the *Aussenkommando* her sister could not work anymore and was taken to the *Revier*, the hospital barrack, from which she never returned. Palomba A. went to look for her in the *Revier* and her number was registered. Some time later her number was called by the *Blockältester*. She did not know whether she 'was to live or to die'. She was assigned to the *Schuhkommando* while the others 'who stayed don't live any more'. This is the first instance in her narrative of chance survival. 'It was luck. Because of this [her visit to the *Revier*] I live, because I went to see my sister' (Af1).

The second event which she recounts also deals with her narrow escape from death. While working in the *Schuhkommando* Palomba A. managed to get hold of shoes which she wanted to exchange for bread. On a Sunday she and some of her fellow prisoners from her block went to the other *Lager* to sell some shoes. Suddenly they (the German guards) closed the gates and she and the others were caught with the shoes ('we were standing like fools near the closed gates with the shoes in our hands', Af1). She was taken with the others to Block 25, convinced she was going to die because Block 25 was the block in which prisoners were kept before being taken to the gas chambers (Kounio-Amariglio 2000: 74).

> We all went together to Block 25, to die. We were there three days and two nights without food, without any food. I was cold. I knew I was going to die. During the third night at 5 o'clock in the morning we were given a soup, this was the soup for the ones about to die, the last soup before death. (Af1)

But she did not die and was taken back to her block. This happened due to the intervention of the *blockova*, a Jewish woman from Czechoslovakia, who talked to the Germans on behalf of the ten woman from her block. This is one of the points in Palomba A.'s interview where the narrative of death and the arbitrariness of survival is interwoven with a narrative of comradeship and help.

After hearing this [that the *blockova* managed to get them out], we hugged and kissed each other and we went back to our Block ... All the girls had thought that we had died, being away for three days. Kisses from one side, hugs and embraces from the other side, *trela, trela, trela* [crazy, crazy, crazy], I will always remember that day. One gave us some bread, the other one a bit of butter. We lived. (Af1)

After the arrival of the Hungarian Jews Palomba A. was transferred from Birkenau to Auschwitz. She was twice supposed to go to Block 10, where Mengele performed medical experiments on the prisoners, but she managed not to go. In contrast to the other times when she speaks about the situation in which she seemed doomed and was saved, she does not give any explanation how she managed not to go to Block 10. She just repeats a phrase which she uses in similar versions a number of times in the interview: 'You could lose your head' (*C'était une chose du perdre la tête*'). We need to realise that each testimony contains these silences and that they are intrinsic to the narrative of traumatic experiences. Silence is an important way of dealing with extreme humiliation, it protects the self-dignity and the dignity of the other victims with whom the survivors identify (Abels 1995: 316).

Death is also present in Hella K.'s testimony. In contrast to Palomba A., Hella K. was working in the administration, the *Politische Abteilung*, first in Birkenau and then in Auschwitz. Her main task was to register the transports from Greece and to administer the files of the prisoners. She had to write death notices for the prisoners who had not come to Auschwitz by transports organised by the RSHA, and together with her co-workers was responsible for typing the lists of the prisoners who had not passed the daily *Selektion* and were destined for SB, *Sonderbehandlung* (the code word for the gas chambers). When I asked Hella K. whether she knew what SB stood for, she answered: 'We knew everything, we had all the files. It was all documented in the files' (Af5). While the leitmotiv in Palomba A.'s testimony is the permanent fear of death, Hella K.'s leitmotiv is the 'overcoming' of death. Through her position Hella K. 'knew' much more about the general situation in Auschwitz and Birkenau than Palomba A. and most other Greek Jews. She and her daughter were the only two Jews from Greece in the *Politische Abteilung*. In contrast to the ordinary prisoners, she worked in an 'office' environment and had personal contact with the SS officers who on a number of occasions helped her to pass messages to her husband and son in the *Männerlager*. She recounts one of these occasions:

'Herr Unterscharführer my ear hurts.' He said: 'The ear is called your husband, isn't it? So let us go to the *Männerlager* to Dr Wasilevski.' He immediately told Wasilevski to call my husband … I was very happy to see that he had warm shoes … Since we had come from Thessaloniki in the summer we did not have good shoes. We were not ready for winter. (Af5)

In her narrative Hella K. comes across as a strong woman who perceives herself more as a 'witness' to death rather than a possible victim. As a witness she describes the arrival of children from Sosnowitz in the most emotional part of the interview.

At the *Selektion* people were sent right or left, right was life, left was death. All the women with their children in their arms and the old women with children went straight to the gas. The worst was the transport with the children from Sosnowitz. Black lorries came with children and you could see weak children's hands. It was terrible. They had dissolved the Lager Sosnowitz and they brought the inmates to be annihilated in Auschwitz. I had to look for a file and thus managed to go to the window and observe what was going on. I saw the waving hands of these starved children, begging for help. (Af5)

It is interesting that the 'worst' event Hella K. describes above has nothing to do with herself or her family and friends. In the interview there are many silences: she does not talk about the death of her father (who came in a later transport because he had given himself up to 'join' his daughter), and she does not talk about the time when she had typhus. When she tells us about the meeting with Dr Wasilevski and her husband she does not mention that Dr Wasilevski operated on her without any anesthetics. These events are mentioned in her daughter's account (Kounio-Amariglio 2000: 85). I suggest that these silences allow her to 'replay' the role she perceives herself in at Auschwitz. Her daughter recalls what her mother said to the newly arrived Greek Jews who inquired about their parents: 'They are fine. Don't think about them. Do whatever you can in order to survive, that is your duty' (Kounio-Amariglio 2000: 68). Her narrative reflects her mode of survival. Her memory focuses on episodes of strength rather than episodes of weakness and vulnerability. Through this narrative strategy the 'world of Auschwitz' becomes much more 'normal' than in the other testimonies. In some parts of the interviews she describes conversations between herself and some SS officers as if they were 'colleagues' rather than perpetrator and victim. She recalls one encounter with an SS officer which happened shortly before the evacuation of Auschwitz:

> I told him that I need to talk to him. I told him he should not ask why but he should just follow my advice. I told him he should send his wife and his two children back to the Reich ... He looked at me, amazed, and thanked me for my advice. (Af5)

By focusing on incidents such as the one described above, the narrative conveys a sense of empowerment which is completely missing in other testimonies. Her narrative is thus diametrically opposed to the more common narrative of 'chance survival', which conveys a complete sense of disempowerment, dependency and vulnerability. This narrative continuously questions the reasons for the speaker's own survival and presents a past which can never be really made sense of and which will continue to 'haunt' the speaker. Hella K.'s daughter writes:

> Often I am tortured by the thought, why did I survive and not May, Dorin, Rita? ... What fate separated us and why? Was it all just a coincidence? (Kounio-Amariglio 2000: 156)

> Auschwitz is so much in me that I cannot grasp it now after 50 years ... I look at that and say: it is incredible. It is not possible. As if I did not live it.' (Yad Vashem Testimony 033C/1424 Erika Kounio-Amariglio)

The statements illustrate some of Langer's points on Holocaust testimonies. They illustrate the extreme difficulty of assimilating the past of the camp experiences into the whole life history. This creates what Langer calls a 'permanent duality' (Langer 1991: 95). On the one hand the experience of Auschwitz is constantly present ('Auschwitz is in me'), on the other these experiences of an 'abnormal' past resist normalisation and cannot be integrated into the post-war normality ('It is not possible. As if I did not live it'). The life histories of survivors are thus often narrated in terms of a 'simultaneity' (rather than sequence) of two unconnected worlds, the 'world of Auschwitz' and the 'world before and after'.

This does not apply to Hella K.'s narrative. She tells her life history as a sequence of chronological events which are not completely dissociated from each other. When I ask her whether her daughter had to lie about her age in Auschwitz she replies: 'We never lied. If one was found out to have lied it was much worse than telling the truth' (Af5). Her reply seems to suggest that the rules which she had lived by 'before' and 'after' were also valid in Auschwitz. Her narrative therefore posits a continuity of moral behaviour which is absent in most testimonies.

There are a number of interpretations which could account for the particularity of Hella K.'s life history, which constitutes a narrative of survival which represses incidents of victimisation and humiliation. The relevant point in this context is the fact that her cultural background enabled her to function as a 'middleman' in Auschwitz and her language ability made it possible for her to work in the *Politische Abteilung* which entailed direct contact with SS officers. Her specific position in Auschwitz allows her to construct her specific narrative of survival. This narrative shares an important feature with what Langer calls 'heroic memory'. It 'honours the connection between agency and fate' (Langer 1991: 193) and is thus juxtaposed to the memory which records the absence of this connection, the 'unheroic memory' (expressed in the narrative of 'chance survival', discussed above). One incident which illustrates this notion in Hella K.'s interview is the sending of postcards to relatives in which she informed them by using Greek words of what was going on in Auschwitz.

> One day they gave us postcards to write to relatives and friends. Erika and I sent six postcards ... We sent one to my brother-in-law Vital. We wrote: 'We heard that you want to change flats. Aunt *Pina* [Greek word for hunger] and Uncle *Tromo* [Greek word for terror] are at the place where you would like to go' ... I also wrote to my cousin who was half Jewish ... 'Dear Edith, we are well and Aunt *Pina* and Uncle *Thanatos* [Greek word for death] are with us.' If the Germans had asked me what *Thanatos* means I would have told them it is an abbreviation. But I carried out the control myself. An Austrian SS officer came, glanced quickly at the postcards and said: 'It's all right.' (Af5)

This brings us back to Handeli's point about the Greek Jews who 'could not understand them [the Germans]'. To know German (and Greek), and more importantly to have grown up in a German-speaking environment, empowered Hella K. in the world of Auschwitz although she was as much a victim as the other Salonikan Jews. The way she narrates the above incident shows that she believed in her ability to outwit the Germans.

The other interviewees could not have written postcards in German. They all learned German in the concentration camp. They recall the orders and the day-to-day routines in German (*Zählappell, raus, raus*) and some tell me their camp number in German. The ordinary Salonikan Jew spoke Ladino, some Greek and some French, languages which were not useful for survival in the camp.[3] Interestingly the issue of the language problem is not given much attention by the interviewees although it is clear that not knowing German rendered them more helpless than the other prisoners. It is presented as simply 'another fact' in the reality of Auschwitz. Sam P. refers to Birkenau as 'the biggest university for foreign languages'. The next sentence reveals that it must have been difficult not to be able to communicate well. 'We had to learn all the languages. We had to talk with our feet, our eyes, and our hands' (Am26).

To have contact with 'other Greeks' was therefore more important for the Greek Jews than with prisoners from other countries. In Palomba A.'s interview we find a number of references to her contact with other Jews from Greece. The first one appears in the description of when she was caught trying to exchange shoes in the *Männerlager*. In that incident she was together with 'a couple of friends' who 'loved each other a lot there'. She then adds that they were 'other Greek Jews' (Af1). The next two references to Greek Jews also have to do with the topic of comradeship in the camp. After Palomba A. was transferred to the *Aussenkommando* she fell sick and was sent to the *Revier*. There she met Frieda, another Jewish girl from Salonika. The Germans had started to evacuate Auschwitz (in January 1945) and Palomba A. embarked together with Frieda on the 'Deathmarch':

> 'At 5 o'clock in the morning I saw that the whole *Lager* started to leave. They told us that the ones who stay will be shot. We did not have shoes, clothes. What were we supposed to do? We had to do something. Only a few stayed. The two of us went to an empty block, we collected some broken shoes, some clothes. What are we going to do? They are going to kill us. Are we going to die after two years and three months? It was very difficult. After some time a car came with bread and sugar. Frieda and I took some bread and sugar and I put some in a sack and we left with the others, the last ones. With the dogs and the soldiers. It was night. We left for the forest, in the direction of Germany. The ones who could not walk. Dung, Dung, they were finished *kato* [on the floor]. It was cold and there was snow. You could see all

the people who were killed in these last minutes. Then we left. Three nights and three days ... The two of us had a blanket, a bit of bread, and a bit of sugar. I told her to hide under the blanket and that we are not going to speak to anyone, we will eat a bit of bread, a bit of sugar, to stay alive. One wanted to kill the other for a bit of bread to survive. You cannot imagine what it was like, one could have gone mad. After three nights and three days, it was so cold that we could hardly walk, we saw something that looked like a crematorium. *Schnell, schnell*, the dogs, the Germans. It was night. We did not know what to do. We took each other's hands. We were on our own, the only two Greeks.' (Af1)

Throughout this passage Palomba A. talks about 'we'. She had found a companion in the midst of the horrific turmoil. The last sentence expresses both a sense of solidarity and comradeship ('we took each others hands'), and the feeling of total isolation ('We were on our own, the only two Greeks'). Since they were with other prisoners she can only be referring to the fact that there were no 'other Greeks'. It is very interesting that Palomba A. refers to other Jews from Greece as 'Greeks'. When she talks about the pre-war or post-war time she refers to Christian Orthodox Greeks as 'Greeks' and to Jewish Greeks as 'Jews'. This shows that attribution of identity is, of course, context dependent. In pre-war Salonika 'Greeks' and 'Jews' stood for different ethnic groups. In the world of Auschwitz the Jews from Salonika became 'Greeks'. They were regarded as 'Greeks' by the Germans and by the other prisoners (Primo Levi talks about Mordo Nahum as 'the Greek' in *The Truce*, p. 209) and they regarded themselves as Greeks. Nobody differentiated between Greek Jews (Romaniotes who were Greek speaking) and Sephardi Jews (Ladino speaking). Although the interviewees do not state whether they spoke Greek or Ladino to each other a language shift seems to have taken place in the camp. Sitton describes one of the ballads which was sung in Greek which laments the harsh life in the concentration camp and recalls the place of birth left behind (Sitton 1985: 252). Another factor which added to this 'unintended Hellenisation process' was the longing for 'home' and the 'homeland'.

Marcel Nadjary's diary, which was found in 1980, attests to the strong feelings of patriotism. He wrote: 'I die content since I know that in this moment our Greece is liberated. I am not going to live but let my last words live: Hurrah for Greece' (Marcel Nadjary 1990: unpublished translation of manuscript by Sisi Benvenisti: 6).

In the world of Auschwitz the contact with other Jews from Greece was a link to the pre-war home. Erika Kounio-Amariglio describes throughout her book how she and her mother tried to find other Greeks (Kounio-Amariglio 2000). She also writes about how proud she was when she found out that 'Greeks were in the front rank' when a crematorium was blown up in the 'Auschwitz rebellion' in 1944. 'The Greeks, our own people, had raised their heads and stood up to them? … I felt so proud of them. "Definitely they will not escape," I thought, "but what a noble death." They have chosen death in the way they wanted!' (Kounio-Amariglio 2000: 115).

After the evacuation of Auschwitz, Palomba A., Hella K. and her daughter all arrived in Ravensbrück, the biggest women's concentration camp in Germany, and were then taken to Malchow, a smaller work camp. Palomba A. recalls:

> We had arrived in Ravensbrück … It was very dirty. The previous day they put us in a block where there were a lot of people who were about to die … I said to Frieda: 'Patience, patience. If God wants we will live, if not we will die.' That was our life in Ravensbrück … We were hungry and there was no food … One morning after eight days they told us *Zählapell*, *Zählappel* [roll call]. I told Frieda to make ourselves look proper … and God will be with us. We all were outside and a German came: you out, you out, you out. Frieda and I were among the ones he called out. They put us on a bus, we did not know where they were taking us, we did not know whether we would live or die. Nobody spoke. After six, seven hours in the bus we arrived in Malchow, another *Lager* …There was one guy from Greece who knew German very well. He heard that they will make us work and he asked: 'Who is Greek here? I want to talk to you. Whatever you will be asked you will answer: "I know"' … We were not lucky. 'Who knows how to make shoes?' I said: 'I know.' They took me and six other people but not Frieda. She was put in the *Aussenkommando*. She was not lucky. After that I never saw her again. (Af1)

In the transient world of the camp the advice of the 'guy from Greece who knew German very well' helps Palomba A. to survive but not her friend Frieda, the only person in the narrative about the camps whom she recalls by name.

Baruch S. also describes how he was saved by a young Salonikan boy called Isakino. After the evacuation from Auschwitz he came to Buchenwald and was subsequently taken to a small work camp in Strocholz. Isakino worked in the kitchen and had heard that the Germans were planning to shoot all the Jews the following day. Baruch S. recounts:

> I told him to keep quiet about this. Luckily they had not taken the number on our arms since we had arrived there. These were the last days of the war. So Isakino and I opened a locked door and went to hide in the second floor. The next morning they took all the Jews and killed them. This was a couple of days before the war ended. (Am23)

Baruch S. was close to death ('I thought, this is the end, *petit* Baruch') but was saved by the help of his Salonikan friend and by luck ('luckily, they had not taken the number). The arbitrariness of survival and the unexpected help of a friend or a stranger are themes which are found in many survivors' testimonies.

Hella K. and her daughter also left Auschwitz with three other Greek Jewish girls. They all eventually arrived in Malchow. Erika Kounio-Amariglio writes that they lived in the same barrack in Malchow and that 'together with the three Greek girls we formed a little family' (Kounio-Amariglio 2000: 127). The conditions in Malchow were much better than in Auschwitz, especially the food situation. Hella K. worked in the garden, her daughter in the kitchen, and Palomba A. in the *Schuhkommando* until the beginning of May 1945.

Liberation

Langer reminds us that the notion of 'liberation' commonly implies 'survival, the beginning of renewal, the end of oppression' (Langer 1991: 175). This language is often not the language of the interviewee but of the interviewer who subscribes to a chronological historical narrative of pre-war, war, and post-war. Langer's interviewees often refuse to comply with this narrative, because for them liberation did not bring about the end of 'their' war, nor did it bring about any form of 'closure'. This becomes painfully clear when we look at Palomba A.'s story of liberation.

On 1 May 1945 the Germans decided to evacuate the camp. In a state of chaos, with the Russian army approaching and the Germans withdrawing, Palomba A. found herself with other prisoners in the forest:

The night came, we walked and walked and walked. We did not know where to go. We saw many soldiers but we did not want to meet soldiers because we were scared of the soldiers. At some point we saw a shed and went to sleep there … One girl said that we should take a piece of wood with a piece of white cloth. We then all left, one by one with the piece of wood in our hand. All over the mountains you could find red flags. We felt happy, very happy with the little piece of wood in our hand. Then the Russians came. 'Who are you?' We could not speak and just showed them our little white flags. 'Go inside, inside'. The war was still going on, it was 5 May. All of us went inside. The minute we arrived we were put to work by the Russians. *Rabot, rabot* [work]. We had to peel potatoes and clean vegetables. We did not know why we had to work like this, why they looked on us as workers. After work we got some potatoes to eat, a bit of bread, and we went to sleep in a room with blankets on the floor. In the middle of the night somebody bangs on our door. Boom, Boom, Boom. The Russians wanted women. They were drunk, they had been drinking a lot of vodka. They all came to me. '*Chora, chora*' [Polish word for sick], I said. I am sick. I pretended to be sick. One wanted me, one took another girl. Then came other soldiers. I screamed '*chora, chora*'. I was still a virgin. Ukrainian soldiers with beards, like old men. The third opened his belt and screamed. I said 'no, no, *chora, chora*'. 'Palomba, they will kill you', said the others. 'Let them kill me. I am virgin, how can I let these old men do this?' They took me there where the horses and the cows were and pointed the gun at my head. I was so scared that I thought I am dead. I did not understand what was happening. How that is possible I don't know. When I woke up there was blood. I will never forget this. It was morning. All the girls thought that I am dead because I had not come back. Then the girls saw me, without shoes, knocking my head against the wall, like a madwoman. I did not speak to anyone. One girl approached me and took me by the arm: 'We thought you are dead. Since you are alive, don't say anything', she said. It has to stay inside me. After this I did not want to stay. The next day we left. The girls ran but I could not run. Suddenly I did not see anyone. What am I going to do, all on my own? Then I saw six, seven French soldiers, prisoners of war. They spoke French. That's why it is good to speak languages. 'Please, help me, I lost my friends', I said in French. They told me to come with them. They were good, they gave me things to eat. (Af1)

The 'haunting past' is not restricted to the experience of the concentration camp but also to the experience of liberation ('I will never forget this'), as the extract of Palomba A.'s interview illustrates. The Russian soldiers did not acknowledge the plight of the women concentration camp survivors. They were put to work and sometimes raped or sexually assaulted. Palomba A. comments on this experience in the same fashion as she commented on the camp experiences: 'Another five kilometres and I would have been liberated by the Americans. This is life. It's all a question of luck' (Af1). After this ordeal with the Russian soldiers she remained alone again ('What am I going to do, all on my own?'). Together with the French POWs she was taken to a place where she could recuperate for the next couple of months, before returning to Salonika at the end of September 1945. Only after returning home she realised that nobody had survived from her family. At this point her narrative of survival is transformed into a narrative of deprival. Palomba A. found herself in post-war Salonika, deprived of her family and of choices. The theme of the lack of personal choice after her return from Auschwitz runs throughout the rest of her life history.

Hella K. and her daughter also found themselves in the forest after having left Malchow. Together with the three other Greek girls they met some French POWs and hid with them in a barn. They stayed in the barn for a couple of days until the arrival of the regular Soviet occupation army. After being put up in barracks by the Soviet army they decided to go with some Serbian POWs to the American zone, thinking that this would enhance their chances of returning quickly to Salonika. With the idea of an immediate return in mind they went on the first transport to the Balkans which brought them to Belgrade. At the end of August Hella K. and her daughter managed to cross the border and get back to Salonika, where her husband and son were waiting for them (they had been liberated by the French and had returned to Salonika earlier). Hella K.'s post-war narrative continues to be a narrative of strength which focuses on 'helping others'. In the immediate post-war years she helped her children to finish school while her husband became active in the community and helped 'to bring the Jews out of their misery', that is, he organised help and support for the young Jews, such as Palomba A. who had come back to Salonika to find neither family members nor any means of subsistence. In contrast to her mother, Erika Kounio-Amariglio describes her 'coming home' in both her interview and her autobiography as an event which she associates with feelings of great comfort and happiness and feelings of loss and absence, sentiments which the 'heroic memory' needs to suppress.

My heart beat joyously like the chiming of a bell, and I wanted to hug and kiss the pebbles, the sea, the sky, the sunset. It did not matter that we had nothing any more, we were together again, alive, in our house, that was what mattered. (Kounio-Amariglio 2000: 141)

Two paragraphs later she continues:

I went in search of the houses where my classmates Dorin, May, and Rita had lived, but it was as though they no longer existed. Strangers had moved in, and they did not even know who the previous owners were and how their houses had come to be deserted. How could I not feel the absence of my uncles, my aunts and my cousins … Twenty-three members of our family had perished. (Kounio-Amariglio 2000: 142)

THE PARTISANS

With the assistance of Italian diplomats some Jews managed to flee to the Italian occupied zone while others joined the resistance in the mountains. The communist National Liberation Front (EAM) with its military wing ELAS, and non-communist resistance groups, the largest of which was the National Republican Greek League (EDES), had been active since 1941. Since it was only possible for young people to 'go to the mountains', many did not take up this opportunity because they did not want to be separated from their families.

Four interviewees spent the time from 1943 until 1944 (when the German forces withdrew) as partisans (*Andartes*) in the mountains. The two women were in their early to mid-twenties when they left the ghetto. Some other interviewees were helped by partisans, as will be seen below.

The war memories of the partisans are very different from the 'memories of death' of the camp survivors. While the camp survivors mostly perceive themselves as victims with no control over their fate in a world in which it was 'chance' to survive, the partisans perceive themselves as individuals who took part in a 'national struggle' against the German occupation. The partisans can therefore more easily make sense of their war experience than the camp survivors, partly because their experience lies in the realm of the known and communicable. The interviewees were eager to talk about their experience in the mountains, especially the two men. The efforts of all partisans were officially acknowledged by the Greek state in 1981 when PASOK came to power. The interviewees proudly showed me the medals and certificates they received (see Figure 26). In contrast to the camp survivors, their war memory forms part of a larger Greek 'cultural memory'. Mazower estimates that about 650 Jews served in the resistance, in combat units or as interpreters (Mazower 1993: 260), of whom 250 were from Salonika (Matsas 1997: 271).

However, for each interviewee the experience in the mountains plays a different role within his or her general life history. For Elvira F., Alici P. and Michael B., the experience in the mountains was a way of survival, limited to the years 1943 until 1944/45. For Moshe B., becoming a member of ELAS/EAM was the beginning of his political development as a communist which shaped all his later life. This kind of connection between the present and the past (in which the past explains the 'self' in the present) is very different from the notion of a 'haunting past' expressed in the survivors' narratives, in which the narrator has no control over his memory of the past. The time in the mountains does constitute a time which can more easily be integrated into the interviewees' life histories. It is a past with a clear beginning (escape), a middle (in the mountains) and an end (return), of which the return was often most traumatic.

The continuity or the link between the partisan experience and the present in Moshe B.'s case is embodied in the interview situation. I interviewed him first on his own and then together with his best friend, who worked for ELAS/EAM and had helped Moshe B. to escape from the ghetto. The second interview took place in his friend's shop. On the wall one could see a framed photograph of himself and Moshe B. with a group of other people on an island. Moshe B. was the only one of my interviewees who did not sign the *Dilosi* (renouncing the activities of ELAS/EAM) after the war, and he was convicted and exiled together with his communist comrade.[4] Mr Stephanos still addresses Moshe B. with his *nom de guerre*, Viron.[5] The friendship and bond between the two men supports Kenna's description of communality and group identity, developed among exiled communists (during 1936 and 1941) on a Cycladic island (Kenna 1991: 65).

Escape

The majority of Jews remained in Salonika until the deportations. About 3,400 fled to Athens (Kabeli 1953: 286);[6] only a very small number escaped with the help of the partisans. There are three reasons which are normally given to explain the fact that most Jews chose to remain in Salonika. The first, discussed in the previous chapter, is the trust in Rabbi Koretz; the second is the closeness of the Jewish family; and the third is the language deficiency (many Salonikan Jews spoke Greek with a heavy accent which could give them away).[7] The factor of the family is emphasised by every interviewee ('We went where our parents went, the Jewish families were very close', Am17). The sense of responsibility for the parents was reinforced by the belief that young people were especially needed in the new settlement in Poland. We should, however, not underestimate the effect of the orders issued by Dr Merten, the head of the city's German military administration. In order 3766, dated 21 March 1943, Merten announced the execution of 25 Jews as a reprisal for the alleged escape of Dr Cuenca,[8] a Jewish doctor who worked for the Red Cross (Novitch 1989: 25). In early March five men who tried to escape from the ghetto were publicly executed (Af8, Novitch 1989: 65).

Looking at the interviews with the partisans we find that they have one thing in common. In all four cases the interviewees or their families had a personal relationship to somebody non-Jewish either in the resistance or outside Salonika. Michael B. came from a religious family. His grandfather used to be the chief rabbi of Salonika and his father was a *Hazan* at Bet Saul synagogue. His father's first wife had died and following Salonikan tradition he subsequently married Michael B.'s mother, the sister of his late wife. Michael B. had six brothers and four sisters. At the time of the German occupation he was 21 and worked in the wholesale pharmaceutical business of his grandfather's brother. There he met a communist who advised him to escape:

> Among the clientele of this store there was a guy from a village called Giannitsa. It's up about 40 or 50 miles from here … He used to shop there and one of the guys was a real communist. We used to talk together, you know, and one day he says to me 'if you go [to Poland] you are dead.' 'If you go, you are dead,' he says to me. I said 'what can I do?' 'I can pick you up from home and try to take you to some place.' So I said, to make a long story short, I said 'O.K., you come and pick me up. (Am16)

Some time later this communist told Michael B. that somebody would meet him the next day. Without telling anyone in his family, he left and stayed for a couple of days with another communist in Katotoumba. But the 'connection' was not ready and he had to return home. Despite the disapproval of his family he tried to escape again, this time successfully. Some days later he was told to come to a certain place from where he and some other Jews were taken to a derelict cinema on Egnatia Street. After a couple of days they started walking south, towards Langada (Am16). They pretended to be villagers and crossed the Gorgopotamos bridge, patrolled by German guards, in a horse carriage. Then they made their way to Veria.

Shaltiel Gattagno mentions Michael B. in his testimony in Novitch's book (Novitch 1989: 82). They must have left the ghetto in the same group. The importance of personal connections in escaping the ghetto is underlined in Mr Gattagno's interview. He and his brother had desperately explored other options until a friend managed to get in contact with someone from the resistance.

Moshe B.'s friend, mentioned earlier, was such a 'middleman' for the resistance. His job was to gather as many people as possible and bring them to the 'connection' who would take them to the mountains. Together with Moshe B. they went to Jewish houses and tried to convince the families to let the young people go to the mountains, but often in vain. Moshe B. recalls:

> At that time I was involved with the communist youth. There were many Jews, mostly of the poorer classes. When we were supposed to wear the yellow star I did not wear it. I was free and I went from place to place and tried to convince the young people to join the partisans. I had more than 70 meetings like this. But because Koretz had said that we are not going to die and because of the closeness in the families, particularly to the fathers and mothers, the young people did not want to go … One day we left for the mountains. One boy returned. He was almost on the edge of freedom but he chose to return. (Am17)

Of the 15 people who were supposed to meet Moshe B. and his friend in order to escape, only six showed up. While Moshe B. tells his life history in most parts in a 'chronicle mode', he gets emotional when recounting the day of his escape:

> I knew a very beautiful girl. We had a very good relationship. We agreed that when I would leave for the mountains I would take her with me. When we arranged the day I told her that I would pick her up. We left Salonika through the place which is now the Baron Hirsch Hospital. We made the following plan: one person

would go and the next person was 100 metres behind. If something happened to one the other could run away. Then we
arrived at the house of my girl and I told the leader to wait for
me for five minutes, so I can fetch her. I went to her house. She
was ready but her father started to cry. All the family was very
upset. They said: 'You leave us, you are not thinking about us.'
Her father was very sick. 'Who is going to take care of your
father?' She stayed. I went alone and the group carried on. It
hurt very much. In the last moment one could not do anything
[long silence]. (Am17)

The last sentence reveals the life-long burden of the survivors who
stayed in Greece. It is not the question: 'Why did I survive?' but 'Why
could I not persuade my brother, sister, or friend to join me?' Moshe B.'s
case though is quite exceptional. While two of his sisters were deported, the rest of his family, that is, his parents, two sisters and one brother, managed to escape from the ghetto. Through the help of another
friend of his who had a connection to the Greek police his family stayed
behind when the ghetto was being emptied and subsequently left
Salonika in the back of a truck and were taken to Naussa, where his
father, two sisters and brother joined the partisans while his mother
stayed throughout the war in the house of a Christian woman. In his
book, Matsas points to the uniqueness of this family in which a father
and his four children became ELAS partisans (Matsas 1997: 323).[9]
Moshe B. recounts that his friend had told his family after their escape
'now you can live like the Greeks and you don't have to be afraid'
(Am17). This is a relevant comment. Moshe B.'s family could live 'like
the Greeks' because they had come to Salonika from the provinces only
in 1926. They spoke Greek at home and Moshe B. went to a Greek
school. He thus had more contacts with non-Jews than most Salonikan
Jews, a fact which helped him and his family to escape from the ghetto.

In contrast to Moshe B. and Michael B., Alici P. was from a more
middle-class background and met her 'connection' through which she
would escape by pure coincidence. She was in a café with her parents
who started talking to three men at the table next to them. These men
were from Tirvanos, one hour south of Larissa, which was occupied by
the Italians. When Alici P.'s father told them that she spoke fluent
Italian (since she had attended the Italian school), the three men invited her to come to Tirvanos. When the order came that the Jews had to
move to ghettos, Alici P.'s mother urged her daughter to go to
Tirvanos. The two men from Tirvanos came to pick her up and with

the help of another man who worked for the railways she managed to get on the train to Tirvanos. This is her description of her escape:

> We had arranged to meet at the railway station. I put on a pair of sunglasses and walked all the way from Agia Triada to the station. I met the person who worked at the railway and we [she and the two people from Tirvanos] entered the train. At 12 o'clock, just before Platamona, the Germans started to check one's papers … there was an interpreter who made all the young women whom he liked get off the train. After he enjoyed himself with them he gave them the laissez-passer [transit pass] … When I refused to leave the train he immediately called the German who was behind him and said: 'This is the girl I was looking for. Give me your papers.' … I was afraid and started crying. The German came and asked '*Was ist das?*' [what is going on?] I had learnt German from the dictionary and I said: '*Ich habe eine kranke Mutter* [my mother is sick], I have to go to hospital.' The German was impressed with my German and said: '*Gut, gut Fräulein* [it's OK, Miss], you can go.' The interpreter did not say anything and took two other young girls off the train and we arrived in Tirvanos. (Af9)

Her description is interesting because it illustrates both the help of Christian Greeks without which she would not have been on the train and the collaboration of the Greek interpreter who wanted to take advantage of her vulnerable situation. The subject of Greek collaboration (as informers) is not a relevant subject for the partisans because once they joined the partisans they were in danger as 'partisans' and not as Jews. For people in hiding the fear of Greek informers was a more pertinent issue.

In the Mountains

Moshe B. and Michael B. were partisans in ELAS units throughout the time of the occupation while Alici P. remained in Tirvanos and joined the partisans only after the withdrawal of the Italian troops. The partisans led a guerrilla war against the Italian and German occupation forces, committing acts of sabotage (such as the bombing of the Gorgopotamos bridge in October 1942 with the help of the British Military Mission), punishing collaborators, and administering the villages and towns of 'Free Greece' (for the history of the Greek resistance, see Mazower 1993). Mazower estimates that the *Andarte* forces consisted of about 17,000 people in May 1943 and about 30,000 in July 1943, of whom the majority was associated with ELAS. After the capitulation of Italy most of the Greek countryside remained under ELAS and EDES (concentrated in the Epirus region) control, while the Germans controlled the Greek cities. The villagers supported the resistance and had to suffer greatly under the retaliation missions by the Germans. The daily life of the partisans is characterised in the following description by Joseph Matsas, who joined the partisans at a similar time as Moshe B. and Michael B.:

> I decided to become a partisan in March 1943. My enlistment in the units of ELAS in the mountains of Paico, near Giannitsa, coincided with the spring search-and-destroy missions of the Germans ... We were forced to change our mountain hideaway every week. We suffered from hunger, cold, rain and uninterrupted forced marches at night. We were continuously pursued by German units. Many times we marched barefoot, and we had to endure legions of lice. (quoted in Matsas 1997: 312)

The theme of the life of hardship as a partisan is immediately followed by a statement about the 'national struggle': 'Our terrible ordeals were more than compensated for by our strong fighting spirit and a realisation that we were free people who fought the enemy enslaving our countrymen' (quoted in Matsas 1997: 313).

Since the Jewish partisans were part of a larger struggle against the occupation, they share their wartime experiences with the other Greek partisans (and villagers). Their memory of this time thus constitutes a 'shared memory'. This decreases the 'duty' to remember for the individual. In contrast to the camp survivors the partisans were not victims and witnesses of genocide (Erika Kounio-Amariglio, for example, clearly states that she needed to write down her story for her friends who did not survive).The partisans can assume that most people (certainly other Greeks) know what it meant to have been 'in the mountains', in the *Andartiko* (resistance). After discussing his escape at considerable length, Michael B. summarises his time in the mountains in a few sentences.

> My little brother was in the same unit as my father. They were in the area of Veria and Naussa. I was in the centre of Greece, around Gianinitsa and Kilkis. Sometimes we met each other. (Am16)

Sometime later he adds that his sister became famous for her courage and that his brother died in a German ambush.

Michael B. talks in great detail about his partisan experience. Once in a while he stopped his narrative and asked me: 'Do you want the details or do you want me to continue?' It becomes clear to me that he is telling me his story because he thinks that I am interested, not because his experiences in the mountains are of the utmost relevance for his life history. Michael B. is not asking for my acknowledgement of his history (while Palomba A., who survived the camps, did). Furthermore he does not see himself as somebody who played an important role in the mountains. His brother became a 'big one in the mountains'[10] (and after the war served ten years in jail) but he 'didn't know the rules of the army' since he had not served in the war with Italy. He held various positions as a partisan, and was mainly used as an interpreter and administrator (for the distribution of food).[11] His narrative of his time as a partisan tells us about close encounters with the Germans, the strenuous hikes up and down the mountains, and the various tasks he was assigned to. He recounts the first major incident:

> So that same night the Germans came up into the mountains and they started shooting and I was hiding myself behind a tree or something and a couple of guys got hit. One guy got hit here … Another guy was hit. This guy was dead too. I was lucky. Nobody shot at me or they must have shot at me and missed. In the meantime you have to walk and walk and walk and get up to the mountains, you know, up, up, up, up to the hills. (Am16)

It is quite hard to follow Michael B.'s narrative because of the number of different places he went and because of the nature of the events he describes. He does not use any heroic language in the chaotic world he describes, and he talks about his sense of duty with a certain irony:

> So, they put me in one place, one village, where they used to store wheat, rice, beans and oil. And I used to send the stuff to the headquarters, to another village, for distribution. And that's what I was doing. And again, to make a long story short, there was a time when the Germans made up their minds to clean us up … So, everybody had to move. They were after us; we were moving, moving, moving … I was close to Kosani and I picked up all the paperwork and put it in a kind of ditch. They covered it up … and we were walking and walking and going and going. I was so

tired … And then, when they spread the rumours that the *Ekatharistikes Epichirisis* [which literally translated means 'cleaning enterprise'] was over, they left. I started going back … I was very anxious to get the papers, which was a dumb way of thinking for me. I was so anxious to get to the place where the papers were that I did not stop walking until I fainted. When I got to that place for my paperwork, the famous paperwork, somebody told me: 'Hey, somebody else came in, he picked up the whole thing and left.' (Am16)

Michael B., whose *nom de guerre* was Michalis, did not tell anyone that he was Jewish ('they did not ask me'). He only once refers to other Jews in the mountains. While they 'wanted to play clever' and go down the mountains a different way, Michael B. preferred to stay with the group ('I always used to go with the main group. I wouldn't listen to anybody. Where the bulk was, I was there', Am16). When he found out that the Germans had left Salonika in December 1944 he immediately returned to the city.

Alici P. recalls her activities after the escape with a stronger sense of pride. After she had arrived in Tirvanos one of the men who had helped her escape accused her of being a spy (for the partisans). The Italians made inquiries about her, found out that she was 'a Jewish girl from a good family' and gave her an 'important position'. She was responsible for dealing with the laissez-passers to Athens and Larrissa. When she was approached by leaders from the resistance she was willing to help them and to smuggle arms. After the Italians withdrew she was taken by the partisans, who knew that she was Jewish, up to the mountains. She was treated very well because they knew that she had 'saved many people'. Knowing Italian and German enabled her to 'play with the Germans and Italians' in order to save herself. She clearly attributes historical importance to her experiences during the occupation and in the resistance ('when I returned I wanted to write a book about what had happened but I did not write it'). Although Michael B. seems to attach less significance to his own activities in the resistance he mentions that he has written down a detailed itinerary of his journey as a partisan. The important point is that the 'time in the mountains' is a time with a beginning and an end. For Michael B. and Alici P. it ended in 1945 when they returned to Salonika where another, most likely more traumatic, struggle started: the coming to terms with the loss of one's family and the struggle to rebuild one's life.

For Moshe B. this was not the case. After the end of the war he remained with EAM and was exiled to the islands of Ikaria and Makronisos. It is not accidental that he talks much more extensively about the post-war years and his time in exile than his time in the mountains; it was after the war when he became the victim of 'historical injustice'. He, as do many other Greek partisans, perceives it as extremely unjust that they were convicted and declared 'outlaws' after having fought the occupation ('We could not do anything although ELAS/EAM had helped to liberate Greece from the Germans', AM17).

IN HIDING

Half the interviewees survived the occupation, or parts of it, in hiding (five women and seven men). In 'hiding' stands here for a variety of experiences. We need to bear in mind that the age of the interviewees varies greatly. The youngest were born during the occupation, the oldest were in their early forties. All the interviewees were either with their parents, children, or spouses during the time of the occupation, except for one man who hid in Athens on his own and one woman who was given as a baby to a Christian family. It was the entire family or a couple who decided to go into hiding and not, as in the case of the partisans, the individual. Only six of the interviewees were born in Salonika. The others came from provincial towns, such as Larissa, Trikkala and Kavalla. We can distinguish between three experiences of hiding: hiding in Athens, hiding in villages (in Thessaly) or on islands (Skopelos), and hiding in Salonika. Two women spent only limited time in Athens and subsequently escaped with their husbands and children by boat from the coast of Euboea to Turkey and then to Palestine. In general the narratives of the interviewees in hiding are narratives of help and support rather than of betrayal and opportunism. Most people who were betrayed and denounced by Jewish informers or Greek collaborators did not survive to tell their story (see Matsas 1997: 109).

Hiding in Athens

It is estimated that about 3,500 Jews from Salonika made their way to Athens, which was under Italian control until September 1943. In the Italian zone there was no discrimination against Jews and the Italian command did not comply with German demands for the deportation of Greek Jews. The Italian consulate actively helped Jews from

Salonika by giving them Italian naturalisation papers and laisser-passers (Mazower 1993: 240).

After the German troops entered Athens, Wisliceny ordered Rabbi Barzilai to provide a list with the name of all the Jews. Following this, the rabbi was taken by ELAS/EAM to the mountains on September 1943 (for an eyewitness report of the escape see Matsas 1997: 91). Having heard of the escape of the rabbi and knowing what had happened to the Jews in Salonika, most Jews did not follow the German registration orders issued in October. Of an estimated 8,000 Jews, only 1,200 registered (Mazower 1993: 251). In total about 1,000 Jews registered at the synagogue. On 23 March 1944 the synagogue doors were locked and all Jews who were present (between 700 and 1,000) for the registration were arrested. They were taken to the Haidari camp and subsequently deported to Auschwitz. At the same time the Jews from other cities were also being deported. Following Barzilai's example, the rabbis of Volos and Larissa also went into hiding and less than half of the Jewish population of Volos and Larissa were captured by the Germans. Most interviewees left Salonika before 1943; only one escaped from the ghetto in March 1943 and made her way to Athens. All the interviewees who were hidden in Athens or went through Athens in order to get the boat from Euboa to Turkey were from middle-class families (most of them had their own businesses). They had the means to sustain themselves or a connection to somebody who could help them in the new place (during the difficult time of the famine) and later to pay for false identity cards and get by in hiding. None of the interviewees registered themselves as Jews in Athens.

The interviewees came to Athens in various circumstances. Rebecca V. had an Italian passport because she was married to an Italian subject. When the war between Italy and Greece broke out her husband was imprisoned. After the Germans entered Salonika he was released and they and their two children subsequently left for Athens (Af11). For a year they survived on the gold coins they had brought with them and in the winter of 1944 they managed to get a boat to Turkey. Eventually they arrived in Palestine.

Felix S. and his father and sister also left for Athens in the early days of German occupation. Since their business was in Salonika, his father returned there and went into hiding with his sisters in a village (it helped that he was from Chalkida and thus spoke flawless Greek). Pavlos S. came to Athens as a 10-year-old boy with his parents and brother and sister from Kavalla. His father had decided that it was better to leave Kavalla, which became part of the Bulgarian occupied zone.

For the interviewees who left Salonika before the ghettoisation, the 'war narrative' usually starts with the arrival of German troops in Athens. Leaving Salonika and life under the Italian occupation was 'uneventful' compared to the later experiences of hiding or escaping (to Turkey). As mentioned above, Lili M. left Salonika in March 1943, when she escaped with her husband from the ghetto. In her testimony the episode of the escape is key to the whole narrative. It is so central (and traumatic) because it is connected to the central themes of her narrative: separation (from her family), and betrayal (by the Jewish leadership and Greek collaborators). After two attempts to give her 2-year-old son to a Christian family had failed, she decided to leave the child behind with her parents and escape from the ghetto with her husband. It was difficult to find a 'way out' of the ghetto and she vehemently denies that there was any organised attempt at helping people escape.

Who went from house to house? There was no organisation. This is what I call stupidities. I never saw anyone going from house to house. Who said so? They must have a big imagination. There was a total lack of organisation. We escaped, my two brothers-in-law, my husband and two other friends, with the help of an Armenian. My brother-in-law, may he rest in peace, he had an Armenian friend and they organised a German truck. We paid money ... They drove us, took the money and left us in Katerini. (Af8)

Lili M.'s memory is shaped by her knowledge that she was the only one to survive because the hiding place of her family was betrayed. When talking about leaving her parents she gets very upset and maintains her composure with great difficulty.

I told my mother that I was leaving and she said, 'What will happen to us?' And my father said [she is crying], 'we have our son and our other daughter, let her go'. He was in bed he couldn't get up ... My mother was sitting by the bed and my father got up and blessed me. [long silence] (Af8)

Leaving her family behind in Salonika (to be deported eventually) created a break in the life of Lili M. which she was not able to mend. This is clearly expressed in the structure and content of her narrative. She repeatedly returns to the episode of leaving her parents, in a manner which indicates the continuous (and haunting) presence of the past: 'It was very hard to leave an older father, in bed with a heart problem, always in bed and yet I had to go, I had to follow my husband. And my mother, still I have her in my eyes, telling me, 'What are we going to do?' It was not easy' (Af8).

The painful and enduring memory of leaving ('still I have her in my eyes') , which Lili M. needs to justify by her lack of choice ('I had to follow my husband') is accompanied by the theme of betrayal. After her parents had managed to find a railworker who brought Lili M.'s son to Athens at the beginning of May, her brother and parents were arrested. She recounts:

> My brother had a Christian girlfriend. I don't know, may I be for-given, they say she betrayed him. He was arrested in the street and never came back. She knew where my parents and my sister and her husband were hidden in Charilao. They were betrayed. We don't know by whom. I never saw her again but my people disappeared. (Af8)

Betrayal is the leitmotiv in Lili M.'s interview. Almost every story of help and support is followed by one of betrayal and injustice (to her family and other Jews). Her own experiences of help and support in Athens seem to take place 'backstage' (in her narrative). They can be summarised as follows: after Italy fell she started looking for a place for her child. Through a connection to the wife of the Belgian consul she was introduced to a Belgian nun who found her a place as a maid and gave the child into the care of a Greek widow who had seven children and lived next to the Monastery of the Divine Providence. Her hus-band joined ELAS/EAM and went to the mountains. Lili M.'s inabili-ty to 'understand' the fate of her family and the other Jews of Salonika is the main theme which guides her narrative. She is aware of the 'bias' of her anguished memory:

> My view is marked by bitterness and anger, terrible anger. How could people, the Germans and the Greeks who were taking advantage of our misery, as human beings, how could they in their own hearts, having babies at home, having wives and moth-ers, do that to other human beings? You see, that is the question. (Af8)

Lili M. points out the difference between Salonika and Athens: in Athens the resistance was 'much better organised and there were more people willing to help' while in Salonika 'they [the Greeks] were not able to hide us even if they had wanted' (Af8). I have discussed Lili M.'s testimony in detail because it stands out among all the interviews. She is most outspoken in her criticism of the Jewish leadership and the Greek bystanders, and she describes both Greek help and Greek antagonism towards the Jews. While most other narratives of interviewees who were in hiding are narratives of survival (focusing predominantly on the help of the Greeks) hers is a narrative of a survival which is constantly juxtaposed to death (of her family). One instance of this parallel narrative occurs when she talks about the letter she received from the headmistress of the American College after the liberation. The headmistress wrote to her that she was sure that Lili M. would survive and that she had prayed for her day and night. Lili M. recalls her reaction: 'I asked "why didn't you pray for my younger sister who was also at Anatolia [the American College]?"' The grief for her family resists chronological order and appears throughout the interview. The structure of her narrative is a structure of parallel existence or permanent duality (Langer 1991: 95). Memory becomes a burden which 'scars' the whole life history of Lili M. ('whether you want it or not there are scars') and it is seen as a process which is beyond the control of the interviewee ('after so many years it comes back, so many years and you are asking yourself won't there be any forgetting?').

Among the interviewees who were in hiding the two women who fled via Athens to Turkey and Palestine (Jean L. and Rebecca V.) also lost their parents and siblings. In contrast to Lili M. they concentrate on their own narrative of survival and just briefly mention that 'their family members were victims of the deportation' (Af11) or that 'all the family was deported' (Af6).

Jean L. comes from a wealthy, middle-class family. Her father was a cotton merchant. When the Germans occupied Greece she was 34, married, and had one son. She told me very early on in the interview that her mother and two sisters were deported, and that one sister survived since she was married to a Spanish subject. When talking about the relations between the Jews and the Greeks in general she very quickly addresses the time of the occupation:

> I was saved by Greeks. Thanks to the Greeks I am alive. If the Greeks had not protected me from the Germans and showed me how to escape I would have died. All the Jews who were saved, were saved by the Greeks. Here [in the *Yerokomiou*] all the nurses are Greek and they are very nice. (Af6)

It is a common feature of the interviews that when it comes to the issue of Greek help towards Jews during the occupation, the intervie-wee generalises from their own experience; discusses the issue of Greek help in the context of Greek–Jewish relations in general; and moves very swiftly from the time of the war to the present. In the same way that 'timelessness' figures in the narratives of anti-Semitism, Jean L. connects the sentence about the past of the occupation 'all the Jews … were saved by Greeks' to a statement about her present 'here', where 'all the nurses are Greek and they are very nice'.

It seems that, on the whole, the interviewees avoid discussing the topic of Greek collaboration. It is often mentioned in an indirect way, expressed, for example, at the end of Jean L.'s description of her escape:

> We went from here to Athens which was occupied by the Italians. The Italians did not touch the Jews and we were OK. Later the Germans came to Athens. The Greek Archbishop Damaskinos gave false Greek names to the Jews. Before leaving I was in a small village and one day they said that the Germans had come and we gathered at a Greek cemetery and the local priest said that we could come to the church because this is the house of God. He told the villagers to bring us some food. There are good people all over the world. We paid a lot of money for somebody to take us to Turkey.[12] The whole group consisted of 15 people. It was very dangerous. In Salonika the villagers were very jealous. They thought the Jews were very rich and all that. (Af6)

The contrast in the degree of collaboration in Salonika and the rest of Greece is often the only context in which the interviewees discuss the theme of Greek collaboration. This is similar to the language issue. Many interviewees talk about the fact that the Salonikan Jews were more disadvantaged than the other Jews because of their limited knowledge of Greek.

Matsas points out that the Germans could not tell the difference between the Jewish and the non-Jewish Greeks but that they relied on informers and interpreters (Matsas 1997: 108). What is thus described as a 'language problem' of the Ladino-speaking Jews ('you could hear from miles away that somebody was Jewish, that was a big problem', Am29) was also a problem of surviving in a society which had numer-ous informers and collaborators. Matsas estimates that about 200 Jews who were in hiding in Athens were denounced and brought to the

Haidari concentration camp (Matsas 1997: 109). There is only implicit mention of the theme of collaborators in the interviews. The fear of denunciation must have been quite substantial because all the interviewees who were in hiding in Athens had to conceal their Jewish identity (in contrast to the Jews who were hiding in villages or on islands) and had to move numerous times while in hiding. Felix S., for example, recalls that he had to leave his room because the neighbours had found out that he was Jewish. Like many other Jews, he then managed to get Christian papers from the police[13] and moved to Piraeus which was more deserted because of the Allied air attacks on German installations. He stayed in Piraeus until the Germans left Athens in December 1944.

Another way of concealing one's Jewish identity was to convert to Christian Orthodoxy. Pavlos S.'s father decided that in addition to the Christian papers he had received from the police the family should convert.[14] Pavlos S. was ten at the time and remembers the ceremony: 'All the family went to the church. We had to say a big prayer and we became Orthodox. For a couple of weeks we continued going to the church' (Am25). While his father went to Egypt and joined the Greek army in exile, his mother stayed with the three children in Athens, pretending to be the family of a Christian Greek officer. They changed places about five times. Pavlos S. recalls himself as a very nervous child who had difficulties at school. He relates this to his experience of hiding. 'I was ten and I could see all the dangers' (Am25).

Two of the interviewees were born during the occupation. Viktoria B. survived in the care of a Christian Orthodox couple, while Leon A. was at first only with his mother in a suburb of Athens and later joined his father who was with the resistance in the mountains. The experience of Viktoria B. is exceptional because she grew up believing that she was the Christian Orthodox child of the Greek couple. The first time she learnt that she was Jewish was when her mother returned from Auschwitz in 1945. In her narrative her idyllic childhood contrasts with the time after the war.

> I remember a very beautiful life with them [the Christian parents]. They were very nice people and took very good care of me … I called them 'Mama' and 'Papa' and I loved them very much. When my mother came back [from Auschwitz] I did not recognise her. I did not know that this woman was my mother and I did not want her. I started to cry, I cried, cried and cried. 'I want

my mother', the Christian woman. This was a crazy story; I still
have psychological problems. (Af30)

Only much later did Viktoria B. reconstruct her family history ('I
collected memories from other people'). In March 1944 a Greek policeman came to the house and told her mother to come to the synagogue.
When she prepared her two children to come as well, the policeman
advised her to leave them behind. Viktoria B. and her sister were first
taken in by the neighbours and then by her mother's sister, who lived
opposite the synagogue and witnessed the arrest of all the Jews, and
managed to escape. When the Christian friends of her parents, who
were childless, found out what had happened they volunteered to take
Viktoria B. while her sister stayed with her aunt and cousins. At the
end of the war Viktoria B. needed to come to terms with two forms of
loss: the death of her real father (and the rest of the family) and the loss
of her adopted parents (when she moved with her mother to Salonika).

Viktoria B.'s experience will be discussed further in Chapter 8 in
considering the childhood of the very small number of child survivors
among the community of survivors in Salonika.

Hiding Elsewhere

This section will present the different experiences of the other interviewees, of whom three are Salonikans, one is from Larissa and one
from Karditsa. Both non-Salonikan interviewees spent the German
occupation (after the fall of Italy) with their families in villages in
Thessaly, an area which was largely controlled by the resistance. Lili
S. survived with her daughter on the island of Skopelos and the other
three interviewees stayed in Salonika throughout the occupation. Two
men were exempted from deportations, Daniel B. because he was married to a Christian woman and Rolli A. because his mother was
Christian. Mois B. was one of the few Jews who stayed hidden in
Salonika but unfortunately he did not want to talk about his experience
(he ended the interview very abruptly, saying: 'the more one talks the
more mistakes one makes. This is the end of the discussion. I have told
you what I know', Am15). Matsas estimated that the number of Jews
who stayed in Salonika after the last deportation was about 72, 15 of
whom were married to Christian women (Matsas 1997: 71).

When I met Daniel B. in the Home for the Elderly one of the first
things he told me was: 'My wife is Christian not Jewish, she saved me
at her house when the Germans came, she saved my life. That's why I
have two daughters today and three grandchildren' (Am13). After a

while it emerged that they had lived together and had a child before the Germans came to Salonika. They were not married, most likely because his family would not have approved of their relationship. When he was arrested by the Gestapo his girlfriend went to a village priest and paid for a wedding certificate which said that they had got married ten years earlier. He was subsequently released. As a Jewish husband of a Christian woman he was responsible for her upkeep and thus exempt from deportation. In the interview he expresses extreme gratitude to his (common-law) wife. This relationship enabled him to survive and 'have two daughters and three grandchildren'.

Rolli A.'s father was in the same category as Daniel B., except he was married to a German woman. As the son of a 'mixed marriage' Rolli A. was not affected by the anti-Jewish laws. From January 1942 onwards he worked as a translator (since he was bilingual in German and Greek) for the fire brigade. He is the only interviewee who recalls Salonika immediately after the deportation of all Jews, a Salonika of deserted Jewish neighbourhoods.

> I used to cycle in the whole city. When I came into the former Jewish neighbourhoods I saw that they were totally deserted and totally looted, even bricks were stolen. It looked as if a bomb had hit the place, doors and windows were off their hinges. All the streets were full of cotton because the Christians thought that the Jews had hid money in the mattresses and had therefore cut open all the mattresses. In the city most of the shops, which used to belong to Jews, were closed. Slowly, slowly the shops were given to the Greeks who had come from villages ... They still have the shops today since the Jewish owners did not return. (Am12)

One should add to this description that the Jewish shops, factories and the land of Jewish neighbourhoods were also given to the Greek collaborators such as Papanaoum and Boudrian (Matsas 1997: 71, also mentioned in interviews Af5 and Af9). Rolli A. is also one of the few interviewees who was in Salonika when the Germans retreated in October 1944. He recalls that on the same day the Germans left, the partisans entered the city, occupied all the offices, and arrested the collaborators.[15]

Let us briefly now turn to the interviewees who went to remote villages and islands. Lili S. had come from Larissa and had settled in Salonika in the early 1920s. She became a Greek teacher at the Alliance School, married (and subsequently divorced) and was living with her daughter at her parents' home when the Germans entered Salonika.

Her family is the only family I came across who decided to leave Salonika as early as 1941. They left Salonika for the island of Skopelos, an island they knew well because they had spent many summer holidays there (it is quite close to Larissa). After a year they thought it was safe enough and returned to Salonika. When the ghettoisation order came Lili S.'s family decided that they needed to leave again. This case illustrates well that the decision to leave Salonika or to go into hiding was often a family decision and not the decision of an individual. Since it had by then become more difficult to find a way to escape, Lili S. left the city with her only daughter. A communist friend and colleague of hers organised the escape. He took her to his village, Vassilika, where she stayed with his family for about two months, pretending to be a Greek widow from Skopelos. After two months her friend decided that they (himself, his wife and child, Lili S. and her daughter) should leave for Skopelos. They went to a village at the Chalkidiki peninsula, where they crossed separately on a small boat to the island (the journey lasted 18 hours). Lili S. had plenty of contacts on the island and therefore settled in quite easily. The Italian commander told her that as a Jew she had nothing to fear from the Italians and she was even able to teach at the local school. When the Germans came to the island she became worried because everyone knew that she was Jewish. She recalls one occasion when she was summoned to the German headquarters with 12 young men who all belonged to the resistance:

> We went up the hill, to the school, the German headquarters. An officer ordered us to stop in the yard and I was the first summoned in. There was the commandant, standing behind a desk. On his side an interpreter. I didn't say that I understood German. 'What's your name, you are Jewish, aren't you?' 'Yes', I obliged, I knew even the informant and it was of no use to deny it. 'And why did you chose Skopelos?' 'I came hiding, because I knew the island and I am sure that the people here love us.' 'Don't be sure', he interrupted. 'You know that I can shoot you on the spot, you know that I can send you immediately to Germany, to Poland, don't you?' He walked me out of the room, gave me a chair near the door and ordered: 'Sit here and keep your mouth shut and don't move.' One by one the others were called in for questioning. When we were all out in the yard the commandant spoke: 'You all go home now and behave, because if not ...', he made a sign with his hand to indicate the cutting of our throats. For a few seconds we did not believe it ... I turned back: 'Can I also go?'

'Yes', he answered. I ran out of the school and the minute I stepped out, I collapsed. People helped me go home, where I broke down and was crying the next two days without stopping. (Shaki, unpublished memoir: 46)

She later learnt that the German commander of the neighbouring island of Skiathos was killed by the resistance and that the German commander of Skopelos was probably ordered to retaliate and kill a certain number of villagers. They carried out the retaliation mission one month after the described arrest. One day in August the German guards left for the island of Alonissos and shot 14 men. Lili S. lived in fear until the retreat of the German army. Thereafter she returned to Salonika.

Lili S.'s story shows that the Jews on the islands and in the provinces were much more part of the day-to-day war between the Germans and the partisans than most Salonikan Jews who had been deported. They were helped by ELAS/EAM and they were denounced by the same informers who denounced partisans. On some occasions people thought it was better to admit to being a Jew than a partisan. Viktor V., who comes from Karditsa, recalls that his uncle was captured by the Germans and admitted that he was Jewish when accused of being a communist. Since the director of the municipality had denied that any Jewish families (of the 12 Jewish families) were still in Karditsa, the Germans then wanted him to identify the houses of other Jews. Convinced that the family of Viktor V. had left Karditsa he took them to their house. When the German officer and the director of the municipality arrived at the house they met Viktor V.'s mother. She realised what must have happened and told them that she was only working there. The director of the municipality knew her well and supported her lie. Soon after Viktor V. and his mother left Karditsa (Am28).

Looking at the testimonies of Manthos V. from Larissa and Viktor V. from Karditsa we understand how different their situation was from the situation of the Salonikan Jews. The description of their families' war experiences are very similar. They spent parts of the occupation in their home town of Larissa[16] and Karditsa[17] and parts in the surrounding villages. Both families continued to trade, which meant that they went back and forth from the villages to the towns. It was relatively easy for both families to have access to the villages because of pre-war personal contacts and because of the strong presence of the resistance in Thessaly. Large parts of both testimonies describe how the families managed to survive economically in these difficult times. Both interviews also emphasise the enormous support and help from the villagers. Although both families had Christian names and false papers, the Jewish identity of the two families was mostly known to the villagers. Manthos V. recalls:

> They knew we were Jewish because we dressed differently and we spoke better Greek than they did. The villagers had a terrible accent. We were well appreciated and, like us, the villagers did not like the Germans. My family is still known in some of the villages. (Am27)

Viktor V. is also very outspoken about the help his family received: 'We had many friends. All houses were ready to accept us. We had given all our things to hide at our neighbours … They were all ready to help us' (Am28). Both men are still in contact with some of the people who helped their families during the occupation and express this with a great deal of pride.

The most traumatic situation Manthos V. remembers of the time in the villages is when the Germans rounded up women and children in the retaliation process for a German being shot by the resistance. He was in this group with his mother. They were told that if nobody came forward to name the person who was responsible for killing the German they would all be killed. Although nobody came forward they were later released. This event left a long-lasting impression on Manthos V. ('I will always remember this event and I have told it many times to my children. I think it will stay in my memory until the end of my days', Am27).

The last episode illustrates the point made earlier. The Jews who spent the occupation on islands or in villages were endangered as part of the fighting between the resistance and the Germans. They suffered not as Jews but as Greeks with the other villagers. In the cities this was not the case. In Athens the Jews in hiding needed to completely conceal their Jewish identity, living in constant fear of being denounced as Jews.

CONCLUSION

This period of war and occupation marks a rupture in all the interviewees' life histories. The narratives of survival vary with the different experiences (and the different personalities of the interviewees). It became apparent in the narratives that it was easier to survive for the interviewees who were more Hellenised, that is to say who spoke better Greek and had more contacts in the non-Jewish world. The experiences of survival in Greece are more 'narratable' and can more easily be connected to the contemporary lives of the interviewees than the experiences of survival in the concentration camps. Therefore, all the interviewees who survived in Greece spoke in great detail about this period of their lives, while only a few of the interviewees who were in the concentration camps talked extensively about their experiences.

NOTES

1. The role of Chief Rabbi Koretz, an Ashkenazi Jew, is highly disputed. He co-operated with the German authorities but he also attempted to stop the deportations by contacting the then Greek Prime Minister Ioannis Rallis. Some people hold him responsible for being too co-operative with the Germans and consider him a traitor. This suspicion is fuelled by the fact that Koretz was taken to Vienna for a period of time and then released.
2. Wisliceny states in his affidavit that the percentage of 'able-bodied Jews' who were 'strong enough for labour' was very small among the Greek Jews, who were considered of 'poor quality' (affidavit Dieter Wisliceny).
3. Apparently the factor of language played a role for selecting French and Greek Jews to be sent from Auschwitz in October 1943 to Warsaw to clear the ruins of the ghetto. According to the testimony of Mr Isaac Aruh, Greek and French Jews were specifically taken for this task because they could not communicate with the local population (Novitch 1989: 39).
4. Matsas mentions the trial in which Moshe B. and 12 other Jews were exiled to the island of Makronisos (Matsas 1997: 325).
5. It was quite popular to adopt names from the Greek Independence struggle among the partisans. Viron is the Greek version of Lord Byron who supported the Greek cause in the nineteenth century.
6. Isaac Kabeli's paper on the resistance of Greek Jews was viewed by many Greek Jews with a great deal of suspicion due to the author's services in the Athens *Judenrat*.
7. An uncle of one of the interviewees found a solution to this problem: he survived the war in Salonika pretending he was mute (Af7).
8. In fact Dr Cuenca was arrested by the SS on 18 March and secretly deported to Auschwitz (Novitch 1989: 25).
9. Matsas writes about 'Leon Bourla of Salonika and his four children ... They were Yolanda, Dora, Charles, and Nikos, who was killed just before the war ended' (Matsas 1997: 323). Either there is a mistake about the name or my interviewee had 'Charles' as another *nom de guerre*.
10. Colonel Dimitros Dimitrou remembers David Broudo as somebody who carried out his missions with 'indescribable courage' (cited in Matsas 1997: 321).
11. Due to their high level of literacy Jewish partisans were especially valued (Mazower 1993: 261).
12. According to the Greek consulate in Izmir about 1,100 Jews reached Izmir before February 1944 (Matsas 1997: 106).
13. Angelos Evert, the commander of the Athenian police, and Dimitras Vranopoulos, police chief of Piraeus, actively helped Jews to obtain Christian papers (Matsas 1997: 94).
14. Archbishop Damaskinos gave clear instruction to the priests to baptise the Jews in order

to help them to obtain Christian documents. Matsas estimated that about 135 converted in Athens (Matsas 1997: 93).

15. Some collaborators, such as the above-mentioned Papanaoum and Boudrian, could not be arrested because by the time of the liberation they had fled to Germany. In 1945 they were tried and condemned to death *in absentia* (Matsas 1997: 406).

16. The pre-war Jewish population in Larissa amounted to 1,120, the post-war to 726 (Matsas 1997: 83).

17. The pre-war and post-war Jewish population amounted to 150 Jews (Matsas 1997: 83).

8

Narratives of Return and Reconstruction

This chapter, which describes the return of the Jews to Salonika and the process of reconstruction, is based on the accounts of the interviewees and on research in the archive of the American Joint Distribution Committee (AJDC) in Jerusalem.

HISTORICAL OVERVIEW OF THE POST-WAR YEARS

The Second World War brought a dramatic demographic change to the city of Salonika. By 1945 the Jewish community had shrunk to 2,000 people, of whom some had survived the concentration camps, some had survived in hiding (in Athens or in smaller villages or on islands in the rest of Greece), and some fighting with the *Andartes* (the resistance fighters) in the mountains. The survivors had to adapt their lives to a totally changed environment. Upon their return from the mountains, from other parts of Greece and from the concentration camps, they found themselves in a different city, a Salonika without Jewish schools, without Jewish shops, without synagogues, without Jewish neighbourhoods and, most importantly, without Jewish families.

Statistics which were published in December 1945 illustrate that the vast majority of the 1,908 people who were registered in the community were young and single. Among the 679 women, 362 had never been married and 103 were widows. Among the 1,229 men, 735 had never been married and 260 were widowers (*Evraiko Vima*, no. 5, 21 December 1945). If we also take the membership numbers by age group into consideration, it clearly emerges that not only was the vast majority of the Jewish population not married but many were left without parents, grandparents, uncles and aunts. There were 1,465 people were between the ages of 20 and 50, 124 aged between 50 and 70 and only 17 between 70 and 100. The number of children was also very small, with 116 children under the age of 14 were registered in the community (*Evraiko Vima*, no. 5, 21 December 1945).

The returnees came back to a city where their homes and their

shops had been taken over by Orthodox Greeks, and all Jewish synagogues (except one) and other educational and cultural establishments
had been destroyed by the Germans. The reconstruction of a Jewish
community in Thessaloniki and throughout Greece was particularly
difficult due to the unstable political climate and the severe economic
crisis Greece was undergoing (Liberles 1984: 105). Immediate help was
given by the AJDC (the Joint), the Conference on Jewish Material
Claims Against Germany (CJMCAG), and the Jewish Agency. These
organisations supplied general financial, medical and welfare assistance
and helped to set up community offices. The rehabilitation programme
of the AJDC proceeded in two phases: from 1945 until 1951 the
emphasis was on emergency relief care, while from 1951 onwards the
focus shifted to the revival of Jewish communal organisations (Plaut
1996: 74).

Records show that 4,000 Greek Jews received financial help from
the AJDC (Plaut 1996: 76). Very practical help was given by the AJDC
to young couples. By setting up a dowry fund, the Joint provided wedding rings, kitchenware and kerosene stoves. A census which was prepared by the AJDC in 1946 estimated the number of Jews in Greece to
be around 10,000, most of whom lived in Athens, where they had fled
during the war; thus Athens became the new Jewish centre in Greece
and Salonika declined in importance.

Several waves of Jewish emigration occurred after the war. Many
young Jews who were the only survivors of their families left immediately after the war for Palestine, North America, or South America. By
1947 the AJDC estimates the number of Jews in the whole of Greece
to have been less than about 8,000 (AJDC Archive, Jerusalem, Geneva
Shipment, 125b). The second wave of emigration took place in 1949
after the Civil War. About 2,000 Jews (from the whole of Greece)
moved to Israel between 1945 and 1951. Among them were also a small
number of communist Jews (sentenced to exile on remote Greek
islands) who were allowed to emigrate to Israel on the condition that
they renounced their Greek citizenship in 1951. According to the correspondence between Abraham Recanati (member of the Knesset) and
the AJDC representative in Israel, there were 23 Jews who were
imprisoned under the charge of communism (AJDC Archive,
Jerusalem, Geneva Shipment, 11c). The third wave of emigration took
place between 1951 and 1956 to the United States, triggered by the
amendment of the Displaced Persons Act, which allowed Greek Jews
to go to the United States. By the end of 1956 about 6,000 Jews
remained in Greece.

The post-war years were characterised by the painful process of reclaiming personal and communal property. In places with fewer than 20 families the communal property was transferred to the Central Board of Jewish Communities (KIS) in Athens which was founded in June 1947. Unused synagogues and schools were sold in order to create income. In Thessaloniki the most important transaction of this sort was the sale of the Baron Hirsch Hospital to the Greek government in 1951. In 1946 the Greek government had passed a law (846/46) which stated that the Greek state gave up its right to heirless Jewish property which would be given to a legal body whose aim would be the relief and rehabilitation of surviving Jews. In conjunction with the Royal Decree 29/29-3-49, the Organisation for the Relief and Rehabilitation of the Jews of Greece (OPAIE) was founded to administer all heirless Jewish property. The work of OPAIE was seriously impeded because of the non-implementation of a law regarding the 'Declaration of Death'. In 1959 the Central Board wrote a letter to the Greek prime minister asking for the implementation of a law on 'mass deaths', stating that 'although 13 years have gone by since liberation the Jewish population of this country is still unsettled'. In the view of the Central Board this law would enable OPAIE to take title to its assets and thus enable the organisation to liquidate its property, the proceeds of which could solve the Jewish rehabilitation problem (AJDC Archive, Jerusalem, Geneva Shipment, 11/A).

The late 1940s and 1950s were characterised by an attempt to revive the communities' educational activities. Looking through the files of the AJDC of the 1950s one realises that Jewish education was also an important point on the agenda of the AJDC. The main problem the AJDC representatives perceived at the time was a lack of Jewish teachers and Jewish textbooks (in Greek). Joseph Blum, who was an AJDC representative of the Reconstruction Department, writes in his 'Greece Report' of 1947 the following about the religious and cultural life:

> Today there is nothing left of it [the Jewish spirit] in any of the communities ... It will suffice perhaps to only point out one fact which has been confirmed to me by several quarters, namely that persons of both sexes under 24 years of age know nothing, absolutely nothing, about Judaism ... The lack of teachers who, except for a very small number, have all been annihilated, is mostly responsible for the fact that the moral life of the youth is in a progress of constant deterioration. (AJDC Archive, Jerusalem, Geneva Shipment, 125b)

In Salonika all Jewish children went to two private primary schools, where they were taught Hebrew and religion through a special agreement with the community. The community also purchased a piece of land in Perea and started to run a yearly summer camp (which now takes place in Litohoro).

THE FIRST TO RETURN: MEMORIES OF ESCAPE AND RETURN

The first Jews to return to Salonika were those who were either with the partisans in the mountains or hidden in other parts of Greece. After the German troops withdrew from Athens in December 1944, fighting between EAM/ELAS and the Greek government supported by British forces broke out, which meant that there was no communication or transport to other parts of Greece. This delayed the return of some of the interviewees to Salonika. There were also other delays. One interviewee, who was eager to return to Salonika to be reunited with his father and sister who had survived in villages in the mountains, was picked up on a street in Athens and drafted into the Greek army for two years.

Michael B., who had been a partisan, found himself near Florina when he heard that the Germans had left Salonika. 'We went on a truck on all kinds of dangerous roads. It took us about a week for eighty or ninety kilometres' (Am16). The first thing he did was to go to his old house:

> I started hitting the door of my house but nobody was there. The door was locked. I am glad nobody was there because I was enraged, I was out of my mind. A neighbour across the street whom I knew before the war, saw me and said: 'you come to my home' ... Well, I did not know if he was from the right or the left and I did not care. (Am16)

After a couple of days, the people who stayed in his house agreed to give Michael B. a room. The reclaiming of apartments and shops was, of course, a necessity which many returnees had to go through. Experiences of betrayal and friendship are often linked to this process.

Lili M.'s husband also came to Salonika quite soon after the Germans had left. He went to see his shop, which was entirely empty: there were 'only the walls'. His wife joined him a couple of months later.

On the very first opportunity (after the revolution in Athens) …
I came with my child on a ship from Piraeus overnight. We were
the first refugees who came from Athens. There was a terrific
storm that night, everybody was sick. The next day we landed on
the quay and my husband was there and we met him. That's how
we started all over. It was a terrible time. We were those who had
survived either in the mountains, or in the city, or like me in
Athens and it was a crazy time. People got in touch with the community. (Af8)

The community, which had re-established itself with the return of the
first Jews from hiding and the mountains, became an important point
of orientation and support for the returnees. Through a certificate, for
example, provided by the community, Lili M. was able to claim a room
in her mother's apartment, which had been occupied.

During this time the early returnees waited, of course, for the
return of the deportees, still in hope that their families might return.
The first deportees were met with shock and disbelief:

We were eagerly awaiting for the people to come back. We heard
that a group was coming from the Vardar. They were saying that
everyone had been burnt and that they had exterminated them
all. We, the people who were here, were thinking that the people
were insane, saying crazy things. It was a very hard time. People
started coming between May and July. When I heard that my
brother-in-law had come without my sister Marcella and with
another wife I went crazy. I did not want to meet him. My people were betrayed. It was a very difficult time. I did not want to
live. I did not feel that it was worth being in a city which was like
a ghost. (Af8)

This statement illustrates the complete sense of betrayal and isolation
the speaker felt and still feels. She feels betrayed by the people who
denounced the hiding place of her parents and her sister, betrayed by
the Jewish leadership, especially by Rabbi Koretz who convinced the
Jews to follow the deportation orders to Poland, and betrayed by
Christian friends or even family members who were given property or
belongings which they did not return.

The feelings of betrayal and shock must have been common to all
the Jews who returned to Salonika in 1945. They not only returned to
a 'ghost city', an image frequently used in the interviews to describe a

city empty of Jews and Judaism, but they also returned to a city in which houses and shops were taken over by Christian Orthodox Greeks, who did not know and did not want to know anything about the previous owners (Kounio-Amariglio 2000: 142).

While the group of people who survived in hiding or in the mountains might have experienced betrayal, they had also experienced Christian help and support. One woman, for example, who had been with EAM/ELAS, emphasises how helpful the Christians had been to the Jews, either by bringing them to villages or by buying food for them while they were in hiding in Athens. In this context, she also tells me the story of the beautiful chandelier in the synagogue. The only remaining synagogue during the German occupation was the Monasterioton Synagogue which was used as a warehouse (some interviewees say it was used as a stable). Before leaving Salonika, the Germans wanted to destroy whatever had remained in the synagogue. When one priest realised what was about to happen, he asked the Germans whether he could have the chandelier for his church. The Germans gave it to him, and after the war he returned it to the Jews who put it back in its place, where it is still today (Af5). In the narrative of my interviewee this is an important story because it proves that Greeks and Jews were 'like brothers and sisters'. As in other interviews, the wartime experience (that is, the perception of one's own and other experiences) almost becomes a yardstick for general questions about the relationship between Greeks and Jews in particular. To have survived in hiding or with the partisans would not have been possible without the help of non-Jews and therefore the theme of Greek help, expressed by the attitude of the Church, the partisans, and the ordinary public, is a central theme in all the interviews.

The experience of the deportees returning from the concentration camps was very different from the Jews who had been in the mountains or in hiding. Because of their different experiences they formed two distinct groups in post-war Salonika, which is expressed in the following statement by Michael B., who had been with the partisans: 'They thought they were heroes just because they could stay alive after what the Germans did, but they were not heroes. They were begging for a place to sleep when they came back' (Am16).

Both groups, the partisans and the camp survivors, formed their own political parties in the first elections of the community which took place in the early 1950s. The more socialist party of the partisans was called 'Partida Renaisainssia' (which translates from Ladino as the Renewal Party) and the party of the displaced persons was called

'Partida Los Omiros' (which literally translated means the 'party of the hostages') (Am14).[1] Each party thought that they could better represent the Jewish community, the partisans because they had fought against the enemy, the camp survivors because they had suffered most (Bm37).

The self-perception of the partisans was certainly different from that of the camp survivors. Like the camp survivors, the partisans had been expelled from their homes and separated from their families, but they had also fought for the 'real Greece'. Their participation in the 'heroic struggle' and the bonds which they had formed with their fellow Greek partisans during the war helped them to cope with the extreme sense of uprooting that all the returning Jews experienced. The interviewees who had received medals and formal certificates from the Greek state took a great deal of pride in showing them to me (see Figure 26).

THE DEPORTEES: MEMORIES OF LIBERATION AND RETURN

In many interviews with concentration camp survivors the interviewees mention their camp experience and the death of their family members very early on in the interview, which points to the traumatic nature of their wartime experiences and to the importance attributed to this part of their life history. When asked a general question about his family background, Leon B. answers one minute into the interview:

> The whole family was from Salonika, everybody was born here. I had two sisters, one older, one younger. Unfortunately, they went to the concentration camp. They died there. I also lost my aunt with her three children. A young girl my age, a younger girl and a younger boy. They all died in the concentration camp. I was there for two years. Since I was in Auschwitz I knew that my mother, my father and my older sister went straight away to the crematorium. My younger sister worked as a secretary (*Schreiber*), but later got dysentery and died. I was liberated in 1945 by the Americans. Although I knew that nobody had survived I came back. (Am14)

In contrast to the Jews who spent the entire war time in Greece, the concentration camp survivors who returned on their own knew that they were not likely to find any other surviving family members.

Many young men came back without their parents and wives, as indicated by the number of widowers cited above. 'I have lost everybody, my wife and everyone else. I came back alone. I was all alone. The situation was very difficult' (Am13). Others had hoped that at least one family member had survived and therefore returned:

> After seven days we came to Salonika [from Bulgaria]. We were liberated on 5 May and we came here 25 September. I came back for my brother, but nobody had survived, nobody; 55,000 people had left and 900 came back from the *Lager*. If I had known that I was alone I would not have come back. (Af1)

Palomba A., who made the above statement, had participated in the 'death march' from Auschwitz to Ravensbrück and Malchow, near where she was liberated by the Russians. Where the survivors found themselves at the time of the liberation, who liberated them, and their state of health (many suffered from typhus) determined how and when they could return to Greece. Some came from Munich by plane to Athens, some came by bus from Bulgaria, some came through Yugoslavia. Because Palomba A. had been liberated by the Russians she came through Bulgaria. With 25 other Greek Jews she was taken to Salonika by bus. She recalls the first moment when they crossed the border: 'We all fell to the ground and kissed the Greek soil. That was the first thing we did' (Af1).

Once arrived in Thessaloniki the group was taken to a Greek army base on the outskirts of town where they were registered and examined by the Red Cross. Only after the Greek authorities realised that they were not *Kataskopoi* (spies) was the group allowed to leave. Since most concentration camps survivors did not have a place to go back to, the first place they went to for help and support was the Jewish community.

The most important thing the community helped to provide immediately after the return of the survivors was housing. In many cases, the survivors who had come back together stayed together. One of the places where they were temporarily housed was the former Jewish orphanage building in Faliro. People also received some money (one woman tells me that she received 5,000 Drachmas, another one that she received 2,000 Drachmas), clothing and food (for some time free lunches were provided). Because of the bad economic situation of the community their support was limited. Other help was provided by the AJDC.

After the experience of the concentration camps and the return to a 'ghost' city devoid of many familiar references, the Jewish community appeared to many survivors as a shelter and connection to the old world. One man tells me: 'Since our return from the concentration camp we are protected by the Jewish community of Salonika' (Am21). The notion of the community as a 'protector' reveals the high degree of insecurity which many of the survivors felt (as the result of their uprooting), a feeling which has most likely been passed on to their children. The Jewish community was also transformed after the war into a community of people who had suffered together, as the following quotation shows:

> We, the Jews of 1945 Salonika, came back to a city empty of Jews and Judaism. Our only joy was to encounter another Jew in the streets of Salonika. A surprise, an embrace with Jews we had never met before and an eagerness to enquire and weep together. (Af8)

However, the experience of protection and closeness went sometimes hand in hand with the experience of conflict. Leon B., who immediately after his return from the camp worked in the welfare commission of the community, speaks about these difficulties.

> The community did not have much money. All the people who returned needed support and asked for help. It was very difficult. How could I say to somebody: 'I have no money for you'? It was very difficult. Sometimes people got very angry. But all we wanted was to help each other. (Am14)

Not all concentration camp survivors spent their first months in Salonika in communal housing. One of my interviewees shared a room with his cousin and one was able to return to her old house, which had been requisitioned by her husband. Hella K., her husband and their two children constitute a very rare case because they had all survived the concentration camp. While her husband and son came back through France, she and her daughter went to Yugoslavia from where they crossed the border with difficulty to Greece (due to the beginning of the Civil War). Erika Kounio-Amariglio describes in her book how happy she was to return to her old house.

> Father found our old house on Koromila Street empty and in a bad state, but our beautiful house, even if it was empty, was waiting

for us ... It was our house with its veranda, its garden with white
pebbles facing the sea, the beautiful crystal-clear sea, indigo and
turquoise blue, the sea I had dreamt about in the concentration
camp. (Kounio-Amariglio 2000: 141)

This quotation underlines the extreme importance of two aspects of
'return': the return to 'being all together again', to meeting other family members, and the return to 'our house', to the place where one had
lived before the deportations. Most survivors' return, though, was
characterised by not finding other family members and by not being
able to go back to their pre-war accommodation. This caused a sense
of total uprootedness and discontinuity among most returnees.

Palomba A. did not have anywhere else to go but to the housing
provided by the community. She recalls that she was given 2,000
Drachmas, one bed and one blanket. She also recalls that she could not
bear to be with the other camp survivors because they were going out
a lot, they were singing and dancing, wanting 'to live their freedom'.
She contrasts her own mood with that of her friends: 'I had suffered a
lot, also from the Russians [she means Russian soldiers]. I did not want
anything. My friends were going out and came back at two or three
o'clock in the morning. I did not want to see this' (Af1). She subsequently found a job as a live-in nanny with a Christian family.

WELCOME HOME

The memory of returning home is not only associated with the absence
of family members and friends and the help of the community but also
with the reaction of the Greek Orthodox population towards the
returnees. All the interviewees who discuss this topic do so in the context of reclaiming their belongings. People who did not get back what
they had left behind with their Christian friends talk about this issue
more extensively. In most of these cases, where either shop merchan-
dise, furniture, or other valuables were left in the care of somebody
else, the 'caretakers' claimed that it had been taken by the Germans, by
robbers, or that it had to be sold in order to survive. Lili M. received a
letter from the Christian brother of her sister-in-law just two weeks
after they had left Salonika for the mountains, saying that robbers had
taken the entire contents of her husband's shop (material for clothing)
which was left in his care. After her return to Salonika the mother of
her sister-in-law did not return her piano and the other things she had

left with her. Lili M. has no doubt that her Christian family members took advantage of the situation. 'They became millionaires. This happened within our family. Who knows from how many they have taken?' (Af8). Other memories of an unfriendly welcome by the Greek Orthodox population refer to remarks made by 'surprised' acquaintances and neighbours, such as 'Ah, you survived?' or 'What a pity you were not made into soap' (Af8).[2] When talking about these incidents the interviewees stress that people who made remarks like that had 'taken things from the Jews' (Af8).

Other people were luckier and received back some or all the goods which had been under the protection of a Christian friend or neighbour. For them it was easier to re-establish themselves. Although the high number of people who were registered as unemployed in the community (808, according to *Israelitikon Vima*, 23 November 1945) indicates how dire the economic circumstances for most returnees must have been, most interviewees do not talk extensively about their economic situation. Often they summarise this topic by saying: 'Slowly, slowly everyone managed to get his home and his shop' (Af1). It is not clear which time frame 'slowly, slowly' refers to. The topic which clearly dominates the discourse about the time of the reconstruction (construction of a small minority community) is marriage, for many the second one, and the birth of children.

'A NEW LIFE IS BEGINNING'

The themes discussed above illustrate that personal experiences shape the perception of treason and help during and after the war and therefore narratives may vary considerably. This is not the case when it comes to the topic of post-war weddings and births. There seems to be a consensus among all my interviewees that there 'was a special feeling common to all survivors, to get married and make a family' (Am14) or in other words 'to make a family after the catastrophe and to replace all the people who were lost' (Am14). 'They came back and they were all alone and did not find anybody, so they were saying: "*ade, ela, ela*" (come on) and people started marrying quickly. They wanted to be together' (Af2).

In the personal narratives of the interviewees, getting married and having children marks 'the new beginning' of their lives – a new beginning associated with the day-to-day problems of the post-war years.

It was not an easy time, but at the same time it was a kind of 'a new life is beginning'. Everyone started having babies. There were many weddings and births. I could not have babies, I lost two. I stayed nine months in bed to have my daughter. It was like the heart cracking. Every day you did not know. Would you have some news, would you not have some news? Would you have some fights with the court for the problems with the store that you have to get back, the house that you have to have back? (Af8)

It is important to point out that marriages were both a psychological and economic necessity in the post-war years. Women in particular, who were left without any other family members to support them, were under pressure to marry. In many instances they got married to older men whose wives and children had been killed in the camps. One interviewee describes how she got married: 'His first wife was taken to the *Lager*. When he came back he did not find her and he asked me to marry him. What could I do? I did not have anyone. I did not love him'.

After having left the Christian family she worked for because they had accused her of stealing, marriage seemed to be the only option. She moved in with her future husband, who was 12 years older than her, and became pregnant. Since her husband had been married before the war, they had to wait until they could get married. The Jewish community had decided to let a year pass after the return of the camp survivors before widowers and widows could remarry. Eventually, Palomba A. was married on 2 June 1946 in a group wedding ceremony with nine other couples. Between 1945 and 1947 39 similar group weddings took place (22 in 1946 alone) (see photograph on front cover).[3] These weddings took place in the building of Matanot Laevionim, which houses the Jewish School today and was a charity organisation giving meals to poor pupils until the war.

We were very poor. I did not have money to buy a wedding dress. All the girls wanted to get married and make a family, to go to Israel and to America. Therefore they married us all together. I got married with three of my friends. Five couples on one side, five on the other side, the rabbi (Michael Molho) and some men from the community in the middle. (Af1)

These group weddings embody the post-war situation of many Jews in the post-war years in Salonika. The couples married together because they had no relatives to celebrate with, they had only each other for help and support. The weddings are seen both as a means to cope with the feeling of loss and loneliness, and as a sign of a new beginning. Leon B., for example, who has been the president of the community for many years, recalls that these weddings were something very special to the Jewish community of Salonika. After getting married, many couples shared their accommodation with two or three other couples until each one was able to move to their own flat or decided to emigrate. Out of the ten couples who got married in the above-mentioned ceremony, three emigrated to the United States, four to Israel, and the others stayed in Salonika (Af1).

Marriage was viewed both by individuals and the community (which encouraged marriages) as a step forward, either to facilitate emigration or to facilitate re-establishment in Thessaloniki. I was told that the community gave sewing machines to some couples as a dowry (Af10). Since most group weddings took place in 1946, we can assume that most people who took part in these weddings were camp survivors. If we look at the marriage statistics we also notice that the average male marriage age in 1945, when 45 weddings were registered, was 26 (the female was 23), while in 1946, when 151 weddings were registered, it was 36 (the female was 26). These figures indicate that most men who got married in 1945 were young and had come back from the mountains or from hiding, while men who got married in 1946 were older, had mostly come back from the camps and often married for the second time. The wedding statistics reveal another interesting point, 24 brides who got married in 1946 and 1947 had converted to Judaism. Due to the much smaller number of conversions in the following year and various references to this fact in the interviews, this number suggests that a number of Jewish men got married to Christian women who had helped them hide during the war.

Subsequent to the many weddings in the post-war years was a 'baby boom'. Between 1945 and 1951, 402 children were born, compared to 234 between 1951 and 1971, and 205 between 1971 and 1994. The number of new births was so high that the AJDC funded the re-opening of the Pinchas Clinic as a maternity hospital in order to accommodate the medical needs of all pregnant Jewish women. The doctor in charge was Dr Menashe, a concentration camp survivor who was the first president of the community after the war until he emigrated to the United States in 1952 (Am14). The clinic operated from 1947 to 1954.

EMIGRATION

The decision as to whether to stay or leave was probably one of the most important issues for Jewish couples and individuals in post-war Salonika. When talking about emigration one should also bear in mind that not all camp survivors returned to Salonika; some found their way to France, Israel, or the United States (Am14). Some families were already split up during the war.

The deciding factors which impelled people to move to Israel, the United States, or other parts of Greece (mostly Athens) were again both psychological and economic. The most common answer people gave me when asked about post-war emigration was: 'The ones who had nobody and nothing here, they went to Israel and the United States' (Af3). It certainly seems to have been the case that people who had managed to re-open a family business and reclaim family property were less likely to leave than others. For people who had reclaimed their own or their family businesses, the strongest deterrent against leaving seems to have been the prospect of 'being an employee' somewhere else (Am16).

However, one should not underestimate other factors. Lili M., for example, tells me why she did not want to stay in Salonika:

> I wanted very much to go to America. I was sick from the prob-
> lems with my parents (who had been deported and killed). I got
> very melancholic, I could not help it. I started saying, we should
> go. What are we going to do? To raise our children here? (Af8)

The concern for the children was also voiced by another interviewee who emigrated to the United States in 1956. 'I was well off here. I was well paid. I built my own house. But I asked myself: What kind of a future will my children have in Greece? That's what pushed me' (Am16).

Another factor for the emigration in the 1940es which should not be overlooked was the outbreak of the Civil War. The prospect of being drafted into a war in which one 'did not know whether you are an enemy or a friend' (Am14) after having survived the camps must have also contributed to the decision to emigrate.

TRAITORS

For a handful of people, emigration from Salonika was a way out of a community in which they were no longer accepted. This refers to Jews who were perceived as traitors and collaborators. This is a topic which is not widely discussed in the interviews. One person who is commonly perceived as a traitor, and held responsible for the fact that so many Jews were deported to Poland, is Rabbi Koretz. One interviewee tells me that 'when his wife and son came back to Salonika, nobody talked to them' (Af9). They both emigrated to Israel. The only other references to traitors in the interviews concerns the trial in Salonika in which one Jew was hanged for collaboration with the Germans (Af9), and the treatment of children whose father was believed to have been a traitor. The following episode, recounted by a teacher who worked in the community, highlights some of the dilemmas the Jewish community faced after the war.

> After school, every afternoon we used to meet. I used to play little piano pieces and small songs for the children and we used to have chocolate and beverages which were given to us by the Joint (AJDC). One day a mother comes and tells me: 'Madame S., please send away these two children because their father was a traitor, a real traitor, send them away.' I said: 'No Madame, the children have nothing to do with that. The children are children, beautiful children. Why should I send them away?' The woman replied: 'Do you think so? I had four children and they killed them, why should they live?' She was right. He was a traitor and he saved his children, she wasn't a traitor and she lost four children. 'You are right', I said, 'but I am not going to kill these children. They live here.' (Af10)

Flora M., who is very involved with the women's organisation of the community, remembers that immediately after the war some women were not accepted in the club. These were women who were associated with the community leadership during the war, and who had been deported in the last transport to Bergen-Belsen, where they stayed in a separate camp, called the 'Albala Lager' or *'Lager del Los Privilegiados'* (the camp of the privileged). She adds that 'memories fade when the years pass' (Af7) and therefore the issue got resolved over the years.

'WE WERE ALL TOGETHER'

Analysing all the interviews, there is much more emphasis on unity and the narrowing of social distance within the community than on divisions and conflict. This does not mean that the post-war community was not riven by conflicts, disputes, and suspicion. One of the interviewees who emigrated to the United States remembers very clearly that there were many polemics and much fighting between community members and 'that every Jew was a headache for the community' (Am16). Reading the post-war AJDC correspondence we find a lot of material on issues of conflict, although more relates to the whole Jewish community of Greece than to internal fights in each community. The biggest area of conflict seems to have been the question of who should benefit from the communal assets of Salonika and what responsibility the Salonikan community had towards the whole Jewish community of Greece, bearing in mind that many Salonikan Jews settled in Athens after the war (see for example AJDC Archive, Jerusalem, Geneva Shipment, 96a).

We need to bear in mind that individual memory is affected by a) the position of the speaker (was and is he or she politically active in the community?), b) by present experience (at the time of the interview) and perception (of 'community', for example), and c) by the wish to focus on the 'positive' aspects of reconstruction rather than on the 'negative' ones. There is thus little mention in the interviews of the impossibility of reaching decisions in the community and of 'divergent personal interests', which is mentioned in the AJDC files (AJDC Archive, Jerusalem, Geneva Shipment, 64a).

The community undoubtedly played a central role in helping individuals to re-establish themselves. Most community members were involved in the life of the community in one way or other, either in leadership functions, as members of a committee, or as visitors and participants in social and religious communal gatherings. Very soon after the return of the camp survivors the community held elections to constitute the Community Assembly (50 people) and to form a Community Council (9 people) (Jewish Community of Thessaloniki 1978: 39). The fact that there were different parties (Zionist, Partisan/Socialists, and the party of the Displaced Persons) is not seen as a sign of division but as a sign of vitality and survival: 'This small community which had just escaped death showed its vitality. All the parties worked for the same aim, the re-establishment of the Jews. They were all concerned with the return of property and education' (Am14).

The 'reconstruction' of the reconstruction years, for example with regard to the different parties, does not necessarily reflect the experience of party politics at the time, in which many people probably would have liked a more unified community. The stress on community unity on the political level is mirrored by the stress on unity on the social level:

> Here, after the war, we were all one. We did not have different classes. How many were we? When we have a wedding, for example, everybody was invited … To the synagogue everybody is invited; when you have a child, when you have a *Brith Milah* or a Bar Mitzvah everybody is invited. (Af2)[4]

The unity or the irrelevance of social boundaries among the few Jews in post-war Salonika is certainly an important topic in all narratives about the post-war years, although it is presented in different lights in the different interviews. Some people see it as a positive phenomenon, some view it with a high degree of embitterment. Leon B. talks about this issue as follows:

> At that time, nobody thought about being rich or poor. The main thing was to be alive, and to enjoy this life. That was the most important thing. At that time we enjoyed life more than today. Today one is rich, one is poor, one is this or that, but at that time we were all together. (Am14)

In contrast to this positive memory Lili M. says: 'We are nobody now. We don't belong to any class. You cannot classify among 800 people' (Af8).

These kinds of statements are clearly linked to personal biographies and personal coping strategies. Leon B. was actively involved in the reconstruction of the community while Lili M. emigrated with her husband and two children to the United States. It seems that people who were actively involved in the reconstruction of the community, tend to stress the notion of social unity in post-war Salonika more than others. This notion of social unity is not only viewed differently by some interviewees, but is also not shared by everyone. One interviewee tells me: 'The rich don't speak with the poor. We are not united. The rich are rich, the middle class are middle class. They never spoke to each other'.

This view was certainly not the majority view of most interviewees, but it might indicate that there are different class perceptions of class distinctions. Class distinctions, mainly defined in terms of income and family background, look different from the perspective of Palomba A., who had to work hard after the war. For her it is clear that the 'rich marry the rich and the middle class, the middle class' (Af1). She includes herself in the latter. In this statement she refers clearly to the more recent situation, but it is interesting that she extends the time period 'after the war' (which I had used in my question) to today.

Class differences among community members after the war were thus not totally eradicated, but social boundaries were definitely blurred and social distance certainly reduced. As one interviewee puts it: 'People belong to different classes but since the Holocaust was very, very recent everything else came second. Jews felt first as Jews and then as belonging to different classes' (Bm37).

The stress on cohesion and unity expressed itself very clearly when it came to the education of the children. With the help of the Central British Relief Fund a Children's Centre was created in Salonika (through the efforts of the Jewish Committee for Relief Abroad (JCRA) field-worker Miss Ann Molho). The community also decided to send all Jewish children to two private Greek primary schools, and arrangements were made with the schools to allow external teachers to come to the school and teach Jewish religion and Hebrew to the children. The community further set up a summer camp (in Perea) for the children in order to 'prevent assimilation and give them a good Jewish education' (Am14).

What is perceived among the older generation as the breakdown of class boundaries and the feeling of togetherness as a result of the catastrophic destruction of the community is perceived in a much more positive light in terms of closeness by the generation which grew up after the war.

GROWING UP AFTER THE WAR

The generation of children who grew up in Salonika after the war were raised as members of a small minority. In contrast to their parents, they did not know what it was like before the war:

> For my father Salonika and the community is something else, a mixture of before the war and after the war. For me it is only what I saw after the war … I know we are only a very small minority. My father did not grow up in a city in which there was a Jewish minority. This is a very big difference. (Af30)

The children who grew up after the war can be divided in two groups: the very few children who had survived the war and the other children who were born in the post-war 'baby boom'. Although these groups differ considerably in size, they describe their socialisation in a very similar way, emphasising the close bond which existed between the children.

Among my interviewees, two were born during the war, both in Athens. Leon A. survived in hiding with his mother while his father was with the partisans in the mountains, and Viktoria B. survived with a Christian couple who pretended to be her parents. Leon A. came back to Thessaloniki with his parents in 1954. Like Viktoria B., whose mother had survived Auschwitz and settled in Salonika in 1947, he regularly went to the community club and the *Kataskinosi* (sometimes also referred to in Hebrew as the *Keitana*), the yearly summer camp for the children. Both remember the activities related to the club and the summer camp in a very positive way. They stress that they felt 'like brothers and sisters', that the club and the *Kataskinosi* was 'like a family' and like a 'second home'. 'I was very happy when I stayed there with all the children. There were about 12 children of my age who had survived. We were like brothers and sisters' (Af30).

The feeling of family is associated with notions of closeness and similarity. 'I really feel nostalgic about the friends I met in the *Kataskinosi* because of one thing. It was like family to me. My name was not strange to them. I was among people that were called Florentin or Coen, names which were similar to mine' (Am29).

The club and the *Kataskinosi* provided the children with a kind of family framework which many did not have because of the Holocaust. For the children the communal atmosphere was perceived in contrast to the atmosphere at home. Leon A. describes how things were at his home:

> I remember my mother crying a lot. I remember very much the feeling of loss we had in the house and I remember my feeling of not being able to compete with the other children because I did not have a grandmother, a grandfather, an uncle, an aunt, a nephew, a niece, a cousin. (Am29)

For Viktoria B., who did not attend the same school as the other Jewish children, the small room in the community centre and the summer camp were not only an escape from the melancholic atmosphere at home but also from the anti-Semitic atmosphere at school, where the other girls used to call her *Evrea* (Jewess).

Apart from the relationship with the other children, most interviewees also remember very vividly the Israeli teachers (*morim*) who were
brought from Israel (with the help of the Jewish Agency) to work with
the children. Learning Hebrew songs and Israeli dances enhanced the
feeling of togetherness among the children (Am29). Because of this
socialisation and personal ties to Salonikans who had emigrated to
Israel, Israel became an important source of identification for the post-
war generation. The community also encouraged young people to
study in Israel, which many (especially the boys) did.

In contrast to the small group of children who survived the war, the
'baby boom' generation constituted 'a rather strong group of Jewish
boys and girls, who did not feel as a minority at all' (Bm37). As a consequence of the community's policy to send the Jewish children to two
schools, there were classes in which 50 per cent of the children were
Jewish. This changed when the children went to high school. 'It was
like a very nice family at elementary school, you felt secure. When I
went to high school I was very shocked at the beginning. I had lost
many of the privileges I had as a protected child in the elementary
school' (Bf33).

This statement illustrates the sense of insecurity some of the second-
generation children must have felt which went hand in hand with the
notion of safety and protection among Jews and a community which
was there to protect its members. The link to the historical experience
of their parents is obvious. One informant recalls what she felt like as
a young girl: 'I felt different. If we are Greeks, why did Greece not
protect the Jews during the Holocaust? Why did nobody protect
them?' (Bf34).

Based on the sample of my interviews it seems that gender needs to
be looked at in this context. There is clearly more stress on vulnerability and insecurity among the women I interviewed than among the
men. Although the men stress the closeness and life-long importance
of friendships among the Jewish children, they also recall that they
rebelled against the 'low-profile mentality' of their parents. They did
not want to 'keep quiet' about their Jewishness, they did not identify
with 'the Jews from the camps, who thought that we cannot sing very
loud or dance very openly'. Instead they wanted to be 'proud Jews'
who 'fight back' (Am29). This element of rebellion is completely missing in the interviews with the women of that generation, and one gets
the impression that the girls developed a more distinct sense of responsibility towards their survivor parents, concerning, for example, the
possibility of moving somewhere else or the choice of spouse.

> A lot of my friends went to Israel (to study). I also wanted to go but my father would not let me because he had already lost one girl in the concentration camp. He did not want to lose me as well. When he said something like this, there was no more question about going. (Bf33)

The sense of duty to their parents as Holocaust survivors is very striking in the reply of a woman in her forties when asked about mixed marriages: 'I felt that I did not have the right to marry a Christian guy because my father went through the Holocaust. It was my feeling that I could not do this to my father who was a believing Jew and has been in a concentration camp' (Bf33).

The most plausible explanation for the development of these kinds of gendered post-war Jewish identities is that, on the whole, the girls grew up more protected than the boys and that there was more pressure on them to marry at a young age within the community. Most women whom I interviewed in this generation talk about the effect of the Holocaust on their upbringing. They attribute the fact that their parents sent them to good schools and wanted to give them a good education to their parents' wartime experiences: 'They prepared us to survive, as if there would be another Holocaust. My father always said: "I survived because I knew some languages." That's why he wanted to teach us foreign languages' (Bf34).

Some people of the second generation describe their parents' feeling of insecurity, others express it themselves. One interviewee remembers that his parents, who belonged to an old Salonikan family, did not take it for granted after the war 'that they as Jews will be here tomorrow' (Bm38). Feelings of contingency and transience do not only relate to place but also to people. The following description of the relationship between the interviewee and her Christian friends illustrates this notion.

> Yes, I live here, I like living here. I have many friends here, but I don't know if there will be another Holocaust if these friends will be friends then ... We are friends now, yes of course, because we have our position, our prestige and all these things. They have to learn from me, I have to learn from them, we exchange ideas and all that, but I don't know if they will be friends in difficult and hard times. (Bf34)

CONCLUSION

The process of return and reconstruction needs to be viewed in the light of the most profound effect of the war on the surviving Jews: the experience of uprooting and dislocation. The war had taken away 'home' from most Jews, both in a narrow and broader sense. Their 'home' was not there any more because of the post-war presence in which families were absent and houses often occupied by strangers; their 'hometown' was also no longer there because of the destruction of most Jewish references to the past, of which the biggest was the destruction of the old Jewish cemetery. After the Jewish cemetery had been destroyed in 1942, Jewish tombstones were scattered throughout the city, having been used as building material for houses, walls, stairs, courtyards and churches. One interviewee talks about visiting a house in which the whole staircase was built of Jewish tombstones; on each stair you could read another Jewish name (Af9). After the war the new university was built on the site of the former cemetery.

These radical changes in the lives of individual Jews and in the landscape of the city brought about a new meaning of Jewish community and Jewish identity in post-war Salonika. The war transformed a heterogeneous and settled population group (who had developed a very strong notion of their Salonikan identity) into a homogeneous, vulnerable, and uprooted minority group. Bereft of a real home, the community became a substitute home, in which relationships between its members were perceived in terms of an extended family framework, providing support, help, friendship and a link to the past. Because of the traumatic experience of the Holocaust and the subsequent experience of dislocation, the community and contact with other Jews provided a 'safe haven' for the older generation and an 'intimate place to socialise' for the younger generation. The concepts of 'being together' or *entre mosotros* (which means 'among ourselves' in Ladino) are distinct expressions of the newly formed post-war minority identity.

As Schneider has shown, ethnic and religious identities are often formulated in terms of symbolic kinship because kinship provides a model of relatedness based on a 'natural connection' and a 'shared essence' (Schneider 1968). In the case of the Jewish community in post-war Salonika, the 'natural connection' between Jews was the shared historical experience, the shared memory of a very different pre-war Salonika, and the shared absence of family. But the family metaphor of community expresses more than the function of a substitute family of community, it also describes the 'privatisation' and marginalisation of the post-war Jewish community. The community became marginal in terms of numbers but more importantly in terms of the public memory of the city. Formulated in the discourse of the Greek nation-state, history was looked at through the looking glass of historical continuity and homogeneity and not through that of multi-culturalism and heterogeneity, which meant that the history of the Jews in Salonika was largely ignored.

In terms of a communal survival strategy this 'privatisation' was reflected in the maintenance of a very low public profile. I suggest that this 'low-profile identity' is an expression of powerlessness and a response to the war and post-war experience, as illustrated in the following quotation: 'We were not like the pre-war Salonikans who had their own MPs and who could influence the local mayor. We knew there was very little we could do. We will always run the risk of provoking, without wanting it' (Bm37).

In conclusion, we can state that the two most important Jewish adaptation strategies in post-war Thessaloniki were firstly, on the individual level, the re-creation of families and secondly, on the communal level, the creation of a community with a low public profile and a high private profile, providing protection, support, help, and a family framework for its members in the changed, non-Jewish environment.

The notion of the Jewish community as family is still relevant today. A young woman describes the relationship to other Jews of the same generation by saying: 'We had no choice. So we were always together as a family' (Cf47). In contrast to their parents or grandparents, many of the younger generation talk about this aspect of community in the context of constraint and pressure. They want a more open community and they are also able to voice their discomfort about the omission of Jews from the public memory more easily: 'We cannot accept the memory loss of our countrymen and we cannot accept that the Jewish presence in our town is ignored, just like that' (Bm37).

The process of the reconstruction of the community started immediately after the war. But the process of the reconstruction of Jewish memory has only recently begun.

NOTES

1. The concentration camp survivors refer to themselves as *omiros* (hostages) who were in *omiria* (taken hostage) in the *stratopedo* (the concentration camp).
2. Kokot writes that the Asia Minor refugees in Salonika whom she researched still sometimes jokingly refer to Jews 'who were made into soap' (*tous kanane sapounaki*) when they speak about the war (Kokot 1995: 197).
3. All the figures to do with marriages are based on my own research in the community archive.
4. *Brith Milah* is the Jewish circumcision ceremony.

9

Identities and Boundaries

Having described and analysed memories of the past in the previous chapters, this chapter will look at articulations of identities and boundaries. It will examine what 'being Jewish' means for the interviewees and what other aspects of identity emerge from their narratives (local, class and gender aspects of their identities).

FROM 'BEING' TO 'FEELING' JEWISH

As stated at the beginning of this study, it is suggested that there is a two-way relationship between memory and identity. On the one hand, memories of the past shape group and individual identities, on the other, present identities determine what we choose to remember or to forget, or, as Henry Lustiger-Thaler calls it, what we choose to 'remember forgetfully' (Lustiger-Thaler 1996: 190). In Antze's terms, 'memories are produced out of experience and, in turn reshape it' (Antze and Lambek 1996: xii). In this process memory and identity are intrinsically linked. Memory serves as 'the phenomenological ground of identity (as when we know implicitly who we are and the circumstances which have made us so) and the means for explicit identity construction (as when we search our memories in order to understand ourselves)' (Antze and Lambek 1996: xvi). Categories of identity, such as gender, class, and ethnicity, are reflected in memories (in content and form) and simultaneously memories reaffirm these very identities. In practice these two processes are intertwined but the distinguishing feature is the element of choice. It is inevitable that class, gender, ethnicity and other social factors shape experiences and the memories of these experiences among individuals and groups, but it is a matter of choice which of these experiences (and in which way) individuals and groups refer to when they present narratives of themselves. Within public and private contexts narratives vary.

As Doumanis has shown in his study of memory of the Italian occupation on the Dodecanese islands, there is a wide gap between official written memory and oral memory. Local written representations of this period emphasise, as does Greek historiography in general, the oppression of the Italian occupation and the manifestations of local resistance (Doumanis 1997: 3). In the interviews people talk about their good relationship with the Italians, about friendships and mixed marriages, topics which do not find any mention in the written sources. They are absent from written and more public narratives because these themes have implications for the reputation of the community. Due to the dominance of 'patriotic history', 'good relations' between the locals and the Italians could be misconstrued as non-patriotic behaviour (Doumanis 1997: 60). Since the islanders want to present themselves as 'good Greek citizens' they select and maintain memories in public which reaffirm their collective self-image. It is their present identity which shapes their 'memory management' (Loizos 1999). In the analysis of the interviews, Doumanis points out that the more educated interviewees always presented the past more in terms of oppression and resistance than the others. The factor of education, as an indicator of social class, is thus pertinent for the articulation of memory. Doumanis' study illustrates very well how conceptualisations of identity shape conceptualisations of memory, as he shows that as 'Greeks' the interviewees want to stress certain aspects of the past, common to all Greeks and in line with the official memory. At the same time their narratives reveal a great deal about their particular experience as Dodecanese islanders. These memories do not fit in with overall Greek historiography. A similar theme among my interviewees was the theme of 'the good relationship between the Jews and the Greeks'. When looking more closely at the narratives, we find counter-memories which complement or contradict these general statements. In Doumanis' study it becomes very clear that memory of the past is conceived as an indicator of identity and thus its articulation, as with articulation of identity, is context dependent. The perceived boundaries between the narrator and the listener/audience are signifnicant. The more distance that lies between them, the more the narrator is concerned with portraying a past which 'fits' with the identity he or she wants to convey.

Particularly in the Greek context the notion of a 'continuing history' is closely linked to a Greek national identity, expressed on the official and personal levels. In his ethnography of Kalimnos, Sutton describes how 'history' is used as a narrative model to understand the present and how individuals perceive a direct link between themselves and ancient history (Sutton 1998: 140, 143). One example of this notion of 'history', perceived as something personal through which the individual is linked by kinship, was evident in my own fieldwork at the time of the 'Macedonia conflict'. When I visited Pella and Vergina, where the tombs of Phillip II were found, the guide told us:

> I am Macedonian. Please let me invite you to the house of my great-grandfather. Welcome to this house after 2,400 years. This is the baptism of Macedonian culture. This is our history and our identity.

The connection Frederick Barth made between ethnicity and boundaries (Barth 1969) can also be applied to memories and boundaries. Memory has different functions in different contexts and in 'in-group' and 'out-group' situations, and memory is important in defining these contexts. The function of memory varies according to the 'boundary context'. Memory as an 'identity marker' is of a different nature when assumed to be shared memory within a group or when assumed not to be shared and presented to an 'outsider'. In order therefore to understand fully the function of memories we need to look at the boundaries in which they are formulated and the extent to which memory plays a role in defining notions of 'insiderness' and 'outsiderness'. Perceived boundaries are crucial to the understanding of memory because the boundary context shapes memory content and function while the boundary narrative reflects 'the other stuff' which leaves a strong imprint on memory (class background, gender, religious orientation, and so on).

As we know from ethnographic studies of Greece (see Chapter 1), notions of 'us' and 'them' are extremely important and can be found in different layers of society (see Hirschon 1998, Kokot 1995, Sutton 1998), linked to segmented notions of 'insiderness' and 'outsiderness': the family versus other families, the neighbourhood versus other neighbourhoods, the village versus other villages, Asia Minor refugees (*Mikrasiates*) versus local Greeks (*Ndopi* or *Palioellines*), and, at the highest level, the Greek nation (*Elliniko ethnos*) versus other nations.

The following section will look more closely at notions of 'insiderness' and 'outsiderness', and at the boundaries and identities which form the context in which memory of the past, discussed in the previous chapters, is articulated, negotiated and adapted. While focusing on the perceived boundaries of the interviewees, we need not forget that identities and boundaries are not only created by individual choice (ascription) but also as a response to the understanding and perception of these boundaries by the larger society (prescription).

Since identities are relational and context dependent, different identities become more or less relevant in different situations. It is therefore not surprising that Jewish identity, or identities, have changed considerably within the twentieth century, in which Salonika became a city of a nation-state and the Jewish population was reduced to a tiny minority. To borrow a phrase from Anny Bakalian, we can speak of a process which involved a change from 'being to feeling Jewish' (Bakalian 1993). 'Being Jewish' connotes a particular lifestyle in a multicultural society with clearly defined ethnic groups, based in varying degrees on religion and language, while 'feeling Jewish' connotes a group attachment in a relatively homogenous nation-state, less clearly defined by 'cultural differences'.[1]

The process of change undergone by the Salonikan Jews can be compared to the 'immigrant experience' of the first, second and third generations of migrants. Although the Salonikan Jews did not migrate, society around them changed to such a considerable degree that the younger generations needed to acquire language and cultural skills 'foreign' to their grandparents. The older generation's identity is still very much based on the reality of pre-war Salonika.

GREEK JEWS AND (CHRISTIAN) GREEKS

The older generation was born at a time when the terms 'Jews' and 'Greeks' referred clearly to two different ethnic groups, distinguished by religion and language. This had historical reasons: as subjects of the Ottoman Empire the Greeks and the Jews were for centuries organised in the *millet* system, which separated them as different ethno-religious groups and certainly accentuated separate cultural identities. When Salonika became part of the Greek state in 1912 the Jews were regarded as a non-Greek minority whose confidence needed to be won by the new state. Following the settlement of about 100,000 Asia Minor refugees the Greek state set out to Hellenise the city of Salonika and its Jewish population (like the rest of Macedonia). The three biggest points of tension between the Jewish community and the Greek state in the inter-war period were:

1) the question of whether Jews should vote in separate ballots (the Jewish community was opposed to this procedure);
2) the introduction of compulsory Greek lessons in non-Greek schools and the introduction of a law which required Greek subjects to attend non-foreign primary schools; and

3) the efforts by the Greek municipality to relocate the old Jewish cemetery.

The second point is of utmost relevance. As Gellner, Anderson and other scholars of nationalism have pointed out, standardised language, disseminated by the introduction of print capitalism (Anderson 1991) and the introduction of state education (Gellner 1983), is extremely important in the building of the nation-state. This was understood by the Greek state which pressed the issue of Greek language instruction in schools and thereby hoped to change the language orientation of the Jews.[2]

Looking at the articulations of individual identities supports this concern with language. Language seems an important factor in the perception of difference and boundaries between Jews and Greeks. A factor which is intertwined with language is social contact, that is, the lack of social contact. Let us look at two statements in which the speakers contrast their own Jewish identity with the Greek identity of the next generation or a spouse. When discussing her Jewish identity Jean L. tells me:

> I talk only about people my age, the young ones are Greek. Today, for example, there was another mixed marriage ... I feel Jewish because our parents did not feel Greek. For the young ones it is different because they go to Greek schools and they have Greek friends. (Af6)

Palomba A. describes her life after the war and characterises her husband as follows:

> For him everything was the dance and the *Bouzouki*. He felt Greek. He always spoke Greek. He wanted to live a Greek life. We never went to the synagogue ... He felt Greek because as a small child he grew up with Greeks. When he was young he lived in a Greek neighbourhood, they were all Greek. (Af1)

Palomba A. portrays her own identity in opposition to her husband's. She told her children that 'we are not Greek, we are Jewish'. In doing so she tried to 'give to her children what her father gave to her' (Af1).

Both Jean L. and Palomba A. articulate their identity in opposition to other identities, the identity of 'the young ones' or the identity of a spouse. 'Being Greek' and 'being Jewish' are characterised as juxtaposed identities. Both women stress similar identity 'markers': language, facilitated by education, and social contact. Palomba A. adds the religious

factor, 'never going to the synagogue' is part of the 'Greek life'. It is interesting that 'Greek life' in this context is negatively defined, something
which I found runs through most interviews. The characterising traits of
a 'Greek life' are the opposites to what is considered a 'Jewish life': not
speaking Judeo-Spanish or any foreign languages, mixing with Greeks,
and not going to the synagogue. Some of the interviewees recall that
their parents had called Greeks *'Grecos engreshado'*, which referred to the
'oily food' Greeks ate compared to the less oily Sephardi cuisine.[3] In a
teasing way this phrase was also used for Jews from the south of Greece
who did not speak Judeo-Spanish and whose cooking was more 'Greek'.
Flora M. recalls: 'I had an aunt from Volos and my father would call her
Greco Engreschada, Emily *Greco Engreschada*. They always told her: "Learn
Ladino, why are you speaking like that? Have you still not learnt how to
speak Ladino?"' (Af7). The 'yardstick' of identity from this perspective
is the perceived cultural distance. Since 'being Jewish' is the primary
identity marker for the interviewees of this generation, other identities
are defined in relation to this primary identity.

Although a Jew can thus lead a more or less 'Jewish' and more or
less 'Greek' life, the boundaries between Greeks and Jews remain
untransgressable. Many women believe that while you can outwardly
convert to Judaism or to Orthodoxy you will always remain what you
were born, Greek or Jewish.

> A Jew cannot become a Greek, nor can a Greek become a Jew.
> The heart remains always Greek when somebody is Greek, and
> the heart of a Jew is always Jewish. (Af1)

> There are some Christian women who converted to Judaism but
> they did not become Jewish. Even after they converted you can
> see them go to church. I will tell you, if you are born and raised
> with a certain religion, how can you from one moment to the
> other change this religion? It is very difficult. (Af9)

Jean L. tells me about a friend's daughter who converted to
Christianity and is now divorced. She used to meet her in the synagogue on Yom Kippur (day of atonement). For Jean L. this is a proof
that it is impossible to become either Jewish or Greek.

> If you go on Kippur[4] to the synagogue early in the morning you
> will find all the Jews who got married to Greeks. Inside they
> remain Jewish. It is the same the other way round. You think that

a Greek who marries a Jew becomes Jewish? It is impossible. (Af6)

It is very interesting that both women use images of the body to describe the core of Jewish or Greek identity, perceived as 'inside' or 'in the heart'. Relating this to what was said before about the 'Jewish' and 'Greek' lifestyles, a concept emerges in which you can have only one 'core' inside identity (transmitted in the home by the family) but other 'outside' identities (transmitted by the school and other social interactions). Palomba A. and Jean L. do not perceive of themselves as Greek because they did not go to a Greek school nor did they have much social contact with Greeks. This was the case for many Salonikan Jews, at both ends of the class spectrum, which Palomba A. and Jean L. represent. Their different Jewish identities were also language-oriented: while the working class was Judeo-Spanish speaking and received a Jewish education, either at the Talmud Thora School or Alliance Israelite Universelle, the upper classes went to French or Italian secular schools and often sent their sons to study abroad (to France or Italy). Many interviewees testify that they had no relations with Greeks in the pre-war period. Lili M., who went to the American School, tells me about her contact with Greek girls which 'never developed into dear friendships. It did not happen on purpose, we just did not have the opportunities and we belonged to other worlds' (Af8). The two worlds were marked by language difference. Asked about the relation between Jews and Greeks, Jean L. answers: 'Before the war we were not so close because we could not speak Greek' (Af6). Gender played a role in inter-ethnic contact. It was often the men who were more likely to have contacts with Greeks in the public realm. The acquisition of a Greek identity was therefore more accessible to men than to women of that generation (see below).

Many interviewees acknowledge a change when 'the younger generation started going to Greek primary schools' (Af8). Of this generation, however, many did not survive the war because they were too young when they arrived in Auschwitz to be taken for labour.

Returning to the notion of an 'inside' and 'outside' identity, the boundaries between Jews and Greeks were so clear-cut because there was an overlap between private and public identities. 'Being Jewish' was something transmitted through family but determined all aspects of social life: where one lived, which school one went to, which youth clubs one frequented, and whom one married. This legacy of the Ottoman *millet* system was reinforced by the fact that the Jews constituted the majority of the city population until 1923. The specific Jewish Salonikan identity was thus very different from Jewish identities in *Palia Ellada* and other parts of Greece, where Jews were in a minority position and thus had more contact with Greeks and were in better command of the Greek language. For Salonikan Jews, other Jews were considered more 'Greek' than themselves. This did not necessarily fit the self-image of the non-Salonikan Jews who were often more religious than the Salonikan Jews and adhered to a more 'Jewish' lifestyle than their urban co-religionists. One can argue that language, that is to say the knowledge of Judeo-Spanish, is often used as the marker of Jewish identity in Salonika because it encompassed all the other differences of the very diverse urban Jewish population and set them apart from the rest of the population.[5] When Flora M. tells me about her uncle who survived the war in hiding in Salonika pretending he was mute, she comments: 'He would not speak. Because if he said only "good morning" it would have been obvious that he was completely Jewish [because of his accent].' At another point in the interview she talks about her mother's generation (born around 1910) who continued to speak French and Ladino in post-war Salonika:

> All my relatives used to speak Ladino at home. It is because of the children that things changed and my mother learnt some Greek. But when she died she still did not know how to speak Greek properly. She was proud of the languages she knew and she did not really want to learn Greek. (Af7)

It is not surprising that Flora M.'s mother had mostly Jewish friends who could speak the 'same language'. Both the older and younger generation acknowledges that many people of the older generation lived in post-war Salonika very much '*entre mosotros*' (among ourselves). The younger ones recall another expression they heard when they grew up: *Los Musestros* (ours) (as opposed to *Los Grecos*, the Greeks). They associate this concept and the Ladino-accented Greek with their grandparents ('we tease our grandfather about the way he speaks Greek', Cf47). The identity of the older generation is founded on the socio-political situation of the pre-war time, and in the history of each family. Although the socio-political situation has changed dramatically, these identities continue to be of real significance for the older generation.

SALONIKANS AND OTHERS

The Jewish Home for the Elderly in Salonika is the only one in the whole of Greece. Because of this, it represents a microcosm of Jews from all over Greece. On each floor there are individual rooms and one common room where people can meet, talk and play cards. The floor on which Jean L. lived was quite exceptional because she had placed some furniture and pictures outside her room and had thus created a sort of 'living room' in the hallway. Her opposite neighbour was Moshe B. and when I visited the Home I could often see them chatting in Jean L.'s 'living room'. In the interview she tells me why she feels quite isolated:

> There are many nouveau riches here and people from *Palia Elada*. Only Moshe B. and myself are from Salonika. What can I talk about with the old people from Trikkala? And there are people from Salonika who are not from 'good families'. That does not mean that they are not good people, it is just that there are diverse categories of people, do not misunderstand me, they are nice but ... let's say for example I want to talk to a lady friend of mine, normally we talk about what she has read and what I have read. But what is there to talk about here? I can not read Greek well. (Af6)

She points out that she is not categorising people according to their economic status but according to their family background and education:

> It is not a question of the *niveau d'argent*, it is a question of the *niveau de famille*. Perhaps they are rich or less rich, they might have lost the money during the war ... I do not have much money but I refer to education and 'family'. Here in Salonika there were very well-known families. (Af6)

Listening to Jean L. one gets an idea of the distinct upper-class Salonikan identity based on family background (of the pre-war time) and education (which went along with the status of each family). The educated ladies are very aware of their difference from the 'other' Jews, both from the provinces and from Athens. Rebecca V., another resident of the *Yerokomiou*, tells me: 'There is a difference. The ones from Athens were more Greek ... In Athens everything was Greek' (Af11).

However, the sense of a distinct 'Salonikan' identity is not restricted to people whose families belonged to the upper classes. Others also voice discomfort about the 'newcomers' who came to Salonika after the war: 'Although we were born here in Salonika, and our parents and grandparents were born here, we have nothing. Others who came from Trikkala, Veria and other places have become very rich. That makes me very sad'.

The feeling of superiority of urban Salonikans towards 'the villagers' is interestingly paralleled among the Asia Minor refugees who
considered the local Greeks as less urban and civilised than themselves
(Kokot 1995: 158 and Hirshon 98: 33).

The 'newcomers' are well aware of the opinions of the Salonikans
and are critical of the snobbery of the Salonikan Jews. An interviewee
who moved to Salonika in the 1960s tells me:

> They call this kind of person [a Jew who is not from Salonika]
> *forastero*,[6] it means somebody who was not born in Salonika but
> only came to live here, since the Jews from Salonika never liked
> the Jews who were not born in Salonika. I was also regarded as a
> stranger, a *forastero* … It was a certain mentality. That's why they
> did not know how to speak Greek. They did not want to speak
> Greek. They did not have Christian Greek friends and they did
> not want to have Christian Greek friends.

The interviewee uses the word 'Christian Greeks' which indicates that
he sees himself as 'Jewish Greek'. He comes from a small town south
of Salonika and his family spoke Greek at home. In a context in which
there was more social interaction between Jews and Greeks, the
boundaries were not as sharp as in Salonika and thus the Jews were
more Hellenised. This is also true of Jews from the provinces who
moved to Salonika before the war and who sent their children to Greek
schools and had more contact with Greeks than the average Salonikan
Jew. Moshe B., for example, whose family had moved to Salonika when
he was six years old, repeatedly insists that he had many Greek friends.
He spoke Greek at home and attended a Greek school.

While not as common as among the older generation, there are also
references to the 'Jews from the villages' in the interviews with the
younger generation. While expressing his discomfort with the lack of
history teaching in the community, Leon A. exclaims: 'They don't know
the history of the Jewish community and most of all they don't respect
it. Do you know why? Because they do not come from Salonika. It is as
simple as that. They have nothing to do with Salonika' (Am29).

Another relevant distinction in pre-war Salonika was the distinction
between Ashkenazi and Sephardi Jews. Hella K., who moved to Salonika
in the 1920s, tells me that it was easier for her to move in 'international
circles' than mix with Salonikan Jews who looked down on 'Jews from
the north' ('they [the Salonikan Jews] thought they were something special', Af5). She recalls that her husband's family did not approve of their

marriage because she was Ashkenazi. As a response to the attitude she encountered she did not want 'to be in contact with them' (the Salonikan Jews) because she considered them quite 'backward', for example in their attitude to women ('Salonika was like a *Türkendorf* [a Turkish village], the women were repressed and had no liberty', Af5). Hella K. found more appropriate social contacts in the 'German Club' where she met German women who were married to Greek men. Her children went to Greek schools and spoke German at home. It was a conscious decision to send the children to Greek schools so they could learn Greek properly. Both she and her husband were convinced that as citizens of a country one has to know the 'national language'. She criticises the disposition of many Salonikan Jews to continue speaking Spanish and not to learn Greek. When I asked her how she would describe her identity after having lived for more than 70 years in Salonika she replies: 'I am a Czechoslovak Jew.' All her life she has been aware that she was an outsider in Salonika. Friends also acknowledge her difference: 'Hella K. never lived like a Salonikan. She has a different mentality. It is a small place and everyone talks about each other. We are a small group and each person knows the history of the other persons. Hella K. did not live like that' (Af11).

The sense of difference as 'Salonikans' is expressed in the interviews not only with reference to 'others' but also with reference to place, that is to say to the city of Salonika. Many interviewees articulate a strong attachment to the city of Salonika. When Lili M. tries to explain why she comes back from the United States every year she says: 'It is *la Patrie*, it is the place of my own religion, it is the place of my ancestors, 500 years they sweated and died here' (Af8).

Lili M. refers to Salonika as *la Patrie*. This encapsulates the historical difference between Salonika and its Jewish population and other cities, both in Greece and the rest of Europe. The Jews felt like Salonikan citizens since they constituted the majority of the population for five centuries. Edgar Morin's father proclaimed to the French authorities that his citizenship was that of a Salonikan Jew, to which the French officer added 'a Jew from the Levant' (Morin 1989: 87). This self-ascription of a Salonikan Jewish identity exemplifies the sense of identity prevalent at the time and the cautious relationship of the Salonikan Jews to the new nation-state which drafted its citizens into its armies.

The connection to Salonika is still often perceived outside the realm of the nation-state since the 'Jewish Salonika' preceded its incorporation into the Greek state. 'I feel *Thessalonikia*, I was born here, I have people in the old cemetery ... I am from Salonika. To whom Salonika belongs is another thing. What I am, I am' (Af8). The identification with the city is expressed through history ('500 years ...') and religion ('it is the place of my own religion'). Let us contextualise these statements by looking at some of the literature on memory.

In his study *'Les Lieux des Mémoires'* (Nora 1992) Nora describes the relationship between memory, spaces and landscapes. He differentiates between *'milieu de mémoire'* and *'lieu de mémoire'* (see Chapter 2). The first category describes places of continuity, the second places of discontinuity which consist of the remains of what ceased to exist. Similarly, Aleida Assmann contrasts the two kinds of places as 'places of generations' (*Generationsorte*) and 'places of memory' (*Erinnerungsorte*) (Assmann 1999: 309). She writes: 'The step from "places of generations" to "places of commemoration" and memory, from *"milieu de mémoire"* to *"lieu de mémoire"*, takes place with the break-up and rupture of cultural frames of meaning and collective contexts' (Assmann 1999: 338, transl.).

Assmann conceptualised places as 'zones of contact'. The nature of the place, which changes over time, determines the nature of its bond: 'places of generations' relate to kinship continuity, 'places of commemoration' relate to reconstructed and transmitted narratives, and 'places of memory' relate to antiquarian and historical interest. Assmann adds one other category of place, the 'places of trauma', which are like scars which cannot heal. She thinks that these places, such as the sites of the former concentration camps in Germany, cannot be accounted for in Nora's paradigm of rupture of tradition and modernity (Assmann 1999: 339).

Without going into further detail of Nora's and Assmann's theories we can apply their conceptualisation to the perception of Salonika among my interviewees. It would appear that Salonika encapsulates all the above-mentioned places for the interviewees. It is generational, commemorative and traumatic. It is generational because most interviewees raised their children in the city, it is commemorative because the pre-war Jewish 'milieu' abruptly ceased to exist, and it is traumatic because it triggers the memory of a past which did not continue into a presence but into an absence.

It is therefore very interesting that most interviewees describe their bond to the city as something unbreakable and eternal, not affected by external circumstances. This notion is expressed by Lili M.'s quote above. 'To have people in the old cemetery' makes Salonika a *'Generationsort'*. Other interviwees share this notion. People told me many times that they, their parents and grandparents were born in Salonika or that they 'were born here and know everything to do with Salonika' (Am19). The city as an abstract entity symbolises the lasting bond between individuals, their families and the place. This bond is embedded in the 'Salonikan tradition' which, in the eyes of the older generation, is 'on the way to dying out'. Some interviewees are very proud of particular Salonikan customs, mostly embedded in the religious context. There was a slight gender bias. Men tended to talk about the synagogue and the prayers, while the women tended to talk about the food and the celebrations of festivals.

Mois A., who has worked as a *Shammas* (assistant to the rabbi) since his return from Auschwitz, urged me to go to the synagogue and observe 'Salonikan folklore'.

> The Ashkenazim have their folklore and we have ours. Our folklore is different. I advise you to take the folklore in the synagogue at the hour of praying because we are on the way to losing it ... One day this folklore will disappear. (Am21)

Other people seem to think that the quality of the religious services in the synagogue shows that the Salonikan tradition has already come to an end. Many people comment on the fact that the acting rabbi was not a qualified rabbi but only a *Hazan* and a merchant who did not know how to do things the 'proper way'.[7]

Although none of the interviewees of the older generation was strictly observant, religion was very much part of their identity, intrinsically linked to their family history. Some interviewees were concerned to emphasise the fact that their grandfathers had been rabbis. When I asked Alici P. whether she felt Greek or Jewish she answered with pride: 'I am 100 per cent Jewish, both my grandfathers were rabbis' (Af9). Michael B. starts the interview by saying that he comes from a rabbinical family, his grandfather had been the chief rabbi of Salonika. After the war he stopped going to the synagogue, partly because he could not bear the way the services were conducted:

> You could not find the kind of services that you had before the war. They were pretty substantial and attractive, there was a choir, there was a *Hazan*, there was this, there was that ... After the war you got disgusted, you got really disgusted. (Am16)

It is very clear to the older generation that the religious services of the community today are only in part a continuation of pre-war traditions, in part they constitute a form of commemoration. As one interviewee puts it: 'Before you could see a Sukkah[8] on all the balconies, decorated with flowers, oranges, and fruits. Today they build a Sukkah in the community, for memory's sake' (Af11).

RICH AND POOR

It is more difficult to write about the categories of 'rich' and 'poor' than about Salonikan and non-Salonikan. While people openly talked about whose family was from Salonika and whose family was not, they were less prepared to talk openly about whose family was considered rich and whose family was considered poor. This was further complicated by the notion of 'good families' and 'bad families' which mostly correspond to the economic categories but not always. Below are two examples of situations where class and family background became an issue of social interaction.

I attended a Friday night service at the synagogue, and sat next to one of my interviewees. Two women walked in and took their seats in the first row. They did not stop talking and the interviewee turned to me and said very angrily: 'You see, these are the rich. They think they can behave like that because they are rich'. On another Friday I found myself at the *Oneg Shabbat* ceremony in the community. After a couple of minutes a row erupted between two women. They shouted at each other and one left the table. The other woman turned to me and said: 'She does not come from a good family.' Some time later she pointed at somebody at another table and said: 'You see, this woman comes from a good family, a very good family.' I knew the family of the woman she pointed out to me. I had interviewed her son. He had acknowledged that his family is a 'good family'. When I asked him what it means to be a 'good family' he answered: 'You have to take into consideration that we are a little bit more intellectual than the other people. So we are something of both, a little bit well read and a little bit well off. We could not be either by itself' (Bm38).

The interviewee also hinted at the close connection between economic status and education in the perception of 'good families'. Another factor which is mentioned later in the interview is family history. If a family is linked to well-known personalities of the past this adds to the good name of the family ('we are bearing extremely important names'). These personalities could have been either of religious, political, or economic importance.

It is interesting that interviewees often used the contrast between two families to explain to me what they mean by 'good families'. One interviewee exclaims very emphatically when speaking of a leader of the community:

> He comes from a very good family, in Greek you would say *Tria Alpha* [triple A]. This is a marvellous, aristocratic family, a family, as you say in Hebrew, which is not *pashut* [simple] ... Mr X comes from a village. He is rich, but he is nouveau riche. (Af9)

As a result of the war, economic success and family reputation did not necessarily go hand in hand in the post-war community. Jean L. states that everything had changed after the war, 'the people who were rich before the war are not rich any more, others have become rich' (Af6).

A younger woman also explains the notion of 'good family' to me by contrasting two families.

> They had Italian citizenship, they were in good positions and they went to good schools, their grandfather was somebody. Today they are not rich any more. Family X is much richer, they think they are upper class. But it is not just money, it is money with a past. (Cf47)

The last two statements are interesting because they illustrate that despite the upheaval of the war, family memories, that is, the reputations of one's own family and other families, were transmitted to the subsequent generations. The small size of the community after the war meant that information about each family was easily accessible and communicable. Gossip and a sense of social control were thus much more relevant to members of the community than to other urban inhabitants. This became apparent in conversations and in the interviews. Many references were made to poorer families whom the community tried to help by employing them, or to rich families who did not come to the community because they thought that the people were beneath their social class. This slightly contradicts the notion that after the war class did not matter, something which was often stated in the interviews. Flora M., for example, recounts:

> Yes, the years went by and people understood there were no more social classes. We came back, we were a few Jews and we had to be together. We had to be strong together. Unfortunately many times you see the way people were brought up, you can't erase that. And many ladies were not so happy to go [to the community] because all the upper classes spoke French before. (Af7)

With this statement the speaker captures the post-war dilemma of the Salonikan Jews: on the one hand the war had made class an unimportant category, on the other hand categories of 'class' and 'family' could not be totally erased and continued to be relevant in the interaction of the members of the community. The breakdown of class also needs to be interpreted as the breakdown of the continuity of social hierarchy. When an interviewee expresses that 'we are nobodies now [and] we don't belong to any class' (Af8), it means that the complex social hierarchy of the pre-war time had collapsed but not that all categories of social hierarchy had disappeared.

Before the war, class membership was more important than community membership; after the war, certainly in the immediate post-war years, the reverse was the case. Therefore, the community participation of all is often seen as an indicator of the breakdown of class. Jilda B. recounts very proudly that every member of the community is invited to wedding ceremonies or Bar/Bat Mitzvahs.[9]

The breakdown of class is visible when it comes to marriage. Although people expressed different views on this issue, it is clear that in the light of the small number of Jews, 'to marry Jewish' is seen as a vital priority, even if that means to marry down or up 'socially'. Jewish marriages are seen to be of vital importance for the survival of the community and a common concern for all members. During my fieldwork I attended four weddings, two in Larissa, two in Salonika. One of the weddings in Salonika was a 'mixed' wedding, the woman had converted to Judaism and another was a 'real Jewish' wedding where both spouses were Jewish. A young woman commented on this wedding as follows:

> The wedding of last Saturday was unbelievable ... The mother of the groom gets a daughter-in-law from a totally different background ... She lived in the city, he lived in Panorama [a rich suburb]. He was in Anatolia [a private American school], she was in a public school, he spent some time abroad ... he had whatever he wanted, she had nothing ... You see, now everything is possible. (Cf47)

In the case of this marriage, 'being Jewish' was considered more important than class difference. However, the above statement shows that this does not mean that class consciousness does not exist, marked by social criteria of education, location of residence, and 'having lived abroad'. Other interviewees insisted that there are very few cross-class marriages and that 'the rich marry the rich and the middle classes marry the middle classes'. One interviewee uses this phrase also in the context of the marriages within the two different groups of survivors, the camp survivors and the people who survived in Greece, which implies that not only class background but also war experience differentiated these two groups in the post-war community. As a reason for the lack of cross-class marriages this interviewee talks about the *prikka* (dowry) which the Jewish families expect. From this point of view, class or economic difference erode the unity of the Jews and the possibility of Jewish survival in Greece. Another interviewee also states that some well-to-do women do not attend the meetings of the women's organisation of the community since 'they feel that the environment is not one they want to be in' (Af7).

She does not understand this behaviour and refers to the deportations to explain why: 'The war showed that it did not matter if you had millions or only thousands, you were in the same train travelling to Poland or to Germany' (Af7). Other people tell me the same about synagogue attendance, namely that the rich people do not attend the services. When I ask an interviewee why he thinks this is the case, he replies: 'Because they are busy with their own things, you need to have a Jewish spirit' (Am23). Despite the fact that class differences (and other factors) are held responsible for the differential participation of Jews in the community, we need to bear in mind that the community does bring people from different backgrounds together, certainly in the Home for the Elderly, at communal celebrations, and in the Jewish School, which most Jewish children attend.

Another way of looking at the importance of class is to look at how class actually structures a life history, apart from the explicit mention of class differences in the narratives. This is clearly detectable through the importance of the narrative of 'economic survival' in some interviews. For interviewees who are better off this issue is often summarised in one or two sentences when talking about the post-war period (such as 'slowly, slowly we managed to get the house and the shop back'). In other interviews this is a recurring theme. Moshe B., who emigrated to Israel and subsequently to the Soviet Union, describes throughout the interview where he worked and how he managed to sustain himself and his family (Am17). He speaks extensively of his financial difficulties when he moved to Salonika in the early 1990s. One of the major themes of his interview is work and his ability to make a living. The theme of 'hard work' and 'getting by' also structures Palomba A.'s life history. She focuses on the constraining factors of her economic situation on her life choices: as the sole survivor of her family she had to get married in 1946, she and her husband had to work

very hard to support a family with three children, and she remarried
after having been widowed because she did not want to be a financial
burden for her children.

The economic situation of families and individuals does feature in
most interviews but the detail with which this issue is mentioned
varies significantly. Since the children of poorer families were involved
from an early age in the upkeep of the family, these interviewees talk in
greater detail about the economic activities of their families. One interviewee for example, whose father was a peddler, recalls how he accompanied his father to the market:

> We always worked, also on Shabbat. I remember that I went with
> my father every Saturday and Sunday to sell jam. Every
> Saturday we went to a small village called Sophades, where there
> was a market. We made some money but we had to get up at 4
> o'clock in the morning during the night in order to arrive in the
> village at about 7 o'clock. We needed to be there early so we could
> choose the best spot to sell our jam ... I was supposed to help my
> father. I remember that it was terrible. I wanted to sleep, it was
> cold, and during the day it became very hot. When we came back
> at night I was always fast asleep. But the next day I had to get up
> again to go to another village. During the week I went to school
> but I remember that I had to work very hard.

The theme of support of his family is central in the entire interview. In
light of the modest background of his parents he speaks very proudly
of his contribution to the economic success of his siblings: firstly he
found a 'good husband' for his sister and secondly he asked his brother to join his successful business. In the narrative of 'finding a husband
for his sister' the interviewee describes why the man he found for his
sister was a 'good man': 'He seemed to be well known in Salonika and
he had a good profession.' He concludes: 'Everyone was happy that a
beautiful girl married someone from Salonika.' The last sentence
underlines the status connected with urban Salonika.

WOMEN AND MEN

The last category of identity we should consider here is gender. As
with class, gender difference is reflected in the structure and content of
memory, that is, narrative representation. In contrast to the juxtaposi-

tion of 'rural' and 'urban, and 'rich' and 'poor', gender differences are not problematised. Therefore it is much more difficult to analyse how the construction of gender, embedded in the general discourse on kinship,[10] shapes the structure and content of the interviews. The following section will concentrate in particular on the relationship between gender and the construction of Jewish identity and 'Greekness'.

While there are significant differences in male and female life histories which reflect gender domains and gender roles, I am hesitant to speak of clearly recognisable 'gendered narratives'. The historical narratives of the pre-war, war and post-war periods express the different experiences of the interviewees but do not clearly vary according to gender. While women tended to speak more about the private domain, centred around the home, and men tended to talk more about the public domain, focusing on their work and their political and communal involvement, there are a few women who discuss their work extensively (Af10, Af8) and a few men who referred in detail to their private lives (Am27).

The first part of this section will focus on gender and Jewish identity, the second on gender and the notion of 'Greekness'. In both cases these constructions seem to be shared by men and women, and cannot be easily classified into gender categories.

The two most fundamental and slightly contradictory concepts when it comes to Jewish identity are a) the close association of 'being Jewish' with a 'Jewish home' and a 'Jewish upbringing', directly linked to women in their role as wives (who are clearly seen as responsible for this domain), and b) the connection between the Jewish surname, mostly transmitted by the men and 'being Jewish', which is almost seen as a prerequisite for being accepted as a Jew. Variations of these themes can be found in all the interviews. Jilda B. touches on these very topics throughout the interview. Jilda B. moved to Salonika from Istanbul in 1947 when she married her first (and only surviving) cousin. Her husband was very involved in the community. She became active in the women's organisation of the community when her three children started going to school. At various points in the interviews she refers to the importance of the 'wife' and 'mother' in transmitting Jewish traditions (and a Jewish identity). In the first instance she remembers her Jewish upbringing: 'My father never went to a synagogue, my mother liked the traditions very much. She used to do everything for the festivals, Kippur and Pessach [Passover] ... That's the way I am with my children. They know everything.' (Af2)

In this depiction the wife and mother is clearly the bearer of Jewish

identity since she is responsible for the transmission of Jewish traditions. Jilda B. is proud of the fact that she told her children to say the
Shema:[11] ('I taught them to say the *Shema* in the evening. Now they
don't say it any more but it does not matter. What matters is that they
know what it is.') She points out that it 'all depends on the mother'
whether the festivals are celebrated at home or not. As a grandmother
she continues to 'keep up the traditions' by having festive lunches
every Saturday for her children and grandchildren. For these occasions
and the Jewish festivals she cooks Sephardic food, such as carp with
walnut and vinegar for Passover. Food is clearly a constitutive part of
the Jewish tradition she talks about. This feeling is articulated by both
men and women, and Jewish food is often referred to in the pre-war
memories and in the general identity discourse. Anthropologists have
underlined the importance of food as an identity marker and as a central component of a sense of collective belonging (van den Berghe 1984,
Fischler 1988), and food can also evoke memories and nostalgia for different times and different places.[12]

Leon A., for example, explains to me that his Jewish wife knew 'by
instinct' to wash the meat before cooking it, a custom which he knew
from his mother but which is not usual in Christian households
(Am29). Women thus form an important part in 'maintaining tradition'
and keeping a Jewish identity alive. Therefore, it is often the women
who 'have the Jewish sentiment' (Af1) and who are seen as responsible
for transmitting Judaism to their children. When Jilda B. talks about
Jewish tradition, she is acutely aware that the younger generation and
especially the younger women do not have adequate knowledge to
'keep a Jewish home'. She says: 'They are trying to write books. They
ask the old ladies about recipes. The young will forget and they won't
do it. And who eats now at home anyway? They go out to restaurants'
(Af2). Like many older people she shares a rather pessimistic outlook
on the future of Jewish identity in Salonika: 'it will all disappear'. She
pauses and continues: 'with the mixed marriage it will all disappear'.
In this view mixed marriages pose the ultimate threat to the continuity
of Jewish identity in Greece.

This conclusion is linked to a specific understanding of gender and
identity, and minority and majority culture. As we have seen in the
previous section on the perception of boundaries between Greeks and
Jews, Jewish identity is conceived in essentialist terms, as something
'deep inside', something which cannot be learnt and hence something
very private. This private identity is perceived as being under threat.
It is under threat because of the lack of knowledge of the younger gen-

eration and because of the strength of the public Greek identity of the majority culture. Since women are seen as the main carrier of the private Jewish identity, Christian Orthodox Greek women who marry Jewish men cannot transmit this identity, even if they convert. They cannot bring the Jewish sentiment into the marriage because it has not been passed down to them by their mothers, and thus their Jewishness seems 'artificial'. One elderly woman recalls that her friends were invited by the Christian wife of her grandson for the celebration of Rosh Hashana (Jewish New Year). Since the 'Greek girl' did not know how to cook the food, they brought the appropriate food to her home. With a sense of irony about the situation the interviewee says: 'so there they were and ate fish and *prassokeftedes* [leek croquettes, a typical Salonikan Jewish dish]'.[13]

It is interesting though that mixed marriages in both gender variations are seen as dangerous to Jewish survival. The reasons for this are very different: one is 'positive' and one is 'negative'. In the first variation, in mixed marriages between Jewish men and Christian women, the active 'bearer' of Jewish identity is missing. In the second variation, when a Jewish woman gets married to a Christian man, the non-Jewish husband, representing majority Greek culture, makes it impossible for the 'weaker' Jewish identity to assert itself. A woman comments on the latter cases of mixed marriages, in which the children according to the *Halacha* (the canon of Jewish religious practice) are considered Jewish:

> I have a friend whose daughter is married to a Greek and has two children. What are the children? Their mother is Jewish, alright, but in Greece? They cannot be Jewish. It is impossible, their name is Greek ... This is a problem we have ... There are many cases of Jewish women who married a Greek and they don't allow these girls to come. Why? Because you cannot have a Jewish child called Papadopolous.

In this concept the Jewish identity is seen as volatile and weak, which cannot stand up against the Greek majority culture, perceived as strong and powerful. This leads to a concept in which women are seen as the bearer of identity but they can only transmit this identity with the support of the husband. Since men in Greece normally do not convert, it means that in practice the women are expected to adapt to the culture of the men.

The husband's name comes to symbolise Greek or Jewish culture. Names in the Greek context are a clear boundary marker because

Jewish and Greek surnames are easily distinguishable. Jews are often asked about their non-Greek names. A friend of mine told me a quite 'typical' story about names. He had to take his brother to the hospital. When filling in the forms, the clerk saw his name and said: 'This is a strange name, you are not Greek, are you?' He answered that he was Greek. The clerk was not happy with the explanation and asked again. When my friend said that he was Jewish, the clerk said: 'You see, I told you that you are not Greek.' This story brings out the 'ethnic character' of names and the the importance of names and naming traditions in Greece. In the discussion of the dispute about the name of the Republic of Macedonia, David Sutton points to the importance of personal names in Greek culture (Sutton 1998: 183). By giving a child the name of its grandparents a link between the past and the present and an inter-generational continuity is established. On mainland Greece it is the custom to give the first child the name of the paternal grandparent and the second one of the maternal grandparent. The same custom is practised among Salonikan Jews. When a Jewish woman thus marries a Christian man, the first child carries not only the Christian surname but also the Christian name of the husband's mother or father. In this patrilineal system of naming a marriage to a Christian man thus interrupts the inter-generational continuity and the link to the past provided by the name(s) of a Jewish man (and his parents).

I interviewed one man whose Christian partner had recently died. They had lived in the Jewish Home for the Elderly. He tells me that she saved him in the war and that they never got married. It is important for him to point out that his children are Jewish and they were accepted in the community: 'the children had my name and were registered in the community … both children have my name' (Am13).

This is a rather unusual case. Somebody else told me that his children were accepted as Jews because 'who could say no to the children after the Greek woman had hidden their father during the war'. There are, however, a fair number of women in the community who converted to Judaism when they got married. They are fully accepted in the community although they are considered different and treated sometimes with caution, as the following quotation illustrates:

> The converted women in the women's organisation are the best …
> We receive them very well but sometimes we put them in a difficult position because we speak like *entre mosotros* … They speak highly of the Jewish education of the children. Is it fake? Is it true? I don't know but I know that the children go to the school, the chil-

dren go to the camp, the children have the Jewish names and they are members of the community … they are not lost. (Af7)

The effect of these concepts of gendered ethnicity is that mixed marriage has different consequences for Jewish men and Jewish women: while the men stay in the community if their wives convert, the women have to leave because men generally do not convert in Greece. Many young Jewish women think it is not fair that the converted women can go along to the community activities, while the women cannot if their partner is non-Jewish (Cf41).[14]

For most interviewees of the older generation the only way to guarantee some kind of Jewish continuity is Jewish marriages. Mixed marriages are seen as vehicles of loss and assimilation which will bring about the end of the community:

Eighty per cent of the children of mixed marriages are lost. I tell the young men it is their obligation to marry somebody Jewish, otherwise we are lost. We are in distress, we are at the minimum right now. We have to fight assimilation. (Am14)

During an encounter with some community members in 1998, several people reported very happily that two 'proper' Jewish weddings had just taken place. These weddings come to symbolise the continuity of Jewish families and the Jewish community because of the perceived weakness of Jewish identity in the younger generation.

Finally, we should consider gender and perceptions of 'Greekness', first as a contrast to the perception of Jewishness and secondly in relation to citizenship. The notion of a 'Greek life' has been discussed above. This lifestyle choice was not available for most women of the older generation because it is situated outside the home ('have fun', *kefi*, go to the coffee shop, *kafenio*, and go to bars, *bouzoukia*) and thus clearly associated with the male domain. It is also used in a more metaphoric way to denote an immoral lifestyle, a life without responsibilities which stands in juxtaposition to the demands of conjugality as a 'family man' (see Loizos and Papataxiarchis 1991: 18). This conceptualisation of a clearly male identity comes out in the next quotation. Although Leon L. does not speak of a 'Greek' versus a 'Jewish' way of behaving this juxtaposition is implicit in the narrative. He explains to me the difference between a 'good Jew' and a Jew who is 'not so good':

A good Jew is somebody who believes in God, somebody who is good to his family, somebody who respects his father, mother and grandfather, who respects the elder ones. Somebody who is not a good Jew is somebody who spends every night in a cabaret, spends the fortunes of his father and spends it on women and in the *kafenia*. He spends his father's money who worked for 50 years to build a house. The Jew who embraces his religion and family is a good Jew. (Am20)

It is not only because the speaker is male that he conceptualises a 'good Jew' and a 'not good Jew' as male identities. This has to do with the fact that men are seen to have private and public identities, while women are seen mostly in the context of their private identities. A Jewish man can thus be Jewish and lead a Greek life (outside the home) in a way in which a Jewish woman cannot.

There is another important aspect which deserves mention which also has to do with the difference between public male identities and private female identities. When asked about feeling and being 'Greek' most men refer to the fact that they served in the army during the Second World War, most women refer to language ability and social contacts with Greek women. Flora M. told me, for example, that her mother did not have a Greek identity. When I asked what she meant by that she replied: 'She wouldn't mix with Greeks' (Af7). Military service is a tangible proof of the Greek loyalty and patriotism of Jewish men. Leon B. recounts what he says when somebody has a problem with his Jewish identity: 'I say, look I fought in Albania … I was in Albania. It was the Jews who fought in Albania' (Am14).

Since loyalty and citizenship are embedded in the realm of politics, which in Greece traditionally has not been part of the female domain, the theme of the Jew as 'good patriot' does not feature much in the life histories of the women. The mention of military service in connection with 'Greekness' can reflect a) the integrative power (in terms of belonging to the Greek nation state) of the experience of serving in the army for the individual Jewish man and b) the fact that the accusation of minority disloyalty is rather directed against the men as public polit-ical beings. Many men are very proud of the fact that they fought in Albania and also mention their position in the army as a proof of their acceptance in Greek society.

CONCLUSION

In conclusion, we return to the theme of memory and identity and their intricate relationship. The descriptions of identities of the older generation have certainly illuminated how deeply rooted these identities are in the pre-war reality of each individual and the pre-war reality of Salonika. Their identities as Jews, as Salonikan Jews, as Greek Jews, as upper-class or working-class Jews, were created in the pre-war past and reinforced by their war experience. While explaining their identities, the interviewees constantly refer to this past, that is to say to the memory of this past. It is very likely that in a more public context some of these identities would not have been discussed.

Through their identities the survivors thus formed and continue to form a link to the past which, until recently, was not complemented by any institutional memory. In contrast to the private memory of the interviewees, the recently developed public communal memory is subject to current political and identity pressures in which the past is remembered through a specific looking glass (of the 'good Greek–Jewish relationship'). With the imminent death of the older generation and the realisation that the memories of the people who actually still remember pre-war Salonika has not been sufficiently recorded, the community began actively to do something about memory of the past. The opening of a Jewish Museum, the erection of a public Holocaust monument, the organisation of a number of international Judeo-Spanish conferences and the collection of survivors' testimonies manifest this new interest in memory.

When we turn to the responses of the second generation we understand that the parents transmitted to their children a 'sense of the past' rather than articulated memory. In the foreword of her book, Rena Molho, who was born after the war, explains why she wrote a Ph.D. on the history of the Jews of Salonika. 'The whole world they [her parents] had lived in was destroyed ... I wanted to pull down the wall which separated us and discover this world they had belonged to. This was not easy: the survivors did not want to discuss this' (R. Molho 2000: 13).

One interviewee, also born after the war, attests to the same difficulty: 'We didn't want to ask questions in those days, we did not want to bring back the sad memories of my father' (Bm37). The powerful presence of this past is certainly acknowledged by the younger generation. In a discussion about the difference between Jewish and non-Jewish families a young woman states: 'Our families are different. All families who have experienced the Holocaust are different'(Cf47).

Renée Hirschon underlines 'the importance of shared memory for any uprooted group' (Hirschon 1998: 15). I would add that this is not always the case, especially if survivors return to the place from which they were uprooted, that is, the location of 'before' and 'after' is the same and there is no 'distant home' to look back to. In these cases the contrast of 'what was' and 'what is' can be very painful and thus a 'shared silence' or a 'shared absence' can replace articulated memories. Kirmayer argues that only if a larger community agrees that a traumatic event occurred will collective memory survive and give space to individual memory (Kirmayer 1996: 189). Since the Greek nation-state and the city of Salonika did not (until the mid-1990s) actively acknowledge the Holocaust, Jewish memory remained private, articulated within the community and within each family, and often not articulated at all. One of the consequences of 'shared silences' is, for the following generations, that the past could not be found in articulated memories but in the observed identities and behaviour of the older generation. So one could say that the identities and perceptions of boundaries among the older generation, discussed above, attest to the importance of the past in the present, while the newly acquired public communal memory attests to the importance of the present in the past.

NOTES

1. Young people often struggle with what their Jewish identity means to them. One of my interviewees, who was in her mid-twenties and married to a Christian, told me: 'my Jewish identity is very Jewish, not when it comes to religion but when it comes to identity. I mean ... I don't know how to put it in words ... I feel different' (Cf41).
2. This process also happened in other countries, such as Turkey. One interviewee who grew up in Istanbul told me that she remembers signs at the post office and at the school saying '*vatandas turkce konus*' (citizen, speak Turkish).
3. One informant told me that the term '*Grecos ensgreshado*' referred to the fact that Greek children are baptised with oil.
4. In the Sephardi world this holiday is called Kippur (atonement) while in the Ashkenazi terminology it is Yom Kippur (day of atonement).
5. This is not to say that only Jews spoke Judeo-Spanish. But only Jews spoke it as their first language, outside and inside the home.
6. *Forastero* in Spanish means stranger.
7. In 1995 the community appointed a rabbi who was brought from Israel. Today the community employs two rabbis, a young Greek rabbi, Mordechai Frizis, and one from Israel.
8. See Chapter 5, note 8.
9. This seemed to have changed very recently. I went to a wedding in the summer of 1999 and it appeared that not every community member was invited to attend the ceremony. During my fieldwork all the members of the community were invited to the weddings which took place.
10. In *Contested Identities* (1991) Loizos and Papataxiarchis discuss two contexts and discourses of kinship, one in which domestic kinship is the dominant metaphor of gendered personhood and one in which the domestic model is transcended or negated (p. 5). In the context of my study the discourse of kinship and gender falls clearly into the model of domestic kinship.
11. The *Shema* is one of the main Jewish prayers. It is called *Shema* because it starts with the words *Schma Israel* which translates as 'hear, people of Israel'.
12. For a brief discussion on food as a marker of identity see Vasiliki Krava 1999.
13. Stavroulakis refers to this dish in Judeo-Spanish as *Keftikes de Prassa* (Stavroulakis 1986: 75).
14. In recent years this situation has changed.

Conclusion

This study has explored articulations of Jewish memory and Jewish identity. The following section will summarise the findings and arguments on the nature of Jewish memory and Jewish identity in post-war Salonika. Irwin-Zarecka uses the notion of 'frames of remembrance'. Here we will consider the identity 'frames', pertinent to the management of Jewish individual and communal memories, and look at the changes which have taken place in recent years.

The analysis of Jewish Salonikan memory clearly supports Halbwachs' idea that memory is linked to group membership.[1] In this understanding memory is structured by group identities and its survival is linked to the survival of the group which perpetuates this memory. In the case of Salonikan Jews, the community and its institutions constituted for many years the only memory space in the city which provided 'memory practices' through which individuals could engage with their past. Most of these memory practices are embedded in Salonikan Jewish culture.

The 'frames' of present identities are of the highest importance for the construction and telling of life histories. Memories are always narrated from the current perspective of the narrator. In the case of the interviewees in this study, this means that we are talking about an older generation whose social, class and religious identities were shaped in pre-war Greece. In Boyarin's terminology they represent a 'transitional' generation (Boyarin 1991) in two ways. Firstly, they experienced the loss of family members and friends, and secondly, they experienced the loss of a culture and 'cultural heirs'. The cultural loss was experienced differently by different people depending on family orientation (for example towards schooling) and family background ('old Greece'/'new Greece') and war experience (help, support, denunciation, deportation). The stronger the interviewees' Greek identity, the stronger the wish to stress the themes expressed in the communal memory (Greek help and good Jewish–Greek relations). The weaker the interviewees' Greek identity, the more likely an inclusion of 'sensitive' topics, such as Greek pre-war and post-war anti-Semitism, Greek collaboration, and post-war difficulties. Silence on sensitive topics cannot only be only explained by the strength of Greek or Jewish identities, but also needs to be looked at in terms of 'insecure belonging'. Within the lifetime of the interviewees the nature of Jewish identity and the meaning of Jewish identity has drastically changed. While Jewish identity on the whole constituted the core identity for the older generation, their grandchildren's core identity is Greek. This cultural 'displacement' is reflected in apprehension over talking about certain experiences. Interviewees who grew up in 'old Greece' have a much stronger sense of continuity and are more able to present their lives as 'consistent and unidirectional' (Langness quoted in Boyarin 1991). Whether individual recollections accept, challenge, or ignore communal and national representations of the past has very much to do with the present identities of the narrators which, however, were shaped in the past of pre-war Greece.

From the excerpts of the interviews quoted above it should have become clear that the experience of the war and the Holocaust have had a deep impact on people's life histories. The most encompassing effect can be considered the narrative division of lives into a 'before the war' and an 'after the war', which goes hand in hand with a presence (or silence) of the traumatic past which defies the chronology of past, present and future in a life history. The experience of the Holocaust entailed, for some, the 'breakdown of *homo narrens* who tries to cast his life as a story with a unified plot' (Meyerhoff quoted in Boyarin 1991). The difficulty of telling a 'story with a unified plot', that is to say to look at the past, the present and the future of the Jewish community of Salonika, was also expressed in the communal post-war memory.

It has been shown that the post-war community was perceived in terms of family and kinship. One can argue that the way the past was remembered after the war corresponded to the notion of family and was thus very similar to a kind of 'family memory'. Within Salonikan Jewish families the two most important memory practices are a) naming (after the paternal and maternal grandparents) and b) the commemoration of deceased family members (which also forms an important part of the religious services in the synagogue, see Chapter 4). As the community and individuals were engaged in their economic reconstruction, the main focus of communal memory constituted for many years the commemoration of the dead. From 1948 onwards, the community commemorated the victims of the Holocaust in a yearly ceremony at the synagogue (Day of Great Mourning).[2] This day is referred to as *Mnimnosino*, the Greek name for the remembrance day of the deceased (see Figure 18). In the early 1960s a Holocaust memorial was erected at the Jewish cemetery. In the 1980s tablets with the names of all Salonikan synagogues were put up in the Yad Lezikaron Synagogue. Memory of the past was expressed through Jewish mourning rituals in the spaces where mourning rituals are performed: the synagogue and the cemetery. By commemorating the victims of the Holocaust through Jewish communal mourning rituals, the nature of the commemoration remained communal and 'private'. Despite the presence of Christian Greek political and Church representatives at the Holocaust commemoration ceremonies and the inauguration of the Holocaust monument, the memory of the Holocaust was in essence a private memory, shared by Jews as Jews and acknowledged by the Greek state in private (communal) spaces. The memory remained private because the Greek state and the municipality of Thessaloniki did not include Jewish history in its official memory. The communal form of commemoration did not challenge the lack of public recognition of Jewish history and Jewish victims of the Holocaust.

The community itself had an ambivalent relationship to its history. After an initial interest in history (the community published a number of books on the history of Salonikan Jews by Rabbi Michael Molho and Joseph Nehama), the community in the post-war years focused on the creation of a 'positive', forward-looking Jewish identity. The past was 'put behind'. Neither Ladino nor the history of Jewish Salonika was given much attention in Jewish education. Although the community formed a 'community of memory' through the shared past of its members, the transmission of knowledge about this past was not seen as necessary condition for Jewish survival. Rather than knowledge about the past, it was contact among Jews and Jewish marriages which were seen to guarantee a Jewish future. I suggest that we cannot understand the importance given to Jewish marriages if we do not relate it to the 'management of memories'. Since memory of the past in the post-war Jewish community was conceptualised in terms of 'family memory', mixed marriages were not only perceived as a threat to the continuity of Jewish customs in the family (such as circumcisions and Bar/Bat Mitzvahs) but as a threat to the continuity of Jewish memory (through the disappearance of Jewish names, for example).

The community thus presented a bridge to the past through religious services and facilities for social encounters, rather than through its articulated 'cultural memory'. As quoted above Hirschon talks about the significance of 'shared memories' for uprooted groups (Hirschon 1998: 15). We also need to acknowledge the importance of shared silences among survivors of traumatic events.

Within the last years we could witness a change in the 'memory status' of the Jewish past inside the community. By 'embodying' Jewish memories through the recording of testimonies and Ladino music, the creation of a Jewish museum and the high-profile public ceremonies on the National Day of Remembrance of the Greek Jewish Heroes, the community began to be engaged in a 'cultural memory' which, in contrast to before, is not confined to the private realm. The *topoi* of remembering and forgetting appeared on the letterhead of the community which showed a menorah (seven-branch candlestick) with the following text underneath: 'God remembers what men forget' (in English) or *'O theos thimate osa oi anthropoi xechnoun'* in Greek. This process can be seen, in Nora's terminology, as a change from *'milieux de mémoire'* to *'lieux de mémoire'*. As the carriers of memories of pre-war Salonika and the Holocaust are about to die, the community takes on a new role. In this new role the community represents memory of the past to its members and is more assertive about the Jewish past to the outside. The community today publishes a lengthy newsletter called *El Avenir* (The Future) in Greek and English. As Connerton has pointed out, 'we will experience our present differently in accordance with the different pasts to which we are able to connect' (Connerton 1989: 2). The newly expressed communal memory illustrates not only the desire to connect to a specific past but also to connect pasts of different collective memories. This means that the community presents Jewish history in a way which incorporates official Greek memory.

The communally articulated memory must be seen in the context of contemporary Greek Jewish identity. I have quoted Gillis at the beginning of this work: 'what is remembered is defined by the assumed identity' (Gillis 1994: 1). One should add here that how something is remembered is shaped by an assumed identity. The newly articulated 'cultural memory' is the outcome of three different processes. Firstly, it represents a more Hellenised Jewish generation which has been fully socialised into Greek culture and thus can look back confidently to its Sephardic past and is able to challenge historical narratives formulated by different agencies. Secondly, it reflects the post-war insecurity of Salonikan Jews as a minority who participate in the collective memory of the majority culture, such as the Macedonia evening, in order to be accepted by Christian Greeks as 'real Greeks'. Thirdly, it reflects the change of Greek 'cultural memory' which has started to acknowledge the Jewish past.

In 2003 two monuments were erected in honour of the Greek Jewish soldiers who were killed in the Greek–Italian War of 1940–41, one in Thessaloniki and one in Larissa. One of the biggest challenges the public memory of the Holocaust faces in contemporary Greece is that of vandalism. In 2002 the Holocaust monument in Salonika was covered with red paint and the word 'Palestinians' was painted next to the memorial. In 2003 swastikas were sprayed on to the memorial. Other Jewish monuments, such as the Holocaust memorial at the cemetery in Ioanina, were also desecrated with the slogans 'Death to the Jews' or 'Jews out'.

We need to look at these recent manifestations of Holocaust remembrance also in the light of international developments. Memory politics are no longer only a matter of nation-states but part of international developments of dealing with particular pasts. The Holocaust has, in recent years, received a great deal of attention in many different countries. The legal issues of slave labour compensation, Nazi gold, compensation for lost property, and stolen art have made a dialogue between different states necessary. The erection of the Holocaust monument in Salonika in 1997 and the establishment of a Holocaust Remembrance Day in 2004 therefore also need to be seen as statements of Greek foreign policy.

We should not underestimate the value of memorials, museums and remembrance days, both for Jewish and Christian Greeks. They provide public spaces where Holocaust remembrance ceremonies can take place. Jewish mourning and remembrance is no longer restricted to the private space of the community and Jewish suffering is thus publicly acknowledged. This is important for survivors and their descendants. For many Christian Greeks these monuments could provide spaces through which they are confronted with Jewish Greek history, unknown to many. This process could eventually lead to an understanding of Greek history which includes Jewish history, rather than treats it as a separate entity. For example, in the case of Salonika this would mean that tour guides not only provide 'Jewish interest' tours to special groups (mostly Israelis and Americans) but incorporate references to the presence of Jews in the standard tour of the city.

In a conversation with one of the interviewees, Lili M. asked me: 'Have you heard the Greek saying: "what was, is behind us?"' She paused and continued: 'But the experience of the Holocaust marks our heart like the tattoo on our arm. It is 50 years ago when I left my parents and sister behind in the ghetto. For me, it seems only a couple of hours ago.'

The Holocaust was, and continues to be, as present in the communal post-war memory as in Lili M.'s statement. The form of commemoration though has changed. The new 'cultural memory' has transformed a traumatic past of rupture and discontinuity into a narratable past which offers hope and continuity. The following excerpt of a message by Mr Andreas Sefiha, the former president of the Jewish community, entitled 'We do exist', is an example of a narrative of continuity:

> Salonika though, has also the tragic privilege to be the city in Europe which had the highest rate of Jewish victims in the Holocaust. Less than 2,000 survived out of 50,000. Ninety-six per cent of the Jewish population perished. And yet, in spite of all the efforts dedicated to our extermination, we exist. We exist and we create, being thus an example of vitality and spiritual power. We take from Salonika and give back social, cultural, and economic offerings. We co-exist harmoniously with our Christian fellow-citizens. We are always present in Salonika's good and bad moments, in its time of sorrow and its time of happiness and glory. Although we are relatively few we are proud of the important personalities that come from our ranks. (November 1998)[3]

As survivors attempt to restore unity and coherence to their narrated lives (Skultans 1998: 26), so does the community. By using the present tense in conjunction with the word always ('we are always present') this message evokes a clear sense of continuity. On the website of the Jewish Museum in Thessaloniki, Jakov Benmajor finishes his essay about the history of the community with a clear vision of the future: 'We are following the steps of our forefathers who created this Jewish town, and hopefully we can become one day a new centre of Judaism, a new Ir vaEm beIsrael.' Apparently, the generation that deals more confidently with the ruptures of the Jewish past in Salonika can look more confidently into the future.

NOTES

1. I prefer to speak of individual and communal expressions of memory rather than use the notion of 'collective memory'. In this way we can situate memory and focus on the interactive aspects of different memory agencies rather than imply a static concept of group memory.
2. In 1948 the Central Board of Jewish Communities established an official day of mourning for the victims of the Holocaust. The Israeli state proclaimed the 'Holocaust and Ghetto Uprising Remembrance Day' three years later, in 1951.
3. This message was distributed, along with articles on the history of the community, a CD of Ladino music and Salonikan Jewish recipes, at a fundraising dinner for the Jewish Museum.

Bibliography

PRIMARY SOURCES/ARCHIVES

AJDC Archive, Jerusalem: Geneva Shipment, 11c, 11/A, 64a, 96a, 125b.

Yad Yashem, Jerusalem: DIV/54-1, Wisliceny affidavit, Bratislava 1947.
Testimony 033C/1424 Erika Kounio-Amariglio.
Testimony 03/7093 Elisa F.

Wiener Library, London: 'Abschlussbericht of the Sonderkommando Rosenberg' in unsorted materials deposited by Mark Mazower.

PAMPHLET MATERIAL

Jewish Community of Thessaloniki (1978) *Short History of the Jewish Community of Thessaloniki.*
Jewish Community of Thessaloniki (1992) *Jewish Community of Thessaloniki.*
Jewish Community of Thessaloniki and The Simon Marks Museum of the Jewish History in Thessaloniki (ed.) (1998) *Thessaloniki.*
Organisation for the Cultural Capital of Europe (1994) *Thessaloniki.*

UNPUBLISHED MEMOIRS

Shaki, L. (date not known) Unpublished Memoir.
Marcel Nadjary (1990) Unpublished translation by Sisi Benvenisti.

MAGAZINES AND NEWSPAPERS

Chronika, September/October 1984.
Chronika, January/February 1998.
Elefterotipia, 30 January 1995.
Evraiko Vima, 21 December 1945.
Israelitikon Vima, 23 November 1945.
Jewish Chronicle, 22 October 1999.
Jewish Chronicle, 21 January 2005.
Thessaloniki, 25 May 1999.

BOOKS AND ARTICLES

Abatzopoulou, F. (ed.) (1993) Jomtov, Jakoel *Apomimnonevmata (Memoires) 1941–1943*. Thessalonika: Paratiritis.
Abatzopoulou, F. (1997) 'The Holocaust: Questions of Literary Representation', in Hassiotis, I.K. (ed.) *The Jewish Communities of South-Eastern Europe. From the Fifteenth Century to the End of World War II*. Thessalonika: Institute for Balkan Studies, pp. 1–21.
Abels, H. (1995) 'Zeugnis der Vernichtung. Über strukturelle Erinnerungen und Erinnern als Leitmotiv des Überlebens', in Platt, K., Dabag, M. (eds) *Generation und Gedächtnis. Erinnerungen und kollektive Identitäten*. Opladen: Leske und Budrich, pp. 305–37.
Alter, P. (1985) *Nationalismus*. Frankfurt-am-Main: Suhrkamp.
American Jewish Committee (1982) *The Jewish Communities of Nazi-Occupied Europe*. New York: The American Jewish Community.
Anderson, B. (1991) *Imagined Communities*. London: Verso.
Angel, M.D. (1978) *The Jews of Rhodes*. New York: Sepher Hermon Press.
Antze, P. and Lambek, M (eds) (1996) *Tense Past. Cultural Essays in Trauma and Memory*. London: Routledge.
Asser, A. (1983) La Communauté Juive De Salonique–Une Communauté de Survivants: Identite Collective ou Sentiment D'Appartenance. Unpublished thesis: écoles Des Hautes Etudes en Sciences Sociales.
Assmann, A. (1999) *Erinnerungsräume. Formen und Wandlungen des kulturellen Gedächtnisses*. Munich: C.H. Beck.
Assmann, J. (1997) *Das kulturelle Gedächtnis. Schrift, Erinnerung und politische Identität in frühen Hochkulturen*. Munich: C.H. Beck.
Avdela, Efi (1993) 'O Socialismos Ton Allon: Taxiki Angones, Ethnotikes Synkrousis Kai Tavtotites Filou Stin Meta-Othomaniki

Thessaloniki' (The Socialism of Others: Class Struggle, Ethnic Conflicts and Gender Identity in Post-Ottoman Thessalonika), in *Ta Historika*, No. 18/19, June–December, pp. 171–203.

Bakalian, A.P. (1993) *Armenian-Americans. From Being to Feeling Armenian*. New Brunswick, NJ: Transaction.

Bal, M., Crewe, J. and Spitzer, L. (eds) (1999) *Acts of Memory. Cultural Recall in the Present*. Hanover, NH: University Press of New England.

Banks, M. (1996) *Ethnicity: Anthropological Constructions*. London: Routledge.

Barth, F. (1969) *Ethnic Groups and Boundaries*. Boston, MA: Little Brown.

Bauer, Y. (1989) *Out of the Ashes*. Oxford: Pergamon Press.

Baum, W.K. and Dunaway, D.K. (eds) (1984) *Oral History. An Interdisciplinary Anthology*. Nashville: American Association for State and Local History.

Bell, D. (1975) Ethnicity and Social Change, in Glazer, N., and Moynihan, D.P. (eds) *Ethnicity: Theory and Experience*. Cambridge, MA Harvard University Press, pp.160–71.

Bell, D., Caplan, P. and Jarim, W.K. (eds) (1993) *Gendered Fields: Women, Men, and Ethnography*. London: Routledge.

Bertaux, D. and Thompson, P. (eds) (1993) *Between Generations. Family Models, Myths and Memories*. International Yearbook of Oral History and Life Stories. Oxford: Oxford University Press.

Blinkhorn, M. and Veremis, T. (1990) *Modern Greece: Nationalism and Nationality*. Athens: Sage-Eliamep.

Blok, A. (1992) 'Reflections on Making History', in Hastrup, K. (ed.) *Other Histories*. London: Routledge, pp.121–7.

Bottomley, Gillian (1992) *From Another Place. Migration and the Politics of Culture*. Cambridge: Cambridge University Press.

Bowman, S. (1989) 'Introduction' to Nahon, M. *Birkenau, The Camp of Death*. Tuscalos, Al: niversity of Alabama Press.

Bowman, S. (1995) Book review in *Bulletin of Judeo-Greek Studies*, No. 17, p. 24.

Boyarin, Y. (1991) *Polish Jews in Paris. The Ethnography of Memory*. Bloomington, IN: Indiana University Press.

Braude, B. and Lewis, B. (eds) (1982) *Christians and Jews in the Ottoman Empire*. New York: Holmes and Meier.

Brettell, C.B. (ed.) (1993) *When They Read What We Write. The Politics of Ethnography*. Westport, CA: Bergin and Garvey.

Breuilly, J. (1982) *Nationalism and the State*. Manchester: Manchester University Press.

Campbell, J. and De Pina-Cabral, J. (eds) (1992) *Europe Observed*. London: Macmillan Press.

Campbell, J.K. (1964) *Honour, Family and Patronage*. Oxford: Oxford University Press.

Campbell, J. and Sherrard, P. (1968) *Modern Greece*. London: Ernest Benn.

Canetti, E. (1989) *Die Gerettete Zunge. Geschichte einer Jugend*. Frankfurt-am-Main: Fischer Verlag.

Caruth, C. (ed.) (1995) *Trauma. Explorations in Memory*. Baltimore, MD: John Hopkins University Press.

Chapman, M., McDonald, M. and Tonkin, E. (eds) (1989) *History and Ethnicity*. London: Routledge.

Clogg, R. (ed.) (1983) *Greece in the 1980s*. London: Macmillan.

—— (1986) *A Short History of Modern Greece*. Cambridge: Cambridge University Press.

—— (1992) *A Concise History of Greece*. Cambridge: Cambridge University Press.

Cohen, A. (1958) *Solal*. Paris: Editions Gallimard.

—— (1969) *Custom and Politics in Urban Africa*. London: Routledge.

—— (1985) *The Symbolic Construction of Community*. London: Routledge.

Cohen, R. (1997) *Global Diasporas. An Introduction*. London: UCL Press.

Collard, A. (1989) 'Investigating Social Memory in a Greek Context', in Tonkin, E., Macdonald, M. and Chapman, M. (eds) *History and Ethnicity*. London: Routledge, pp. 89–103.

Comaroff, J. and Comaroff, J. (1992) *Ethnography and the Historical Imagination*. Boulder, CO: Westview Press.

Connerton, P. (1989) *How Societies Remember*. Cambridge: Cambridge University Press.

Constantopoulou, P. (1998) 'Prologue' to *Documents on the History of the Greek Jews. Records from the Historical Archives of the Ministry of Foreign Affairs*, published by Ministry of Foreign Affairs of Greece and University of Athens: Kastaniotes Editions.

Cowan, J.K. (1997) 'Idioms of Belonging: Polyglot Articulations of Local Identity in a Greek Macedonian Town', in Mackridge, P. and Yannakakis, E. (eds) *Ourselves and Others. The Development of Greek Macedonian Cultural Identity Since 1912*, Oxford: Berg, pp. 153–71.

Danforth, L.M. (1995) *The Macedonian Conflict*. Ethnic Nationalism in a Transnational World. Princeton, NJ: Princeton University Press.

Dashevsky, A. (ed.) (1979) *Ethnic Identity in Society*. Chicago, IL: Rand McNally.

Davis, D. (1993) 'Unintended Consequences: The Myth of "the Return" in Anthropological Fieldwork', in Brettell, C.B (ed.) *When They Read What We Write. The Politics of Ethnography*. Westport, CA: Bergin and Garvey.

Davis, J. (1977) *People of the Mediterranean*. London: Routledge.

—— (1992) 'History and the People without Europe', in Hastrup, K. (ed.) *Other Histories*. London: Routledge, pp. 14–28.

De Vos, G. and Romanucci-Ross L. (eds) (1975) *Ethnic Identity*. Palo Alto, CA: Mayfield Publishing.

Delamont, S. (1995) *Appetites and Identities. An Introduction to the Social Anthropology of Western Europe*. London: Routledge.

Deshen, S. and Zenner, W.P. (eds) (1996) *Jews among Muslims. Communities in the Precolonial Middle East*. London: Macmillan Press.

Deutsch, K.W. (1966) *Nationalism and Social Communication: An Inquiry into the Foundations of Nationality*. Cambridge, MA: MIT Press.

Douglas, M. (1987) *How Institutions Think*. London: Routledge.

Doumanis, N. (1997) *Myth and Memory in the Mediterranean. Remembering Fascism's Europe*. London: Macmillan.

Dubisch, J. (1986) *Gender and Power in Rural Greece*. Princeton, NJ: Princeton University Press.

Durkheim, E. (1964) *The Division of Labour*. New York: Free Press.

Elazar, D.J., Fiedenreich, H.P., Hazzan, B. *et al*. (eds) (1984) *The Balkan Jewish Communities*. New York: University Press of America.

Eley, G. and Suny, R.G. (eds) (1996) *Becoming National. A Reader*. Oxford: Oxford University Press.

Encyclopedia Judaica (1996) Vols 1–17. Jerusalem: Keter Publishing House.

Epstein, A.L. (1978) *Ethnos and Identity. Three Studies in Ethnicity*. London: Tavistock Press.

Epstein, H. (1979) *Children of the Holocaust*. New York: Putnam Sons.

Epstein, M.A. (1980) *The Ottoman Jewish Communities and their Role in the Fifteenth and Sixteenth Centuries*. Munich: Klaus Schwarz Verlag.

Eriksen, T.H. (1993) *Ethnicity and Nationalism*. London: Pluto Press.

—— (1995) *Small Places, Large Issues*. London: Pluto Press.

Faubion, J.D. (1993) *Modern Greek Lessons. A Primer in Historical Constructivism*. Princeton, NJ: Princeton University Press.

Feldman, S. and Laub, D. (1992) *Testimony. Crises of Witnessing in Literature, Psychoanalysis, and History*. London: Routledge.

Fentress, J. and Wickham, C. (1992) *Social Memory*. Oxford: Blackwell.

Fischler, C. (1988) 'Food, Self, and Identity', in *Social Science Information*, Vol. 27, No. 2, pp. 275–92.

Fleischer, H. (1986) *Im Kreuzschatten der Mächte: Griechenland 1941–1944*. Frankfurt-am-Main: Lang.

—— (1991) 'Griechenland', in Benz, W. (ed.) *Dimensionen des Völkermords*. Munich pp. 241–74.

Fox, R. (ed.) (1990) *Nationalist Ideologies and the Production of National Culture*. Washington, DC: American Anthropological Association.

Fox, R.G. (1977) *Urban Anthroplogy. Cities in their Cultural Setting*. Englewood Cliffs: Prentice-Hall.

Friedl, E. (1962) *Vasilika: A Village in Modern Greece*. New York: Holt, Rinehart, and Winston.

Frisch, M. (1990) *A Shared Authority: Essays on the Craft and Meaning of Oral and Public History*. Albany, NY: State University of New York Press.

Fromm, R. (1992) 'We Are Few: Folklore and Ethnic Identity of the Jewish Community of Ioaninna, Greece'. Unpublished thesis: Indiana University Department of Folklore.

Gellner, E. (1983) *Nations and Nationalism*. Oxford: Blackwell.

—— (1986) *Culture, Identity, and Politics*. Cambridge: Cambridge University Press.

Gillis, J.R. (ed.) (1994) *Commemorations. The Politics of National Identity*. Princeton, NJ: Princeton University Press.

Glazer, N. and Moynihan, D.P. (eds) (1975) *Ethnicity*. Cambridge, MA: Harvard University Press.

Glenny, M. (1999) *The Balkans 1804–1999. Nationalism, War, and the Great Powers*. London: Granta Books.

Golde, P. (1970) *Women in the Field: Anthropological Experiences*. Chicago, IL: Aldine Publishing.

Goodenough, W. H. (1957) 'Cultural Anthropology and Linguistics', in Garvin, P. (ed.) *Report of the Seventh Annual Round Table Meeting on Linguistics and Language Studies*. Washington, DC.

Govers, C. and Vermeulen, H. (eds) (1994) *The Anthropology of Ethnicity. Beyond 'Ethnic Groups and Boundaries'*. Amsterdam: Het Spinhuis.

Greenspan, H. (1998) *On Listening to Holocaust Survivors. Recounting and Life History*. Westport, CA: Praeger.

Grele, R.J. (1991) *Envelopes of Sound. The Art of Oral History*. New York: Praeger.

Halbwachs, M. (1925) *Les Cadres Sociaux de la Mémoire*. New York: Arno Press.

—— (1980) *The Collective Memory*. New York: Harper and Row.

—— (1985) *Das Kollektive Gedächtnis*. Frankfurt-am-Main: Fischer Verlag.

Hammar, T. (1990) *Democracy and the Nation State*. Avebury: Gower Publishing.

Hammersley, M. and Atkinson, P. (1983) *Ethnography*. London: Routledge.

Handeli, Y. (1993) *A Greek Jew from Salonika Remembers*. New York: Herzl Press.

Hannerz, U. (1989) *Exploring the City. Enquiries Toward An Urban Anthropology*. New York: Columbia University Press.

Hareven, T. (1984) 'The Search for Generational Memory', in Baum, W.K. and Dunaway, D.K. (eds) *Oral History. An Interdisciplinary Anthology*. Nashville, TN: American Association for State and Local History, pp. 248–63.

Hart, L.K. (1992) *Time, Religion, and Social Experience in Rural Greece*. Lanham, MD: Rowman and Littlewood.

Hartman, G.H. (ed.) (1994) *Holocaust Remembrance. The Shapes of Memory*. Oxford: Blackwell Publishers.

Hassiotis, I.K. (ed.) (1997) *The Jewish Communities of South-Eastern Europe. From the Fifteenth Century to the End of World War II*. Thessalonika: Institute for Balkan Studies.

Hastrup, K. (ed.) (1992) *Other Histories*. London: Routledge

Herman, J.L. (1992) *Trauma and Recovery. From Domestic Abuse to Political Terror*. London: Basic Books

Herman, S.N. (1977) *Jewish Identity. A Social Psychological Perspective*. London: Sage Publications.

Herzfeld, M. (1982) *Ours Once More. Folklore, Ideology, and the Making of Modern Greece*. Austin, TX: Austin University of Texas Press.

—— (1987) *Anthropology Through the Looking-Glass: Critical Ethnography on the Margins of Europe*. Cambridge: Cambridge University Press.

—— (1991) *A Place in History. Social and Monumental Time in a Cretan Town*. Princeton, NJ: Princeton University Press.

—— (1992) 'Segmentation and Politics in the European Nation-State: Making Sense of Political Events', in Hastrup, K. (ed.) *Other Histories*. London: Routledge, pp. 62–81.

—— (1997) *Cultural Intimacy. Social Poetics in the Nation State*. London: Routledge.

Hinchman, L.P. and Hinchman, S.K. (eds) (1997) *Memory, Identity, Community. The Idea of Narrative in the Human Sciences*. Albany, NY: State University of New York Press.

Hirsch, M. (1997) *Family Frames. Photography, Narrative, and Postmemory*. Cambridge, MA: Harvard University Press.

Hirsch, M. (1999) 'Projected Memory: Holocaust Photographs in Personal and Public Fantasy', in Bal, M., Crewe, J. and Spitzer, L.

(eds) *Acts of Memory. Cultural Recall in the Present*. Hanover, NH: University Press of New England, pp. 3–23.

Hirschon, R. (1998) *Heirs of the Greek Catastrophe. The Social Life of Asia Minor Refugees in Piraeus*. Oxford: Berghan Books.

Hobsbawm, E. and Ranger, T. (eds) (1983) *The Invention of Tradition*. Cambridge: Cambridge University Press.

Horowitz, D.L. (1975) 'Ethnic Identity', in Glazer, N. and Moynihan, D.P. (eds) *Ethnicity. Theory and Experience*. Cambridge, MA: Harvard University Press, pp. 111–40.

Hunt, J.C. (1989) *Psychoanalytic Aspects of Fieldwork*. London: Sage.

Hutton, P.H. (1993) *History and the Art of Memory*. Hanover, NH: UniversityPress of New England.

Irwin-Zarecka, I. (1989) *Neutralizing Memory: The Jew in Contemporary Poland*. New Brunswick, NJ: Transaction.

—— (1994) *Frames of Remembrance. The Dynamics of Collective Memory*. New Brunswick, NJ: Transaction Publishers.

Jenkins, B. and Sofos, A.S. (eds) (1996) *Nation and Identity in Contemporary Europe*. London: Routledge.

Jenkins, R. (1999) 'Ethnicity Etcetera. Social Anthropological Points of View', in Bulmer, M. and Solomos, J. (eds) *Ethnic and Racial Studies Today*. London: Routledge, pp. 85–97.

Judd, C.M., Smith E.R. and Kidder, L.H. (1991) *Research Methods in Social Relations*. Chicago, IL: Holt, Rinehart, and Winston.

Just, R. (1989) 'Triumph of the Ethnos', in Tonkin, E., Macdonald, M. and Chapman, M. (eds) (1989) *History and Ethnicity*. London: Routledge.

Kabeli, I. (1953) 'The Resistance of the Greek Jews', in *Yivo Annual of Jewish Social Studies*, Vol. 8, pp. 281–8.

Kaplan, R. (1994) *Balkan Ghosts. A Journey Through History*. New York: Vintage Press.

Karakasidou, A. (1991) 'Politicizing Culture: Negating Ethnic Identity in Greek Macedonia', in *Journal of Modern Greek Studies*, Vol. 11, pp. 1–27.

—— (1997) *Fields of Wheat, Hills of Blood. Passages to Nationhood in Greek Macedonia 1870–1990*. Chicago, IL: University of Chicago Press.

—— (1997) 'Women of the Family, Women of the Nation: National Enculturation among Slav-Speakers in North-West Greece', in Mackridge, P. and Yannakakis, E. (eds) *Ourselves and Others. The Development of a Greek Macedonian Cultural Identity Since 1912*. Oxford: Berg.

Karpf, A. (1998) *Remembering for My Parents: The Experience of the Second Generation*. Unpublished lecture given at the Wiener Library.

Kedourie, E. (1960) *Nationalism*. London: Hutchinson.

Keesing, Roger (1981) *Cultural Anthropology. A Comparative Perspective*. New York: Holt Rinehart and Winston.

Kellas, J.G. (1991) *The Politics of Nationalism and Ethnicity*. London: Macmillan.

Kenna, M.E. (1991) 'The Social Organization of Exile: The Everyday Life of Political Exiles in the Cyclades in the 1930s', *in Journal of Modern Greek Studies*, Vol. 9, pp. 63–81.

Kirmayer, L.J. (1996) 'Landscapes of Memory. Trauma, Narrative, and Dissociation', in Antze, P. and Lambek, M. (eds) (1996) *Tense Past. Cultural Essays in Trauma and Memory*. London: Routledge, pp. 173–98.

Kitroeff, A. (1990) 'Continuity and Change in Contemporary Greek Historiography', in Blinkhorn, M. and Veremis, T. (eds) *Modern Greece: Nationalism and Nationality*. London: Sage, pp. 143–72.

Kitromilides, P. (1990) 'Imagined Communities and the Origins of the National Question in the Balkans', in Blinkhorn, M. and Veremis, T. (1990) *Modern Greece: Nationalism and Nationality*. Athens: Sage-Eliamep, pp. 23–66.

—— (1994) *Enlightenment, Nationalism and Orthodoxy: Studies in the Culture and Political Thought of Southeastern Europe*. Aldershot: Variorum.

Kleinmann, S. and Copp, M.A. (1993) *Emotions and Fieldnotes*. London: Sage.

Klötzel, E.S. (1920) *In Saloniki*. Berlin: Jüdischer Verlag.

Koch, G. (1991) 'The Angel of Forgetfulness and the Black Box of Facticity: Trauma and Memory in Claude Lanzmann's Film Shoah', in *History and Memory*, Vol. 3, No.1, Spring 1991, pp. 119–14.

Kohn, H. (1967) *Prelude to Nation-States*. New York: Macmillan.

Kokot, W. (ed.) (1990) *Stadtmosaik*. Bonn: Holos.

—— (1995) *Kulturelle Modelle und Soziale Identität in einem Fluechtlingsviertel in Thessaloniki*. Unpublished Habilitationsschrift: University of Cologne.

Kounio-Amariglio, E.M. (1996) *Damit es die ganze Welt erführt. Von Saloniki nach Auschwitz und zurück*. Konstanz: Hartung-Gorre.

Kounio-Amariglio, E. and Nar, A. (eds) (1998) *Proforikes Martiries Ton Evraon Tis Thessalonikis* (Oral Testimonies of Salonikan Jews) Thessalonika: Paratiritis.

Kounio-Amariglio, E. (2000) *From Thessalonika to Auschwitz and Back. Memories of a Survivor*. London: Vallentine Mitchell.

Krava, V. (1999) *Food as a Marker of National Identity: A Case Study*. Unpublished M.Phil./Ph.D. proposal: Goldsmith College, London.

Kroeber, A.L. and Kluckhohn, C. (1952) *Culture: A Critical Review of Concepts and Definitions*. Cambridge, MA: Harvard University Press.

Kulick, D. and Willson, M. (eds) (1995) *Taboo. Sex, Identity and Erotic Subjectivity in Anthropological Fieldwork*. London: Routledge.

Kuper, A. and Kuper, J. (eds) (1996) *The Social Science Encyclopedia*. London: Routledge.

Kvale, S. (1996) *Interviews. An Introduction to Qualitative Research Interviewing*. London: Sage.

LaCapra, D. (1994) *Representing the Holocaust. History, Theory, Trauma*. Ithaca, NY: Cornell University.

Langer, L. (1991) *Holocaust Testimonies. The Ruins of Memory*. New Haven, CT: Yale University Press.

Langness, L.L. and Frank, G. (1981) *Lives: An Anthropological Approach to Biography*. Novato, CA: Chandler and Sharp.

Laub, D. (1995) 'Truth and Testimony', in Caruth, C. (ed.) *Trauma. Explorations in Memory*. Baltimore, MD: John Hopkins University Press, pp. 61–75.

LeGoff, J. (1988) *History and Memory*. New York: Columbia University Press.

Leroy, B. (1987) *Die Sephardim. Geschichte des iberischen Judentums*. Munich: Nymphenburger Verlagsbuchhandlung.

Levi, P. (1994) *If This is a Man. The Truce*. London: Abacus.

Lewis, B. (1987) *Die Juden in der islamischen Welt*. Munich: Beck.

Lewis, I.M. (ed.) (1968) *History and Anthropology*. ASA Monograph. London: Tavistock Publications.

Lewkowicz, B. (1990) 'Das Selbstverständnis Junger Juden in Thessalonika', in Kokot, W. (ed.) *Stadtmosaik*. Bonn: Holos, pp. 81–96.

—— (1994) 'Greece is my Home, But … Ethnic Identity of Greek Jews in Thessalonika', in *Journal of Mediterranean Studies*, Vol. 4, No. 2, pp. 225–40.

Liberles, A.W. (1984) 'The Jewish Community of Greece', in Elazar, D.J., Fiedenreich, H.P., Hazzan, B. *et al.* (eds) (1984) *The Balkan Jewish Communities*. New York: University Press of America.

Liebkind, C. (ed.) (1989) *New Identities in Europe*. Aldershot: Gower.

Loizos, P. (1981) *The Heart Grown Bitter. A Chronicle of Cypriot War Refugees*. Cambridge: Cambridge University Press.

—— (1992) 'User-Friendly Ethnography?', in Campbell, J. and De Pina-Cabral, J. (eds) *Europe Observed*. London: Macmillan Press, pp. 167–96.

—— (1994) 'Confessions of a Vampire Anthropologist', in *Anthropological Journal of European Cultures*, Vol. 3, No. 2.

—— (1999) 'Ottoman Half-Lives: Long Term Perspectives on Particular Forced Migrations', *in Journal of Refugee Studies*, Vol. 12, No.3.

Loizos, P. and Papataxiarchis, E. (eds) (1991) *Contested Identities. Gender and Kinship in Modern Greece*. Princeton, NJ: Princeton University Press.

Lowenthal, D. (1985) *The Past is a Foreign Country*. Cambridge: Cambridge University Press.

Lustinger-Thaler, H. (1996) 'Remembering Forgettfully', in Amit-Talai, V. and Knowles, C. (eds) *Re-Situating Identities*. Peterborough: Broadview Press, pp. 190– 217.

Macdonald, S. (1993) *Inside European Identities*. Oxford: Berg.

Mackridge, P. and Yannakakis, E. (eds) (1997) *Ourselves and Others. The Development of a Greek Macedonian Cultural Identity Since 1912*. Oxford: Berg.

Malinowski, B. (1961) *The Dynamics of Culture Change: An Inquiry into Race Relations in Africa*. New Haven, IL: Yale University Press.

Malkki, L. H. (1995) *Purity and Exile. Violence, Memory, and National Cosmology Among Hutu Refugees in Tanzania*. Chicago, IL: The University of Chicago Press.

Marcus, G.E. (1992) 'Past, Present and Emergent Identites: Requirements for Ethnographies of Late Twentieth Century Modernity Worldwide', in Lash. S. and Friedman, H. (eds) *Modernity and Identity*. Oxford: Blackwell.

Marcus, G.E. and Fischer, M.J. (1986) *Anthropology as Cultural Critique: An Experimental Moment in the Human Sciences*. Chicago, IL: University of Chicago Press.

Marketos, S. (1994) 'Ethnos Choris Evreos: Apopsis Tis Historiographicis Kataskevis Tou Ellinismou' (A Nation without Jews: Perceptions of Historiographic Constructions of Hellenism), in *Synchrona Themata*, Vol 52–53, No. 17, pp. 52–69.

Matkovski, A. (1982) *A History of the Jews in Macedonia*. Skopje: Macedonian Review Editions.

Matsas, M. (1997) *The Illusion of Safety. The Story of the Greek Jews During the Second World War*. New York: Pella Publishing.

Mavrogordatos, G. (1983) *Stillborn Republic: Social Coalitions and Party Strategies in Greece 1922–1936*. Berkeley, CA: University of California Press.

Mazower, M. (1993) *Inside Hitler's Greece. The Experience of Occupation 1941–44*. New Haven, CT: Yale University Press.

—— (1995) 'The Jews of Northern Greece: A Review Essay', in *Bulletin of Judeo-Greek Studies*, No. 17, pp. 40–4.

—— (1996) 'Introduction to the Study of Macedonia', in *Journal of Modern Greek Studies*, Vol. 2, No. 14, pp. 229–35.

—— (2004) *Salonika. City of Ghosts. Christians, Muslims and Jews 1430–1950*. London: Harper Collins.

McCready, W.C. (ed.) *Culture, Ethnicity and Identity*. New York: Academic Press.

Medding, P.Y. (1983) 'The Politics of Jewry as a Mobilized Diaspora', in McCready, W.C. (ed.) *Culture, Ethnicity, and Identity*. New York: Academic Press.

Megas, Y. (1993) *Souvenir. Images of the Jewish Community. Salonika 1897–1917*. Athens: Kapon Editions.

Meinecke, F. (1969) *Weltbürgertum und Nationalstaat*. Munich: Oldenbourg.

Melhuus, M. (1997) 'Exploring the Work of a Compassionate Ethnographer. The Case of Oscar Lewis', in *Social Anthropology*, Vol. 5, No. 1, pp. 35–54.

Messinas, E. (1997) *The Synagogues of Salonika and Veria*. Athens: Gavrielides Editions.

Messinas, E. (2000) 'Athens Holocaust Monument', in *Kol haKehila*, Vol. 2, No. 3.

Meyerhoff, B. (1978) *Number Our Days. A Triumph of Continuity and Culture Among Jewish Old People in an Urban Ghetto*. New York: Simon and Schuster.

Middleton, D. and Edwards, D. (eds) (1990) *Collective Remembering*. London: Sage.

Ministry of Foreign Affairs of Greece and University of Athens (1998) *Documents on the History of the Greek Jews. Records from the Historical Archives of the Ministry of Foreign Affairs*. Researched and edited by P. Constantopoulou and T. Veremis. Athens: Kastaniotes Editions.

Moerman, M. (1965) 'Who are the Lue? Ethnic Identification in a Complex Civilization', in *American Anthropologist*, Vol. 67, pp. 1215–29.

Moewe, I. (1988) Parea: Eine Studie zur Ethnographie der Geselligkeit. (unpublished MA thesis: Hamburg)

Molho, A. (1991) 'The Jewish Community of Salonika: The End of a Long History', in *Diaspora*, Vol. 1, No. 1, pp. 100–22.

Molho, M. (1988) *In Memoriam. Hommage Aux Juives Des Nazis En Grèce*. Thessalonika: The Jewish Community of Thessalonika.

Molho, R. (1986) 'Venizelos and the Jewish Community of Salonika', in *Journal of the Hellenic Diaspora*, Vol. 13, No. 3/4, pp. 113–123.

—— (1988) 'The Jewish Community of Salonika and its Incorporation into the Greek State, 1912–19', in *Middle Eastern Studies*, Vol. 24, pp. 391–403.

—— (1993a) 'Education in the Jewish Community of Thessaloniki in the Beginning of the Twentieth Century', in *Balkan Studies* 34/2, pp. 259–69.

—— (1993b) 'Le Renouveau', in Veinstein, G. (ed.) (1993) *Salonique 1850–1918. La 'Ville des Juifs' et le Réveil des Balkans*. Paris: Editions Autrement, pp. 64–78.

—— (1997a) 'The Zionist Movement in Thessalonika, 1899–1999', in Hassiotis, I.K. (ed.) *The Jewish Communities of South-Eastern Europe. From the Fifteenth Century to the End of World War II*. Thessalonika: Institute for Balkan Studies, pp. 327–50.

—— (1997b) 'Les Juifs de Salonique, 1856–1919: Une Comunaute Hors Norms'. Unpublished Ph.D. thesis: Université des Sciences Humaines de Strasbourg.

—— (1998) 'The Jews in Salonica and Their Role in the Seafaring Trades', in The Simon Marks Museum of the Jewish History in Thessalonika (ed.) *Thessalonika*. Thessalonika: The Jewish Community of Thessalonika, pp. 13–16.

—— (2001) *Oi evraioi tis Thessalonikis, 1856–1919: Mia Idiaiteri Kinotita.* (The Jews of Thessalonika, 1856–1919: A Unique Community). Athens: Themelio.

Molho, R. (1994) *They Say Diamonds Don't Burn. The Holocaust Experiences of René Molho of Salonika, Greece*. Berkeley, CA: Judah L. Magnes Museum.

Morin, E. (1989) *Vidal et les Siens*. Paris: Editions Du Seuil.

—— (1994) 'Vidal and his People', in *Journal of Mediterranean Studies* Vol. 4, No. 2, pp. 330–43.

Nar, A. (1997) 'Social Organisations and Activity of the Jewish Community in Thessalonika', in *Thessalonika. History and Culture*. Thessalonika: Paratiritis.

Nathan, N. (1964) 'Notes on the Jews in Turkey' (1964), in *The Jewish Journal of Sociology*, Vol. 6, No. 2, pp. 172–89.

Nehama, J. (1935–78) *Histoire Des Israélites De Salonique*. Vol. 1–7. Thessalonika: The Jewish Community of Thessalonika.

—— (1989) 'The Jews of Salonika and the Rest of Greece Under Hellenic Rule: The Death of a Great Community', in Barnett, R.D. (ed.) *The Western Sephardim*. London: Gibraltar Books, pp. 243–82.

Niethammer, L. (1995) 'Diesseits des Floating Gap. Das kollektive Gedächtnis und die Konstruktion von Identität im wissensch-aftlichen Diskurs', in Platt, K. andDabag, M. (eds) *Generation und*

Gedächtnis. Erinnerungen und kollektive Identitäten. Opladen: Leske und Budrich, pp. 25–50.

Nora, P. (ed.) (1984–92) *Les Lieux de Mémoire*. Paris: Editions Gallimard.

Novitch, M. (1989) *The Passage of the Barbarians. Contribution to the History of the Deportation and Resistance of Greek Jews*. Hull: Glenvil Group.

Olick, J.K. and Robbins, J. (1998) 'Social Memory Studies: From "Collective Memory" to the Historical Sociology of Mnemonic Practices', in *Annu. Rev. Sociol.*, Vol. 24, pp. 105–40.

Papacosma, S.V. (1978) 'The Sephardic Jews of Salonika', in *Midstream*, Vol. 24 December.

Paserini, L. (1987) *Fascism in Popular Memory. The Cultural Experience of the Turin Working Class*. Cambridge: Cambridge University Press.

—— (1996) *Autobiography of a Generation. Italy, 1968*. Hanover, NH: Wesleyan University Press.

Patterson, O. (1975) 'Context and Choice in Ethnic Allegiance', in Glazer, N. and Moynihan, P.P. (eds) *Ethnicity*. Cambridge, MA: Harvard University Press.

Pattie, S.P. (1997) *Faith in History. Armenians Rebuilding Community*. Washington, DC: Smithsonian Institution Press.

Perahia-Zemour, E. (1997) Le Particularism des Juifs de Grèce durant la Deportation. Unpublished Masters thesis: Department of Sociology, Université des Science Humaines de Strasbourg.

Perdurant, D. (1995) *Antisemitism in Contemporary Greek Society. Analysis of Current Trends in Antisemitism* (No. 7). Jerusalem: Vidal Sassoon Center for the Study of Antisemitism.

Peristiany, J.G. (1965) *Honour and Shame. The Values of Mediterranean Society*. London: Trinity Press.

Perks, R. and Thompson, A. (eds) (1998) *The Oral History Reader*. London: Routledge.

Petropoulos, E. (1983) *Les Juifs de Salonique, in Memoriam*. Paris: Atelier Merat.

—— (1985) *A Macabre Song. Testimony of the Goy Elias Petropoulos Concerning Anti-Jewish Sentiment in Greece*. Paris.

Platt, K. and Dabag, M. (1995) (eds) *Generation und Gedächtnis. Erinnerungen und kollektive Identitäten*. Opladen: Leske und Budrich.

Plaut, E.J. (1996) *Greek Jewry in the Twentieth Century, 1912–1983*. Madison, NJ: Fairleigh Dickinson University Press.

Poliakov, L. (ed.) (1978) *Ni Juif Ni Grec. Entretions sur le Racisme*. Paris: Mouton Editeur.

Pollak, M. (1988) *Die Grenzen des Sagbaren. Lebensgeschichten von KZ-*

Überlebenden als Augenzeugenberichte und als Identitätsarbeit. Frankfurt -am-Main: Campus.

Pollis, A. (1992) 'Greek National Identity: Religious Minorities, Rights, and European Norms', in *Journal of Modern Greek Studies*, Vol. 10, pp. 171–95.

Popular Memory Group, (1998) 'Popular Memory. Theory, Politics, Methods', in Perks, R. and Thomson, A. (eds) (1998) *The Oral History Reader*. London: Routledge, pp. 75–86.

Portelli, A. (1991) *The Death of Luigi Trastulli and Other Stories. Form and Meaning in Oral History*. Albany, NY: State University of New York Press.

Rapaport, L. (1997) *Jews in Germany after the Holocaust. Memory, Identity, and Jewish-German Relations*. Cambridge: Cambridge University Press.

Read, P. (1996) *Returning to Nothing. The Meaning of Lost Places*. Cambridge: Cambridge University Press.

Reilly, J. (1998) *Belsen. The Liberation of a Concentration Camp*. London: Routledge.

Rex, J. and Mason, D. (eds) (1986) *Theories of Race and Ethnic Relations*. Cambridge: Cambridge University Press.

Richter, H.A. (1973) *Griechenland zwischen Revolution und Konterrevolution 1936–1946*. Frankfurt-am-Main: Europäische Verlagsanstalt.

Roden, C. (1997) *The Book of Jewish Food. An Odyssey From Samarkand and Vilna to the Present Day*. London: Viking.

Rogers, A. and Vertovec, S. (eds) (1995) *The Urban Context. Ethnicity, Social Networks and Situational Analysis*. Oxford: Berg Publishers.

Roper, M. (1996) 'Oral History', in Kuper, A. and Kuper, J. (eds) *The Social Science Encyclopedia*. London: Routledge.

Roosens, E. (1989) *Creating Ethnicity: The Process of Ethnogenesis*. London: Sage.

Rosaldo, R. (1986) *When Natives Talk Back. Chicano Anthropology Since the Late Sixties*. Tuscon, AZ: University of Arizona.

Rosenthal, G. (ed.) (1998) *The Holocaust in Three Generations. Families of Victims and Perpetrators of the Nazi Regime*. London: Cassell.

Rudolph, W. (1988) 'Ethnos und Kultur', in Fischer, H. (ed.) *Ethnologie. Einführung und Überblick*. Berlin: Dietrich Reimer, pp. 39–60.

Salamone, S.D. (1987) *In the Shadow of the Holy Mountain. The Genesis of a Rural Greek Community and its Refugee Heritage*. Boulder, CO: Columbia University Press.

Samuel, R. and Thompson, P. (1990) *The Myths We Live By*. London: Routledge.

Schieder, D.M. (1968) *American Kinship: A Cultural Account*. Englewood Cliffs, NY: Prentice-Hall.

Sciaky, L. (1946) *Farewell to Salonika. Portrait of an Era*. London: W.H. Allen.

Segre, D.V. (1980) *A Crisis of Identity*. Oxford: Oxford University Press.

Sevillias, E. (1983) *Athens-Auschwitz*. Translated and edited by N. Stavroulakis. Athens: Lycabettus Press.

Seymour-Smith, C. (1986) *Macmillan Dictionary of Anthropology*. London: Macmillan.

Shain, Y. (1989) *The Frontier of Loyalty*. Middletown, CI: Wesleyan University Press.

Shaw, S.S. (1991) *The Jews of the Ottoman Empire and the Turkish Republic*. London: Macmillan Press.

Sherrard, P. (1978) *The Wound of Greece*. London: Rex Collings.

Sitton, D. (1985) *Sephardi Communities Today*. Jerusalem: Council of Sephardi and Oriental Communities.

Skultans, V. (1998) *The Testimony of Lives. Narratives and Memory in post-Soviet Latvia*. London: Routledge.

Solomon, N. (1994) 'Judaism in the New Europe: Discovery or Invention?' in Webber, J. (ed.) *Jewish Identities in the New Europe*. London: Littman Library of Jewish Civilization, pp. 86–98.

Smith, M.G. (1969) 'Institutional and Political Conditions of Pluralism', in Kuper, L. and Smith, M.G. (eds) *Pluralism in Africa*. Berkeley, CA: University of California Press, pp. 415–58.

Smith, A.D. (1986) *The Ethnic Origins of Nations*. Oxford: Blackwell.

—— (1991) *National Identity*. London: Penguin.

—— (1995) 'Gastronomy or Geology? The Role of Nationalism in the Reconstruction of Nations', in *Nations and Nationalism*, Vol. 1, No.1, pp. 3–23.

Smith, A.D. and Hutchinson, J. (1994) (eds) *Nationalism*. Oxford: Oxford University Press.

—— (1996) (eds) *Ethnicity*. Oxford: Oxford University Press.

Spillman, L.P. (1997) *Nation and Commemoration: Creating National Identities in the United States and Australia*. New York: Cambridge University Press.

Spitzer, L. (1989) *Lives In Between: Assimilation and Marginality in Austria, Brazil, West Africa 1780–1945*. Cambridge: Cambridge University Press.

—— (1994) 'Andean Waltz', in Hartman, G.H. (ed.) *Holocaust Remembrance. The Shapes of Memory*. Oxford: Blackwell, pp. 161–74.

—— (1999) 'Back through the Future: Nostalgic Memory and Critical Memory in a Refuge from Nazism', in Bal, M., Crewe, J. and Spitzer, L. (eds) *Acts of Memory. Cultural Recall in the Present*. Hanover: University Press of New England.

Stavros, S. (1995) 'The Legal Status of Minorities in Greece Today: The Adequacy of Their Protection in the Light of Current Human Rights Perceptions', in *Journal of Modern Greek Studies*, Vol. 13, pp. 1–32.

Stavroulakis, N. (1986) *Cookbook of the Jews of Greece*. Philadelphia: Cadmus Press.

Stewart, C. (1994) 'Syncretism as a Dimension of Nationalist Discourse in Modern Greece', in Stewart, C. and Shaw, R. (eds) *Syncretism/Anti-Syncretism*, pp. 127–44.

—— (1998) 'Who owns the Rotunda? Church versus State in Greece', in *Anthropology Today*, Vol. 14, No. 5, pp. 3–9.

Stroumsa, J. (1993) *Geiger in Auschwitz. Ein Jüdisches Überlebenschicksal aus Saloniki 1941–1967*, edited by E.R. Wiehn. Konstanz: Hartung-Gorre.

Sutton, D. E. (1998) *Memories Cast in Stone. The Relevance Of the Past in Everyday Life*. Oxford: Berg.

Tentokali, A. (1999) 'Families from Thessaloniki: The Howells', in *Close Up*, No. 26, pp. 128–36.

Thomas, W.I. and Zaniecki, F. (1984) *The Polish Peasant in Europe and the United States*, edited and abridged by Eli Zaretsky, Urbana: University of Illinois Press,

Thompson, P. (1988) *The Voice of the Past. Oral History*. Oxford: Oxford University Press.

Tonkin, E. (1992) *Narrating our Past. The Social Construction of Oral History*. Cambridge: Cambridge University Press.

Tonkin, E., Macdonald, M. and Chapman, M. (eds) (1989) *History and Ethnicity*. London: Routledge.

Tsimouris, G. (1995) *The Long-Term Embodied Memory of Refugees and the Language of Nationalism: the Case of Mikrasiates Greeks*. Paper given at 'Anthropological Understandings of the Politics of Identity' Seminar, Queens University, Belfast.

Tylor, E.B. (1871) *Primitive Culture*. New York. Reprinted as *Religion in Primative Culture* (1958) New York: HarperTorchback.

Valensi, L. and Wachtel, N. (1991) *Jewish Memories*. Berkeley, CA: University of California Press.

Van den Berghe, P.L. (1984) 'Ethnic Cuisine: Culture in Nature', *Ethnic and Racial Studies*, 7 (3), pp. 386–97.

Varon-Vassard, O. (1999) 'L'intérêt pour les Juifs de Grèce', in *Historein*, Vol. 1, pp. 157–60.

Varouxakis, G. (1995) *A Certain Idea of Greece: Perceptions of History as an Impediment to Fuller Integration into Europe*. Unpublished Paper.

Vassiliadis, I. (1997) 'La Communauté Juif d'Athèns. De la Persécution au Redressment', in Hassiotis, I.K. (ed.) *The Jewish Communities of South-Eastern Europe. From the Fifteenth Century to the End of World War II*. Thessalonika: Institute for Balkan Studies, pp. 571–78.

Vassilikou, M. (1993) 'The Anti-Semitic Riots in Thessalonika and the Greek Press: A Case Study of "Scapegoating" Theory'. Unpublished MA thesis: King's College, London.

Veinstein, G. (ed.) (1993) *Salonique 1850–1918. La 'Ville des Juifs' et le Revéil des Balkans*. Paris: Editions Autrement.

Verdery, K. (1994) 'Ethnicity, Nationalism, and State-Making', in Govers, C. and Vermeulen, H. (eds) *The Anthropology of Ethnicity*. The Hague: Het Spinhus.

Vermeulen, H. (1983) 'Urban Research in Greece', in Kenny, M. and Kertzer, D.I. (eds.) *Urban Life in Mediterranean Europe: Anthro-pological Persectives*. Urbana: University of Illinois Press, pp. 10–132.

Volkgenannt U. and Röttger, E. (1995) *Thessaloniki bei Tag und Nacht. Wissenswertes über eine Vielseitige Stadt*. Essen: Clemon Verlag.

Voutira, E. (1991) 'Pontic Greeks Today: Migrants or Refugees?' in *Journal of Refugee Studies*, Vol. 4, No. 4, pp. 400–20.

Wallman, S. (1979) *Ethnicity at Work*. London: Macmillan.

Wardi, D. (1992) *Memorial Candles. Children of the Holocaust*. London: Routledge.

Watson, L.C. and Watson-Franke, M.B. (1985) *Interpreting Life Histories. An Anthropological Inquiry*. New Brunswick, NJ: Rutgers University Press.

Wayne, H. (ed.)(1995) *The Story of a Marriage: The Letters of Bronislav Malinowski and Elsie Masson*. London: Routledge.

Webber, J (ed.) (1994) *Jewish Identities in the New Europe*. London: Littman Library of Jewish Civilization.

Weiker, W.F. (1992) *Ottoman, Turks, and the Jewish Polity*. Lanham, MD: University Press of America.

Wente, Bettina (1990) 'Das Fenster zur Strasse. Anmerkungen zum städtischen griechischen Saloniki', in Kokot, W. (ed.) *Stadtmosaik*. Bonn: Holos, pp. 13–25.

Whitehead, T.L. and Conaway, M.E. (eds) (1986) *Self, Sex, and Gender in Cross-Cultural Fieldwork*. Urbana, IL: University of IIllinois Press.

Williams, B.F. (1989) 'A Class Act: Anthropology and the Race to Nation Across Ethnic Terrain'. *Annual Review of Anthropology*, Vol. 18, pp. 401–44.

Wintle, M. (1996) *Culture and Identity in Europe. Perceptions of Divergence and Unity in Past and Present*. Aldershot: Avebury.

Young, J.E. (1988) *Writing and Rewriting the Holocaust: Narrative and the Consequences of Interpretation*. Bloomington, IN: Indiana University Press.

—— (1993) *The Texture of Memory. Holocaust Memorials and Meaning*. New Haven, CT: Yale University Press.

Zenner, W.P. (1988) *Persistence and Flexibility. Anthropological Perspectives on the American Jewish Experience*. Albany, NY: State University of New York Press.

Zonabend, F. (1984) *The Enduring Memory. Time and History in a French Village*. Manchester: Manchester University Press.

Index

Page references to footnotes have the letter 'n' appearing after the footnote number, while references to any tables are in *italics*

Recently published by Vallentine Mitchell

Jewish Resistance in Wartime Greece
Steven Bowman

While the murder of nearly 90 per cent of Greek Jews by the Nazis has begun to enter the Holocaust story, the participation of Greek Jews in the war against the Nazis is virtually unknown. Greek Jews actively fought in the war against the Italian and German invaders. Veterans and young Jewish males and females went to the mountains to fight or serve in various ways in the *andartiko* among the several Greek Resistance movements. Other Jews remained in urban areas where they joined different Resistance cells, whether as active saboteurs or in leadership roles. A number of Jews appear on the payrolls of Force 133. Additionally Greek Jews participated in the Sonderkommando revolt in the Auschwitz concentration camp in October 1944, while others fought in the Warsaw revolt from August to October 1944. Based on interviews and archival research the author has assembled a preliminary list of over 650 individuals who fought or served with the Greek Resistance forces. These include *andartes* and *andartissas*, interpreters, recruiters, doctors, spies, nurses, organizers and a number of non-Greek Jews who volunteered or were trapped in Greece during the war years.

From Thessaloniki to Auschwitz and Back: Memories of a Survivor from Thessaloniki
Erika Kounio Amariglio

Before the Second World War there was a thriving Jewish community for some 50,000 people in Thessaloniki, Greece. In 1943, under Nazi occupation, virtually the entire community was deported to Auschwitz extermination camp. That Erika Amariglio and several members of her family survived is due only to a series of coincidences, which started with the fact that they were on the first transport to Auschwitz, and of the 2,800 people on the train they were the only ones who spoke fluent German.

Erika Amariglio's story covers the period before the war in Thessaloniki, the German occupation and the gradual tightening of restrictions, the transportation, the two-and-a-half years that she and members of her family spent in Auschwitz, the long death march back to Germany, their escape to Yugoslavia, and the eventual reunion of the family in Greece. It concludes with the author's return to Auschwitz many years later as a delegate to an international conference on the Holocaust.

From Thessaloniki to Auschwitz and Back has previously been published in Greek (a third edition is currently in preparation), German, French and Serbia; a Hebrew edition is due to appear shortly.

Recently published by Vallentine Mitchell

Jews and Port Cities, 1590–1990: Commerce, Community and Cosmopolitanism
David Cesarani and Gemma Romain (eds.)

With studies of Jewish communities in port cities ranging from sixteenth-century Livorno to modern Singapore, this book develops and extends the concept of the port Jew using a blend of conceptual innovation and original research. The first section explores the world of the Sephardi Jews, revealing patterns of mobility and networks that intertwined commerce, community and kinship. Individual case histories based on Livorno, Amsterdam, Curaçao, Charleston, Liverpool and Bristol examine how Jewish identity was formed in the unique milieu of the cosmopolitan maritime trading centre, how the commercial ethos of the bustling port promoted tolerance, and how the experience of civic inclusion was both a boon and a threat to Jewish life and culture. Innovative work on Hamburg, Corfu, Liverpool and Bristol also reveals that it was possible for intolerance to flourish in business circles and that competition could become a threat to ethnic diversity. Challenging research on Charleston and Liverpool shows how slavery cast a shadow over the Jewish population and created an environment of racialized identities in which Jews occupied an ambiguous and ambivalent position. The second section concentrates on the experience of Ashkenazi Jews in the modern era, when the port was less a commercial hub for exchange and more a location of production, transhipment and transmigration. Jews went from being primarily settlers and traders to becoming commodities in the business of mass migration. The studies of Libau, Cape Town, and Southampton show the importance of transmigration in the local and global economy and the limits of cosmopolitanism. A disturbing case study of Hamburg under the Nazis shows that a history of diversity was no guarantor of tolerance. Yet research on Glasgow, with its ethnic and religious fragmentation, shows how far Jews and non-Jews in port cities could get along functionally and amicably. All these contributions explore the concepts of diaspora and identity, probe the links between commerce and inter-communal relations, and map the subtle, shifting contours of language, culture and community in the unique mercantile environment in the world's greatest ports.